THE Alberta Fact BOOK

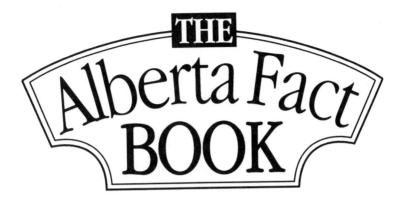

THE Alberta Fact BOOK

Everything YOU Ever Wanted To Know About Alberta

Mark Zuehlke

Whitecap Books
Vancouver / Toronto

The information in this book is true and complete to the best of our
knowledge. All recommendations are made without guarantee on the
part of the author or Whitecap Books Ltd. The author and publisher
disclaim any liability in connection with the use of this information. For
additional information please contact Whitecap Books Ltd., 351 Lynn
Avenue, North Vancouver, BC V7J 2C4.

Edited by Elizabeth McLean
Proofread by Lisa Collins
Cover design and illustration by Rose Cowles
Interior design by Tanya Lloyd
Printed and bound in Canada

Canadian Cataloguing in Publication Data

Zuehlke, Mark.
    The Alberta fact book

    ISBN 1-55110-545-4

    1. Alberta—Handbooks, manuals, etc.   I. Title
FC3657.Z83 1997   971.23   C96-910771—4
F1076.Z83 1997

The publisher acknowledges the support of the Canada Council and
the Cultural Services Branch of the Government of British Columbia
in making this publication possible.

Contents

Acknowledgements

Completion of this book would have been impossible without the assistance of literally dozens of people in federal departments, provincial government ministries, the province's national parks, provincial parks, federal and provincial historic sites, provincial museums, provincial and community tourist information centres, and many other information outlets too numerous to mention.

Rosemary Neering provided some excellent research resources. John and Helen Backhouse were gracious hosts.

Crisscrossing the province with me during a seemingly endless quest for more facts was Frances Backhouse, who provided an essential knowledge of a province she knows well, most welcome company, and much valued friendship.

Introduction

There is a bench in the coulee country on the south shore of the Milk River in Writing-On-Stone Provincial Park where natural grasses reach up to knee height. In August these grasses are dried and bleached pale by hot sun and the seemingly endless brushing of westerly wind. Across the Montana border the Sweetgrass Hills are silhouetted, rendered grey and intangible by sun's white glare. Northward, the muddy Milk winds past a clay cliff on one shore and a grove of cottonwoods on the other. Rimming in the other flanks of the small clutch of trees are the hoodoos Blackfoot called *Áisinai'pi,* or "it is written," because of the ancient art carved or painted on the rock faces.

Although I have never lived there, Writing-On-Stone is one of those places of the heart where, during my first and all subsequent explorations of its starkly beautiful landscape, I have felt entirely, naturally at home. Many of us know such places. We arrive and it is as if we have always known this land. While travelling through Alberta to research this book other homeplaces of the heart were discovered and explored. Several were in the Rocky Mountains, another lay in a foothills montane forest and meadow, the rugged badlands held another, and open prairie sang its own song of eternal welcome.

That Alberta should offer so many landscapes that spoke of home is hardly surprising. This is a complex province, where a few hours spent travelling in any direction will take you some place differing entirely from your starting point. Mountains give way to prairie, prairie melds into seemingly endless reaches of boreal forest, and so it goes.

This book attempts to encapsulate as much factual information about Alberta as possible. Not just its landscape, but also its wildlife, peoples, their history, culture, and present economic and social experience—all the components that woven together form a place's soul. I've tried to unravel and illuminate specific threads of this provincial skein to give some understanding of how Albertans have been shaped by the environment in which they live and of who they are as a people. This process, of course, could be endless so the limiting constraint was that it must all fit into one easily used and read volume. That's the big-picture purpose behind this book, but it's also hoped the facts contained here will make for some enjoyable and informative reading on a subject-by-subject level that will enhance both residents' and visitors' understanding of this always intriguing, amazingly diversified, Canadian province.

It should be noted that there was no attempt to list every Albertan community. The decision to include one community and not another was, however, not completely arbitrary. Communities listed and the details in their descriptions were selected on the basis of what that information contributed to the sense of who Albertans are and how they live now, or have lived in the past.

Alberta Facts at a Glance

- Alberta has a total area of 661,188 square kilometres, including 16,796 square kilometres of inland water. It encompasses about 6.6 percent of all of Canada.

- The province's boundaries are: southern boundary 49° north latitude, northern boundary 60° north latitude, eastern boundary 110° west longitude, western boundary 120° west longitude south from 60° north latitude to just below the 54° north latitude point (at Intersection Mountain) whereafter the western boundary follows the Continental Divide to the southern boundary. Alberta is bordered to the west by the province of British Columbia, to the north by Canada's Northwest Territories, to the east by the province of Saskatchewan, and to the south by the state of Montana in the United States.

- Maximum altitude is 3,747 metres (Mount Columbia); lowest point is in the northeast corner where the Slave and Salt rivers cross the Alberta–Northwest Territories border. Altitude here is about 180 metres above sea level.

- Time zone is Mountain Standard Time (noon Greenwich Mean Time = 5:00 a.m. MST). The province changes to Daylight Saving Time in the spring (noon GMT = 6:00 a.m MST).

- Total population is 2.77 million. Its largest city is Calgary (727,000).

- The capital city is Edmonton.

- The province was formed and entered Confederation on September 1, 1905.

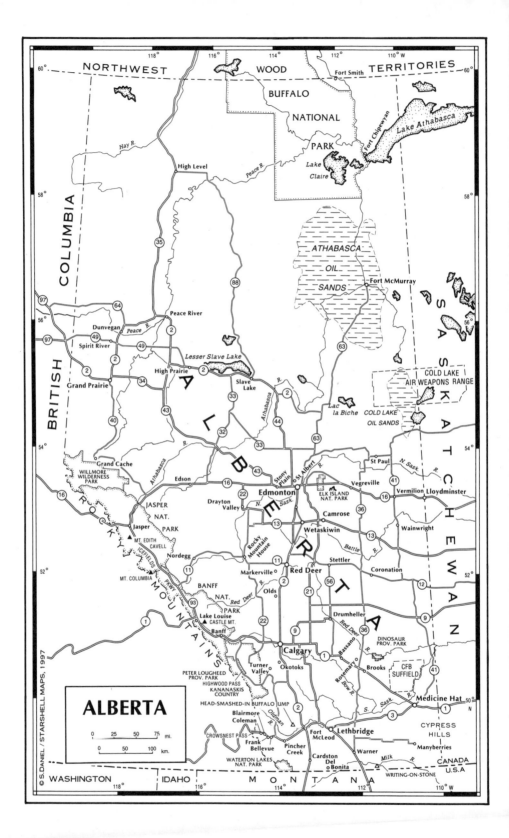

Agriculture

Alberta has one of the world's most productive agricultural economies, producing about 24 percent of Canada's annual output. Approximately 11 million hectares of land are currently under cultivation and a further 8.4 million hectares of uncultivated land are used as pasture and forage for livestock.

Wheat remains Alberta's primary crop and the province maintains the largest livestock population in Canada, primarily beef, cattle, and hogs.

There are more than 57,000 farms and ranches in Alberta, directly employing 96,000 Albertans. Products raised on these farms sell for about $5.85 billion annually. The agri-food sector, consisting primarily of those working directly on farms and ranches plus those in food and beverage manufacturing industries, tallies about 113,500. This sector is the province's third largest employer, trailing only retail trade at 183,000 and health and social services at 129,000.

The agri-food sector comprises 8.3 percent of the provincial **labour force.** Compared to 1994, 16,400 new agricultural jobs were created in 1995, which was the largest gain among all Alberta's major industries. This trend of growth continues. Not surprisingly, given the economic health of this sector, it has the province's lowest unemployment rates, averaging only about 1.5 percent annually.

The number of people working directly in the agri-food sector constitutes merely a thin foundation upon which stands a huge provincial agri-industry that renders the agricultural sector Alberta's major employer. The provincial government estimates that one in three Albertans is either directly employed in agricultural industries or involved in services and activities such as food and beverage processing. Within this sector people engage in wholesaling, packaging, retailing, and transporting farm products, agriculture equipment, and supplies. Others work in agriculture-related fields of communications, professional services, food services, and restaurants.

Alberta's agricultural **economy** is export-oriented, annually exporting about 64 percent of its agricultural commodities to 138 countries. Primary and secondary agricultural exports average about $4.2 billion a year.

The province's top five agricultural commodities are usually as follows: cattle and calves at about $2.2 billion, wheat at $1.1 billion, canola at $690 million, hogs at $390 million, and barley at $330 million. Altogether, livestock and meat products contribute the largest proportion to provincial farm sales, about $3.1 billion annually.

Not all agricultural products are used exclusively as food. Canola, for example, is used in inks, cosmetics, creams and lotions, anti-dandruff shampoos, lubricants, fabric softeners, candles, resins, and drugs used to help fight infections and Acquired Immune Deficiency Syndrome (AIDS). A transgenic canola produces a protein used to treat heart and stroke patients.

Livestock are used just as diversely. More than 100 different medicines used by humans come from cattle. Insulin is one example; it takes the pancreas from 26 cattle to provide a diabetic's yearly supply. Products such as insulation, tennis balls, marshmallows, toothbrushes, bone china, floor wax, emery boards, and numerous surgical supplies are all made from various parts of sheep.

As is true throughout North America's agricultural areas, past agricultural practices have caused many problems in Alberta. Overtilling, cutting of trees and resultant elimination of shelterbelts, draining of marshes and swamps, and damming and diversion of rivers for irrigation purposes have all caused extensive environmental damage in the province and often reduced agricultural land productivity.

Heavy investment in irrigation projects throughout southern Alberta has transformed about 500,000 hectares of dry land into highly productive agricultural land, but the environmental impact from the drawdown of natural rivers and streams has been extreme. **Fish** stocks, natural vegetation and wildlife habitat, and in some cases supplies of potable **water** for communities have all suffered from the development of these irrigation projects.

The agricultural industry, however, has made great gains in protecting the environment in other ways. A technique known as zero tillage, which avoids breaking up the soil for seeding, reduces wind and water erosion of nutrient-rich soil. Leaving stubble from a harvested crop on the fields traps snow and keeps the soil moist. Both the presence of stubble and the zero tillage technique help support wildlife, especially **birds** that nest in the fields. Shelterbelts created by planting rows of trees also help protect soil from wind and water erosion and serve as wildlife habitat. As part of a shelterbelt creation program, Albertan farmers have planted over 17,000 kilometres of new shelterbelts.

Despite these efforts at soil and habitat conservation, the provincial government estimates that about 0.5 percent of wetlands are filled or drained annually for agricultural reasons with adverse effects on the 20 percent of North America's wildfowl population that uses Alberta wetlands. Other wildlife are also adversely affected by wetland loss. Since 1900 more than 65 percent of Alberta's wetland found in settled areas has disappeared; 70 percent of this was lost due to agricultural development.

Alberta's farmers and ranchers are themselves threatened by the on-going expansion of the province's urban centres. Between 1976 and 1990 64,500 hectares of prime agricultural land were paved and covered by urban building. No legislation exists in Alberta to protect farmland from nonagricultural use. The trend of urban expansion continues, with little attention or concern being given to the issue by provincial or municipal governments. (*See also* **Ranching.**)

Air Travel

Alberta has three major airports numbering among the ten largest in Canada. The largest in Alberta is **Calgary** International Airport, which provides weekly direct service to about 20 Canadian destinations, a dozen U.S. cities, and 4 overseas destinations.

Edmonton International Airport provides weekly nonstop service to a half-dozen Canadian destinations, about ten American cities, and several other international destinations. Its sister airport—Edmonton Municipal—provides weekly nonstop links to many destinations in Alberta, Saskatchewan, and British Columbia.

All told more than 2,700 domestic, 200 transborder, and 18 nonstop overseas flights pass through these airports each week.

The two national Canadian airlines (Canadian International and Air Canada) service Alberta's three largest airports and these and other smaller airports are also served by several regional airlines. Canadian, Air Canada, and five U.S. airlines provide flights from Alberta across the U.S. border. One international carrier, along with the two major Canadian airlines, provide links to overseas destinations.

Altogether, Alberta is served by 83 licensed airports, 28 heliports, 8 seaplane bases, and more than 800 unlicensed airports. Almost 80 percent of Alberta's population lives within 100 kilometres of licensed air service.

Alberta's Name

The province of Alberta was named after Princess Louise Caroline Alberta, the fourth daughter of Queen Victoria and the wife of the Marquis of Lorne, Governor General of Canada from 1878 to 1883.

In 1882, Alberta was declared an additional provisional district of the North-West Territories. At that time its borders included only that part of the province south of 55° north latitude and west of 111° west longitude.

The Canadian federal government recognized the province's name by order-in-council on May 8, 1882. Its name arose from a conundrum that the government was unable to solve. The first three districts had been named years earlier after a significant river running through the relevant region (Saskatchewan and Athabasca) or, in the case of Assiniboia, after the **First Nations peoples** living within its boundaries. But this new district extended from **Edmonton** on the North Saskatchewan River to **Fort Macleod** on the Oldman River in the south. Neither river name seemed appropriate and a number of First Nations called the region home.

The previous year, however, during a visit to Canada's west by the Governor General and his wife, the Marquis had proposed naming a Canadian province after his wife, but no new provinces had been in the offing. With the sudden opening for a name of distinction the government accepted with relief the Governor General's proposition. As a Louisiana and two Carolina states already existed in the United States it seemed pertinent to choose Princess Louise's third name—Alberta.

The Marquis was so moved by this recognition of his wife he penned a sonnet, entitled "On The New Province of Alberta."

> In token of the love which thou has shown
> For this wide land of freedom, I have named
> A province vast and for its beauty famed,
> By thy dear name to be hereafter known.
> Alberta shall it be. Her fountains thrown
> From Alps unto three oceans, to all men
> Shall vaunt her loveliness e'en now: and when
> Each little hamlet to a city grown,
> And numberless as blades of prairie grass
> Or the thick leaves in distant forest bower
> Great peoples hear the giant currents pass,
> Still shall the waters, bringing wealth and power
> Speak the loved name—the land of silver springs
> Worthy the daughter of our English kings.

Although there is disagreement over whom **Lake Louise** is named after, one account maintains it too was named in honour of the Marquis's wife.

Alberta Special Waste Treatment Centre

The community of Swan Hills, about 200 kilometres northwest of **Edmonton,** is home to the only hazardous and toxic waste treatment plant in Canada. The Alberta Special Waste Treatment Centre was established in 1987 as a joint venture between the provincial government and a private company specializing in toxic waste disposal. Its mandate was simple: treat all Alberta's hazardous waste, except for radioactive waste and explosives, no matter what treatment process was needed and no matter what volumes of waste required treatment.

Initially the plant could treat about 18,000 tonnes of waste a year. In 1990, the government authorized an $80 million expansion. When the expansion was completed in 1993, the plant was capable of annually processing about 55,000 tonnes of waste.

At the plant's core are two massive incinerators which treat organic waste, such as solvents, paints, pesticides, and polychlorinated biphenyls (PCBs). These incinerators can produce temperatures up to 1,200° Celsius. A patented transformer furnace treats contaminated transformers. This furnace is able to bake an intact transformer weighing up to six tonnes by heating it to the point that the PCBs are driven off the metal. The process enables the PCB-clean metal to be recycled as a clean, uncontaminated substance.

Additional facilities include a chemical plant capable of neutralizing acids and bases. A stabilization plant immobilizes solid inorganic compounds, such as heavy metals, by chemically and physically binding the waste with such materials as Portland cement and flyash.

All waste produced by the plant must be rendered environmentally safe. To achieve this the plant's waste residues are treated to the same procedure meted out to the original waste. Liquid waste is then injected into a 2,000-metre-deep storage well, while solid waste goes into landfill cells designed for hazardous waste containment. By this time, the waste is no longer classified as hazardous, but the process ensures another safety stop.

The plant's existence has enabled Alberta to eliminate all its stockpiles of PCBs, a toxic substance now banned, but for many decades contained in many types of electrical equipment and consumer products, such as refrigerators. PCBs are bioaccumulative, meaning they will not break down in the environment and become concentrated in species high up the food chain, such as bald eagles and humans.

Since its inception in 1983 the plant has caused controversy in Alberta. Many environmental groups and **First Nations peoples** from the Swan Hills area fear its operation is slowly polluting the surrounding black spruce and pine forests and pristine streams. They also fear that toxic wastes en route to the plant along the province's designated dangerous goods routes from within Alberta and from other provinces will be spilled, causing an environmental disaster.

The plant has also been criticized as an expensive, taxpayer-subsidized boondoggle. To break even it needs to treat 40,000 tonnes of waste annually, but in most years of operation it has never managed to operate at more than half its capacity. This is due to a shortage of toxic waste to treat and the fact that many companies in Alberta opt to export their toxic and hazardous waste to cheaper treatment plants in the United States.

Alberta's Toxics Watch, an environmental group, estimates that customers pay $1,450 to burn a tonne of waste at Swan Hills, but that the real cost for this process is $4,800, leaving a shortfall of $3,350.

A unique agreement between the provincial government and Bovar Inc., which operates the plant, provided the company with $141 million in loan guarantees and assured it of realizing an annual profit equivalent to the prime interest rate plus 3 percent on all capital investment for every year the plant stayed open. Consequently, whether the plant loses or makes money the company's return on investment is guaranteed, which critics say gives the plant management no incentive to operate cost-effectively.

Alberta Temple

In 1887, a group of Mormon settlers fleeing U.S. anti-polygamy laws arrived in the North-West Territories district of Alberta and founded the community of Cardston, some 25 kilometres north of the U.S. border. The name referred to the group's leader, Charles Ora Card. The community became the focal point for a substantial migration of Mormon settlers across the border into the western part of southern Alberta.

Bearing a profound and deliberate resemblance to the Mayan-Aztec temples of Central and South America, the Alberta Temple dominates Cardston's skyline. (Mark Zuehlke photo)

Three years after the first Mormons arrived in Canada, the Church of Jesus Christ of Latter-Day Saints banned polygamy and future migration of Mormons into Alberta was motivated primarily by economic considerations. The major draws were the availability of abundant agricultural land, good irrigation possibilities, accessible coal and timber, and proximity to the Blood Indian reserve, which Card and other Mormons thought ripe for missionary work.

Soon the population of Mormons in Alberta was sufficient to justify constructing in Cardston the first temple outside the United States. The temple was to be no modest structure, but rather one as significant as any of its kind erected anywhere by the church.

Its architects, Hyrum Pope and Harold Burton of Salt Lake City, were greatly influenced by Frank Lloyd Wright, who advocated a form of "organic architecture." Accordingly, Pope and Burton's 1912 design entailed a geometric composition of white granite blocks that blended ancient and modern themes. The result was a massive structure reminiscent of Mayan-Aztec temples, but softened by the Prairie School of Architecture's emphasis on clean lines and the use of natural materials, such as the uniformly cream-coloured granite blocks selected for the temple's construction.

Completed in 1923, the temple became Cardston's centrepiece. The special rooms inside reserved for sacred ceremonies were richly embellished with woodwork, murals, and fine furnishings.

By 1991, the building was deteriorating alarmingly. A major restoration project, conducted with meticulous care and an eye for original detail, was undertaken and the temple restored to its former grandeur. It is now designated a national monument, recognizing the Mormon contribution to Canada and the pre-eminent position the temple plays in Mormon religious life.

American Pronghorn. *See* **Pronghorns.**

Amphibians

There are about 4,250 amphibian species in the world. Forty are native to Canada, but only ten of these are known to live in Alberta. Another species—the tailed frog—may occur in suitable lake habitats of **Waterton Lakes National Park** and along Castle River, but its presence is unconfirmed.

Three of Alberta's amphibians number among the seventeen species on the province's red list for threatened species—those considered either no longer viable or at immediate risk of declining to nonviable levels in the province. The great plains toad, long-toed salamander, and **northern leop-ard frog** are red-listed.

The plains spadefoot toad and spotted frog appear on the province's blue list, which means they are believed to be vulnerable but not in immediate jeopardy.

Amphibian species, especially toads and frogs, are noted to be in decline throughout the world. Scientists are unsure why. It may involve unusual local conditions, such as drought, frost, disease, acid rain, and loss of habitat combining with worldwide changes caused by global warming, higher ultraviolet radiation levels, and increased contamination of air, soil, and **water.** Loss of habitat is definitely a factor in Alberta, with clearcut logging in subalpine areas and draining or other changes to wetland areas the primary causes of amphibian habitat loss.

Besides the five amphibians listed as endangered, Alberta is home to the tiger salamander, western toad, Canadian toad, striped chorus frog, and wood frog.

The long-toed salamander occurs in Alberta in subalpine and alpine areas of the **Rocky Mountains.** It favours the undersides of rocks, rotting logs, and other debris near ponds, lakes, and sometimes streams. This species is rarely seen, except in April and May when adults migrate to breeding sites and in September when juveniles leave the nests for hibernation sites. The long-toed salamander feeds on small **invertebrates.**

The tiger salamander is found in short-grass **prairie, aspen parklands, boreal forest,** and subalpine habitats. It is common throughout the province south of **Edmonton,** with an isolated group known near **Grande Prairie.** Tiger salamanders can survive in very dry conditions, but usually live near small lakes, ponds, or dugouts. A large amphibian species with average total length of 14 to 18 centimetres, the tiger salamander feeds on insects, mites, earthworms, molluscs, and small vertebrate species. It is primarily nocturnal.

Distribution of the plains spadefoot toad is confined to a region extending from the U.S. border to a northern line running from the Red Deer River country to the lower **foothills** of Pincher Creek. This toad is rarely seen except during breeding periods, as it commonly buries itself in sand to depths of almost one metre alongside small bodies of water. It feeds mostly at night on moths, ants, and beetles.

In Alberta, the favoured diet of the western toad is beetles and ants, although it will eat other insects and spiders. The western toad inflates itself with air and stands high on all four limbs when threatened. If the inflating display fails, it will urinate on an attacker. The western toad's preferred habitat is ponds, streams, rivers, and lakes up to the 3,000-metre level in the Rockies. It lives along the foothills in the south, and also spreads east across most of the province in the boreal forest region. Naturalists are unsure if western toads live north of **Lesser Slave Lake,** but believe it likely.

The great plains toad frequents irrigation canals, river flood plains, temporary rain pools, and dugouts. It eats moths, flies, and beetles. The species is limited to the extreme southeast of the Red Deer River on a front bordered to the west by Brooks, Vauxhall, and Taber, as well as the South Saskatchewan River and its tributaries.

It is believed that Canadian toad populations in Alberta have declined by more than 50 percent since the beginning of the 1990s. The Canadian toad's Alberta range is north and east of the Bow River to the Northwest Territories, limiting it to the province's eastern half.

The striped chorus frog is widely scattered throughout southern Alberta, except in the foothills and Rockies. Isolated populations also live in parts of northern Alberta. While it will inhabit any body of water, the striped chorus frog favours grassy pools, lakes, and marshes. It eats ground-dwelling insects, snails, and other small invertebrates.

Northern leopard frog populations once thrived throughout southern Alberta below **Red Deer** except for the foothills and Rocky Mountains. They are now confined to several small pockets.

The spotted frog is highly aquatic and usually prefers permanent lakes, streams, and ponds in the subalpine foothills and Rocky Mountain areas of southern Alberta. The species is not found below altitudes of 2,000 metres. It feeds on worms, insects, and molluscs.

One of Alberta's ten confirmed amphibians, the western toad is known to defend itself by urinating on attackers. (Frances Backhouse photo)

Except for the short-grass prairie of the extreme southern part of Alberta, the wood frog lives throughout the province. It favours wooded areas and ponds. The wood frog lives up to the 2,500-metre level and hibernates on land by burying itself under humus and plant litter. It is the only amphibian capable of surviving north of the Arctic Circle.

Ancient Alberta

With its towering mountains, extensive northern forests, and wide expanses of **prairie** in the central and southern regions, Alberta seems a new land. It has, however, undergone phenomenal change in the 4.5-billion-year history of the earth. Over millennia, the landscape of Alberta has experienced and been shaped by immense floods, the intrusion of vast oceans, bombardments by asteroids and meteorites, volcanic eruptions, and the scouring of great glacial ice sheets. During this time a remarkable diversity of plant and animal life has existed here.

Alberta's oldest surface rock is 2.8 billion years old. It lies near Slave River in the province's northeastern corner. This igneous rock is part of the **Canadian Shield.** About 1.7 billion years ago, what is now Alberta was part of a supercontinent lying along the equator. This continent began breaking up and massive continental-sized chunks were set adrift on the ocean. Alberta's western border formed a waterfront flank of a new continent. Scientists believe that what is now Antarctica and Australia lay just across a narrow chasm of ocean from Alberta. Present-day **Calgary** was 240 kilometres inland, part of a great expanse of blowing sand. The continents continued to drift apart. Over 400 million years, water and wind piled layers of sediment along the coastline, creating an 11-kilometre-thick layered cake of sandstone, slate, shale, volcanic rock, and limestone. Evidence of this can be seen today at **Waterton Lakes National Park.**

Throughout the Proterozoic Era, which lasted until 590 million years ago, Alberta's temperatures were tropical but the landscape was barren. Huge rivers, as wide as the Athabasca River today, poured into the great ocean. The first life in Alberta—primitive proalgae—developed in shallow pools along the coastline. Although these were small microbes, they stacked one atop the other by the billions to create ten-metre-high cabbage-shaped colonies called stromatolites. Meanwhile, other primitive life forms were developing, absorbing, and drawing life from the world's increasing oxygen supply.

From these developed a form of life—the eukaryotic cell—from which all of today's life forms developed. Unlike previous bacterial life, which survived through photosynthesis, the eukaryotes fed on other life—either as parasites or predators.

Between 1.2 billion and 760 million years ago a new wave of continental fragmentation and drift occurred. Antarctica and Australia drifted far away and the Pacific Ocean was born. Alberta formed the shoreline of a clearly defined continent—North America. Massive rivers still laced Alberta's landscape, dumping huge quantities of silt and sand into deltas at their mouths. Various life forms lived in the water or along the shorelines—jellyfish-like or worm-shaped creatures and a form of fern.

The continent slowly drifted northward from the equator. Just as slowly, Alberta was being eroded by relentless winds and its great rivers. The land was flattening and this opened it to invasion by the ocean. Over 180 million years, covering the Cambrian and early Ordovician periods, the sea advanced and retreated from Alberta and most of North America more than ten times. Alberta was often completely underwater. Eventually North America's northern flank collided with another continent. Like two cars crashing head-on both continents crumpled back upon themselves. This lifting of land caused the ocean to spill off western Canada and for about 20 million years the land was dry. Even when the ocean covered the land, however, its waters were unlike those of the deep Pacific Ocean pushing against the lesser ocean's western edge. Depths were shallow, temperatures warm, allowing these waters to serve as an incubation tank for the creation of life.

About 570 million years ago the coast of Alberta witnessed what scientists call "the Cambrian explosion." Along the coastline, where the inland ocean met the Pacific, vast reefs formed. Darting in and around these reefs was an ever-growing and diversifying array of creatures. Some were soft-bodied and vulnerable, most developed an armoured mix of shells, claws, shields, and lancelike spines as weapons and protection. Some forms of these creatures survive today. Brachiopods, which look like clams and have calcite shells, still live in the oceans. More than 100,000 species of molluscs, including snails, slugs, mussels, oysters, and octopuses, emerged. So, too, did some arthropods, which today constitute 80 percent of all visible life. These have horny external coverings and jointed legs. Crabs, lobsters, spiders, beetles, and ants are arthropods. Another life form dating to the Cambrian explosion was chordates. These possessed segmented muscles, a tail fin, and a flexible backbone. **Fish, amphibians, reptiles,** and **mammals** (including humans) are chordates. While many forms of life that emerged during the Cambrian explosion survive today, a greater number became extinct.

Eventually marine plants crept from the edge of the oceans onto the more hostile beachfront. The oldest known vascular land plant **fossils** date to 415 million years ago. This plant had neither leaves nor roots. It consisted of simple stalks ending in spore-filled sacs and stood only a few centimetres tall. Meanwhile, the seas covering most of North America continued retreating as the continent was warped and uplifted by further collisions with other land masses.

The Devonian Period, dating from 410 million years to about 360 million years ago, saw Alberta sluiced repeatedly by ocean advances and retreats. With each retreat, large saltwater pools, bigger than Utah's Great Salt Lake, were trapped in basins. Alberta's Devonian climate was as arid as the modern-day Sahara. The stranded salt pools evaporated and left salt pans in their wake. By the Devonian Period's end, Alberta was once again submerged. Crisscrossing the landscape, however, was a spider's web of reefs created by the ocean's rise and fall over 50 million years.

Throughout this period, North America continued to drift northward. Finally Alberta reached about 20° north of the equator and this brought cooler weather to the land, leading to the slow death of the area's reefs. As the Devonian gave way to the Carboniferous Period, land-based plants developed roots and leaves. Swamps, forests, and shrubby plains added **biodiversity.** Insects and amphibians evolved that were no longer dependent on watery environments. Over the next 100 million years thousands upon thousands of species evolved and thrived across the globe. But about 250 million years ago a sudden, still unexplained catastrophe occurred and 95 percent of all these species became extinct. Was earth struck by a massive asteroid? Did some global disaster render earth's atmosphere unbreathable? Scientists remain unsure.

Life is persistent and from the fragment of survivors new species evolved and thrived during the Triassic Period, lasting until about 210 million years ago. During this period reptiles, which evolved on land, developed the ability to live in the oceans. Along Alberta's coastline these fierce marine reptiles lived and died. Some were equally comfortable in the ocean or foraging along the seashore. Small mammals also appeared in the Triassic, offering a good source of food for the larger, more predatory reptiles.

The Triassic ended abruptly when a shower of asteroids bombarded the planet. Many species became extinct. Mammals survived but remained small despite the fact that most of the more predacious reptiles of this period disappeared. Dinosaurs and crocodiles, both formerly relatively small species, rushed to fill the void. For the next 145 million years, dinosaurs ruled.

During this period Alberta was hot and dry. By the middle Jurassic a wetter global climate led to development of forests and swamps along Alberta's coast. North America also reached its current latitude. Southern Alberta, Saskatchewan, and Manitoba lay beneath a warm sea the size of today's Gulf of Mexico. Drifting in from the west to collide with Alberta's coastline, however, were volcanic island arcs. Over millions of years these volcanic islands pressed against the coast, creating immense pressure and pushing up from the ancient sea floor rock layers that were tens of millions of years old. Molten magma escaping from cracks in the earth's crust flowed toward the surface and was transformed into great underground layers of solid granite. As increasing numbers of volcanic island arcs piled up against North America's western shore, British Columbia was born and Alberta ceased to have a coastline. The Pacific Ocean retreated completely from Alberta by the late Jurassic Period, about 140 million years ago.

What had been Alberta's coastline was a land of warm swamps contained in a basin created by the uplifting and folding of the volcanic islands pressing against its western flank. During the final phase of its retreat from Alberta, the last traces of the Pacific Ocean flowed north along this long, narrow basin which extended from northern British Columbia to Montana. Into this basin was deposited sand, silt, mud, and other sediments, which would eventually form huge coal deposits.

With the dawn of the Cretaceous Period 130 million years ago, a process involving the collision of five island arcs with North America's west coast began. Each collision took ten million years to play out and was followed by a calm of several million more years. With each collision massive layers of rock were thrust further eastward. British Columbia widened. Volcanoes spewed ash and lava across the newly formed land mass. The immense forces playing out to the west pushed the Alberta basin eastward from the present-day **foothills** deep into Saskatchewan. With each collision the basin buckled further, eventually becoming lower than the Arctic Sea, which immediately gushed in from the north. The Arctic Sea linked with a sea flowing in from the south to split the North American continent in half for the next 35 million years.

On Alberta's western flank, new mountains were being uplifted from the earth's surface. As these rose, they sloughed great amounts of mud and other debris off their eastern slopes into the basin. Over 50 million years the basin was filled with layer upon layer of sediments which eventually reached a depth of more than three kilometres.

The sea covering parts of Alberta was probably only about 300 metres deep and sustained temperatures ranging between 15° and 25° Celsius. This seaway caused a moist subtropical climate to prevail over Alberta. Magnolias, figs, and other broad-leaved trees grew along its shores. Sediment off the western mountains continued to flow into it, creating a rich gumbo of mud, shale, and volcanic ash. In the **Crowsnest Pass** region volcanoes erupted, spreading ash over the area. Over the course of millions of years the seaway rose and fell many times, creating layer upon layer of geological formations that give present-day Alberta much of its shape and geological texture.

About 100 million years ago a land bridge surfaced between North America and Asia. This bridge would eventually be used by prehistoric **First Nations peoples** migrating from Asia, but during the Cretaceous Period it provided a means for dinosaurs in North America and Asia to roam freely back and forth.

By the middle Cretaceous, flowering plants dominated Alberta's landscape. Toward the end of the Cretaceous Period a relatively modern, deep forest landscape was evolving in Alberta. With the rise and fall of the sea, peat swamps were created throughout the province, which would eventually develop into coal beds.

Seventy-four to seventy-two million years ago, the sea advanced one last time across southern Alberta. This sea is known today as the Bearpaw Sea, after the Bearpaw Mountains in Montana. Forests and swamps were covered. The land between present-day **Medicine Hat** and **Lethbridge** was transformed into a large shallow bay, interspersed with wetlands.

When the Bearpaw Sea began retreating, swamps, coastal deltas, and river plains advanced. The region thrived with land-based dinosaur life.

Sixty-seven million years ago, the climate began to dry and cool. Alberta's climate became similar to that of modern New Mexico. The dinosaur population experienced a sudden decline. About 65 million years ago a catastrophe—probably resulting from asteroid strikes—led to the extinction of dinosaurs and many other species. Crocodiles, birds, reptiles, insects, and fish survived, as did mammals.

It was during the early Tertiary Period, beginning with the extinction of dinosaurs 65 million years ago, that the **Rocky Mountains** developed. Far to the west, off the shore of Vancouver Island, the Pacific oceanic plate bumped into western North America and eventually broke in two. One part ground its way up the coast of British Columbia before sinking into the Alaska Sea. Over 30 million years this northward-drifting plate caused great folding and lifting, with the result that new mountains rose and moved eastward into Alberta. The Alberta mountain string formed part of a long cordillera running the length of North America. The Rocky Mountains were born.

Between 65 and 55 million years ago Alberta was a land of bush and forest. Rivers, lakes, marshes, and swamps added to its lushness. Temperatures ranged from 20° to 25° Celsius and it often rained. No longer easy prey for dinosaurs, mammals were thriving and diversifying.

About 40 million years ago the Bearpaw Sea drained out of Alberta. Sediment washed off the Rockies and covered the emerging plains.

Fourteen million years ago grasses appeared in Alberta and soon dominated the plains. The forests gave way because the earth was cooling, but it took until only two million years ago for the first ice sheets to cover most of North America and Europe. The grinding erosive force of these great sheets of ice transformed most of Canada. The greatest ice sheet to cover Canada is known as the Laurentide. Originating in Hudson Bay, it eventually covered 13 million square kilometres. About 15,000 to 12,000 years ago the Laurentide melted, swamping Alberta with lakes and ice. Eventually, when the waters dried, Alberta passed from tundra to forest, and only slowly back to grassy plains.

Between 20,000 and 9,000 years ago prehistoric First Nations peoples came from Asia south from Alaska along an ice-free corridor into Alberta. At the same time a major extinction eliminated many massive carnivores and hooved mammals that had populated the plains. Woolly mammoths, giant black-bear-sized beavers, sabre-toothed cats, horses, and enormous **bison** all disappeared. Approximately 40 species of giant mammals are believed to have become extinct. The cause of this extinction remains controversial among scientists, but whatever its cause it opened the plains for humans and for the mid-sized mammals—bison, elk, caribou, and deer.

Antelope. *See* **Pronghorns.**

Archaeology

There are about 17,000 known archaeological sites scattered throughout Alberta, but it is believed there may be more than one million sites that remain undiscovered.

To date, archaeological evidence unearthed at these sites indicates the presence of human life in Alberta no earlier than about 20,000 years ago. Primitive stone tools prised from the walls of the Bow River valley at a site in the heart of **Calgary** were embedded in glacial till, left behind by the retreating ice of the last glaciation period approximately 23,000 years ago.

The ice finally withdrew from most of Alberta about 12,000 years ago and archaeological evidence indicates that prehistoric peoples did not establish a significant presence in the province until 15,000 years ago—apparently following the melting ice sheets northward.

The people occupying prehistoric Alberta were hunters and gatherers, who moved their camps up to 50 times a year in quest of new food sources. This way of life made it impossible to construct villages or establish large graveyards in which to bury their dead. For this reason Alberta's archaeological sites are many but they reflect, in the sparseness of artifacts unearthed, the lightness with which the prehistoric peoples lived upon this land.

Most of the archaeological evidence found in Alberta is contained in samples of their tools and the bones of animals they killed. Ceramic artifacts are also often unearthed at the province's archaeological sites, especially in the plains areas. It is from these three broad categories that archaeologists reproduce a sense of prehistoric life in this region.

Prehistoric people made tools out of stone, bones, and antlers. Stones were shaped into tools suitable for cutting meat or hides, finishing an arrow shaft, or helping to shape more complex tools, such as the projectile points that tipped spears, darts, and arrows. The most commonly used materials in Alberta were chert and quartzite stones or pebbles found alongside river beds. Obsidian and chalcedony tools have also been discovered in Alberta but these materials must have been acquired through trading with people as far away as Manitoba and Wyoming.

To make a tool from a piece of chert or quartzite, prehistoric artisans used a technique called percussion flaking to chip flakes off the core. By striking the stone with a stone hammer, large flakes could be broken off. The flakes removed were very sharp and could be used without further modification.

For constructing more elaborate tools, such as arrowheads and spear points, additional shaping and thinning were required. To make a spear point, a larger flake would be selected and shaped by using a stone or antler hammer to strike off several wide, thin flakes. Once the approximate shape had been achieved, a technique called pressure flaking was used to finish the stone. Small, thin flakes were pushed off the edges of the tool with an antler or bone punch—a method that required both great skill and physical strength to produce clean, even edges on all sides.

Moose, elk, and caribou antlers, as well as the leg bones from these animals and **bison,** provided many prehistoric tools, ranging from simple scraping devices to elaborate barbed harpoon points. A leg bone split into a number of pieces yielded a variety of sharp, functional tools. Smaller fragments could be transformed into awls by sharpening one end or using a stone flake to whittle the bone into the desired shape. Bone weapons and fleshers and beamers used for tanning required a finer touch to render the barbs, points, and shafts sufficiently smooth for their intended purpose. These tools would also be polished into a final, precise shape and given a high gloss with a fine-grained grinding stone. Occasionally, these implements were decorated with finely incised lines cut with stone tools.

Most prehistoric peoples of Alberta did not begin using pottery until about 1,500 years ago. Little pottery outside the southern part of the province has been discovered by archaeologists, which suggests it was primarily used by the plains people. Clay taken from the margins of streams and rivers was mixed with a small amount of finely crushed granite to render the clay more easily worked and less likely to crack during the drying process. It was then hand-moulded and set aside to air dry to a leathery consistency. At this stage the pot was often decorated, sometimes by pressing a stick wrapped with cord into the soft clay. Once the pot was completely dry it was fired in a campfire. The finished vessels, coloured buff to black, were used mainly for cooking and storage. Few of these pots have survived, but shards of the pottery are used by archaeologists to establish age and cultural relationships of sites.

Other artifacts found in Alberta sites consist of complex arrangements of stones into cairns, what appear to be ceremonial sites, tipi rings, various complexes of **pictographs and petroglyphs,** and the mysterious **medicine wheels**—the purposes of which remain unexplained to this day.

The Alberta Historical Resources Act protects archaeological sites, providing for fines of up to $50,000 and maximum imprisonment of one year for anyone found willfully destroying archaeological sites. In the past, such sites as the Writing-On-Stone petroglyphs in southern Alberta suffered extreme defacement and damage by vandals, but since the act was proclaimed in 1973 there have been fewer problems of this kind.

Archaeological sites that are readily accessible to the public include **Writing-On-Stone Provincial Park, Head-Smashed-In-Buffalo Jump,** and the Strathcona Archaeological Centre in **Edmonton.** This latter facility provides an opportunity to openly view, and even participate in, archaeological work undertaken at a 5,000-year-old prehistoric site.

(*See also* **First Nations Peoples; Tipis.**)

Athabasca Oil Sands

In 1787, Alexander Mackenzie reached a point about 39 kilometres from the junction of the Clearwater and Athabasca rivers. He noted here the presence of "some bituminous fountains, into which a pole of 20 feet [6 metres] long may be inserted without the least resistance. The bitumen is in a fluid state, and when mixed with gum, or the resinous substance collected from the spruce fir, serves to gum the canoes. In its heated state it emits a smell like that of sea-coal."

The sands of the Athabasca Oil Sands (sometimes called the McMurray Sands or the Athabasca Tar Sands) were formed when the Arctic Ocean pressed inland across present-day Northwest Territories about 120 million years ago. As rivers flowed out of Alberta into the expanded ocean, they shed sediment that formed a massive sandy shoreline. When the ocean withdrew, the sand remained.

How the vast reserves of oil came to be locked into this sand remains unclear. There are probably two causes. First the rivers flowing north across Alberta to the greatly advanced Arctic Ocean must have breached many Palaeozoic Era coral-reef oil pools and pulled the released oil along with them to the Arctic Ocean shoreline's loose sand. More importantly, however, oil was also created by the dropping of literally trillions of minute plants pushed down into the mud that blanketed the sands as the ocean pressed further southward. Millions of years later, this vast rotting mess lying in the mud was squeezed clean of its oil by earth pressure. Once released, the oil seeped into the sand below.

The first attempt to extract oil from the sands was undertaken by J. K. "Peace River Jim" Cornwall in 1905, the same year Alberta became a province. By 1909 he and other oil explorers reported striking oil in the area and Cornwall started subdividing the river flats at **Fort McMurray** to create a modern town. He tried to attract the attention of **Edmonton** commercial interests by dragging a large batch of the sticky sand to the city and using it to pave a sidewalk along a section of Jasper Avenue. It soon became clear, however, that the oil in the sands could not be tapped with conventional drilling techniques. There were no large pools or wells of oil under the surface; instead the oil saturated the sand. Nobody knew how to separate the sand from the oil.

By the late 1920s, the Alberta Research Council's main oil sands researcher, Karl Clark, discovered a technique of water flotation extraction. Oil-bearing sand was mixed with hot water, which forced the bitumen tar to the surface for skimming off. Refined further, the substance could be turned into usable oil. This led in the 1930s to the establishment of a commercial venture, Abasand Oils, which produced synthetic crude oil from 1940 to 1941 to meet increased wartime demand for petroleum products. The plant burned, but was rebuilt and taken over by the federal government in 1943. When it burned a second time in 1945, the federal government— now seeing the wartime demand decreasing—abandoned the operation. Angered by this loss of interest, the Alberta government built a new plant and continued experiments from 1946 to 1949. But the cost of extraction remained too costly compared to world oil prices, so the project languished.

Not until world oil prices began to rise in the early 1960s did extensive extraction of synthetic crude oil from the huge reserves (at the time estimated at 625 billion barrels) become economically feasible. In 1964, the Great Canadian Oil Sands project opened. By 1973, federal and provincial governments and several oil giants had joined forces to create the Syncrude project. Meanwhile, Suncor Inc. had taken over Great Canadian in 1967 and expanded that facility.

Syncrude became the world's largest producer of synthetic crude oil. The massive project also includes a world-scale ore processing and refining plant. Vast open-pit oil mines use immense draglines with booms the length of a football field and bucketwheels for excavation. The draglines are the largest land-bound machinery in the world. The buckets are bigger than a two-car garage. From the open-pit mine the vast machines drop sand onto an enormous conveyor belt for transportation to the processing plant. The plant, which opened in 1978, cost $2.3 billion to build.

In an advancement of the process discovered in the 1920s by Karl Clark, the oil is extracted from the sand by using hot water and steam to force the bitumen to the surface where it can be skimmed off. It is then diluted with naphtha to make it flow more easily and heated to 500° Celsius to produce vapours. When cooled, these vapours condense. The sulphur and gases drawn off are all utilized commercially, but the process is focused on releasing and purifying the liquid oil. The blended oil liquids are injected with an increased hydrogen content to lighten the oil, improving its quality and ensuring it can be piped more easily to distribution points south of Fort McMurray.

Current estimates are that about one trillion barrels of bitumen remain in the vast 31,000-square-kilometre oil sands. This is more oil than exists in all the Middle East's known reserves.

Badlands

Most of Alberta's starkly beautiful badlands were cut into their remarkable shapes during the vast melt resulting from the withdrawal of glaciers from the province some 14,000 years ago. Massive rivers emanating from the melt dug deeply into the soft terrain where the badlands are today located.

The Alberta badlands have a high amount of decayed volcanic ash, or bentonite, in their composition. The bentonite drifted down upon the southern part of Alberta about 80 million years ago after being spewed from volcanoes active in southern British Columbia and the Yellowstone area of Montana and Wyoming. Bentonite seals off rock so moisture can neither get in nor out. Consequently, instead of the rock weathering in normal fashion with little ravines or low slopes, the hills remain steep and the rivulets form flutings.

The erosional forces working on the badlands today are most often heavy rains falling in short-lived torrents that cause flash-flooding down the many ravines, gullies, furrows, small cuts, and minute cracks riddling the badland terrain. Erosion of several millimetres a year is common here. Wind-driven sand helps scour away the surface. This surface erosion is often accompanied by extensive underground fracturing and tunnelling of water through below-ground channels. The undermined surface slopes break away in erratically shaped chunks to create the bizarre-looking **hoodoos** common in many parts of Alberta's badlands.

The badlands of Dinosaur Provincial Park are among the most accessible and extensive examples of this remarkable landscape found in Alberta. (Mark Zuehlke photo)

Alberta's most extensive badland region is the Red Deer Badlands. Their boundary ranges from Atlee, near Steveville, to Nevis in the Stettler district of east-central Alberta. For more than 300 kilometres, these badlands follow the Red Deer River and include the extensive badlands of **Dinosaur Provincial Park.**

The Dinosaur Provincial Park badlands have been principally carved by the Red Deer River. This meandering, muddy stream wound through the badlands to carve out a two-kilometre-wide valley with 120-metre-high walls. The multicoloured layers of various beds through which the river worked were laid down during and since Cretaceous times about 50 to 80 million years ago. Many of the **dinosaurs** now found as **fossils** in the park's soil hunted and foraged here in that era.

Badlands in this park, and most of those elsewhere in southern Alberta, are composed of layers of coal, clay, ironstone, shale, and sandstone. The colour of the layers varies from black through brown to grey and white. Sometimes cliffs are grey-yellow. Often a crust of greyish, spongy bentonite coats layers of underlying rock and soil.

Little vegetation can survive in the poor soil conditions of the water-starved badlands country. But numerous small **mammals,** some lizards, large numbers of **invertebrates,** and many species of **birds** thrive in this harsh landscape.

The name badlands is believed to have derived from the early French explorers and fur traders who were the first Europeans to see these formations and who dubbed them *terres mauvaises* (lands bad). Their English counterparts quickly transposed the two words to create the term badlands.

Banff

Following the discovery in 1883 of the **hot springs** that are today known as **Cave and Basin National Historic Site,** just a few kilometres from the railway station then known as Siding 29, development of the Banff area began. By 1887, the government of Canada had created a bathhouse at the springs and soon other commercial facilities were opened along what is now Banff Avenue to service the influx of tourists coming to enjoy the scenery and to seek the supposed curative powers of the springs. The name Banff derives from Banffshire, the Scottish birthplace of George Stephen, who was the Canadian Pacific Railroad (CPR) president during this early period of development.

In 1888, the CPR opened Banff Springs Hotel, constructed at a cost of about $250,000. At the time this 250-room facility was the largest hotel in the world and rooms started at a nightly rate of $3.50. Other restaurants and less expensive hotels soon followed. Guiding and hunting services were established nearby. By 1900 Banff boasted eight hotels.

From the outset Banff was an unusual community in that it was governed by the Canadian Parks Service in Ottawa. Although this should logically have led to an emphasis on controlled growth, the community became renowned for its haphazard and sometimes unrestrained development. In June 1988, Banff's permanent residents voted to incorporate and sever their links to Parks Canada. The community was formally incorporated in 1990, but Parks Canada retains control over environmental protection matters.

Banff is the largest urban centre in any national park in the world. Its permanent population of about 7,000 people faces some difficult living conditions. Housing demand far surpasses supply, real estate is among the most expensive in Alberta, and every summer day about 50,000 tourists clog the small community's streets and shops. Foreign investment is an issue causing endless debate for which no solution seems evident. More than one-third of Banff's hotel industry, including two of the three largest hotels, are owned by offshore Japanese investors.

The town's commercialism is often criticized by visitors and residents alike but, as both the community and **Banff National Park** were created as commercial endeavours rather than to preserve the environment, it is unlikely the community could have developed in any other manner. Both park officials and the town council, however, face a serious challenge in trying to contain growth so the very environment that draws so many people to the park and town is not overly damaged by the commercialism upon which the community relies for its survival.

In addition to its history as a tourist facility, Banff has an almost equally long history as a centre for the arts. The Banff Centre for the Arts first opened as a summer theatre school in 1933. It has since grown into a multi-faceted independent educational facility. The centre serves as a hub for a host of cultural activities throughout the year. The Banff Festival of the Arts and the Banff Festival of Mountain Films are just two internationally recognized events held here.

The community is also home to four museums: Banff Park Museum, Luxton Museum, Whyte Museum of the Canadian Rockies, and the Natural History Museum. The Banff Park Museum is a taxidermist's dream, featuring stuffed animals native to the park. Luxton Museum traces the history of the region's **First Nations peoples.** Whyte Museum is dedicated to preserving artistic and historical material relating to the Canadian Rockies.

It houses the world's largest collection of Canadian Rockies literature and art. The smallest museum in Banff is the Natural History Museum, which profiles the geological evolution of the Canadian **Rocky Mountains.**

One of the most unique features of Banff is its resident population of about 900 elk (wapiti), which can be found wandering down Banff Avenue and lying about in residential front yards. The population is growing rapidly and conflict between these ungulates, which average 305 kilograms, and humans is increasing accordingly. In 1995, there were nearly 180 elk-human encounters in Banff National Park, with the majority of these occurring inside the town limits. Seven people were injured by elk that year, making them a more serious threat to human life than the park's **bears.**

In 1996 this led to a highly controversial proposal by the federal government to erect a stout fence around the outskirts of Banff to keep elk and other wildlife out of the community. The problem, however, is that Banff sits in the centre of a traditional elk breeding and wintering ground. Researchers are unsure what impact fencing the animals out of their traditional territory would have on the population. Residents of Banff are also of a mixed mind about whether they want to live in a community walled in by a high fence.

Banff National Park

In 1883 Canadian Pacific Railway (CPR) general manager William Cornelius Van Horne visited the **Rocky Mountains** section of the transnational railroad. Van Horne was struck both with the difficulty construction crews faced building the railroad through the mountains and by the wonderful scenery presented by these same obstacles to progress.

As he travelled through the mountain region, Van Horne realized this rugged, spectacular landscape might hold the key to riches for the company. "If you can't export the scenery, you have to import the tourists," he later wrote. Van Horne envisioned a string of luxurious hotels crossing the mountains of Alberta and British Columbia. They would be set in the most scenic locations. They would stand beside the railroad and be owned by the CPR. The tourists coming to stay in them would increase ridership on the railroad and line the pockets of a CPR tourism and hospitality division. If these hotels were set within the boundaries of a series of parks, he further speculated, it would be a simple task to market the mountains and the company's hotels in Britain and the rest of Europe.

That same year three CPR employees prospecting on their days off discovered the **Cave and Basin Hot Springs** near present-day **Banff.** Soon the federal government had to step in to resolve a squabble over ownership of the springs. In September 1885, William Pearce of the Department of the Interior visited the hot springs and, upon his return to Ottawa, was instrumental in lobbying for the passage of an order-in-council to establish a 25.9-square-kilometre reserve around the springs known as the Banff Hot Springs Reserve.

Shortly thereafter reserves were also established in the Waterton Lakes area, the Selkirk Mountains, and at Mount Stephen. In 1886, George A. Stewart was appointed to survey the Hot Springs Reserve. Stewart reported back to Ottawa that the country surrounding the reserve was very scenic and suitable for a national park. He was ordered to undertake another survey. In the end, Stewart surveyed a 673-square-kilometre area extending from Sulphur Mountain north to the end of Lake Minnewanka. Based on his findings, the Rocky Mountains Park Act of June 23, 1887 established the area as Canada's first national park.

The legislation creating Rocky Mountains Park was modelled closely on U.S. legislation that had governed the establishment of Yellowstone National Park 15 years earlier. The park, declared the legislation, was to be "a public park and pleasure ground for the advantage, benefit, and enjoyment of the people of Canada." No leases, licences, or permits that would "impair the usefulness of the park for purposes of public enjoyment and recreation" would be issued.

Stewart became the park's first superintendent. He held the position until 1896, when Howard Douglas assumed the post. Between 1887 and 1908, when Douglas retired, these two men moulded the park and town of Banff. They created a spa and resort area catering to the rich, heavily financed by revenue raised from selling lumber and mining licences.

By 1902 the park had swollen to about twice its present-day size, covering 12,690 square kilometres—encompassing the **Lake Louise** reservation, and the watersheds of the Bow, Red Deer, Kananaskis, and Spray rivers. In 1911, when it became apparent this vast territory was beyond the ability of the small park's staff to administer, the park was significantly reduced.

In 1904, a couple from Boston drove the first motor car into the park boundaries. The following year all cars were banned from the park because of their detrimental effect on wildlife. By 1911, however, park officials recognized that the automobile promised even greater tourism potential for the park and lifted the ban.

Throughout the early 1900s the park underwent systematic development of commercial facilities and a road and trail network that formed the basis of the park's infrastructure. In 1930, the National Parks Act was passed and 17 parks were created throughout Canada. Rocky Mountains Park was officially renamed Banff National Park. The boundaries were again adjusted downward. In 1949, they were further shrunk to the present-day size of about 6,640 square kilometres.

Between the 1940s and 1960s, Banff National Park emerged as an all-seasons resort. Downhill ski facilities, built in 1936, were improved and expanded in 1956 and 1963. The first lift at Mount Norquay opened in 1948, and a gondola went into operation on Mount Whitehorn in 1959. All these facilities have since been expanded several times.

Today, Banff National Park is the most heavily visited park in Canada, with more than four million people passing through each year. Slightly over half of these visitors come in July and August.

The park's natural terrain is remarkable. Within its boundaries are some of North America's largest icefields, spectacular mountain ranges, vast alpine meadows, crystalline rivers, streams, and lakes, and lush forests. More than 1,100 kilometres of trails provide access to many parts of the park.

Abundant wildlife includes elk, moose, deer, wolves, coyotes, **bears,** pika, the rare spotted frog, longnose dace fish, and more than 240 species of birds.

In 1985, Banff, **Jasper National Park,** and British Columbia's Yoho and Kootenay national parks were declared a joint World Heritage Site by UNESCO because of their combined representation of the Rocky Mountain landscape.

Bar U Ranch

From 1882 to 1950, the Bar U Ranch was one of the most famous ranching operations in Canada. It was one of a small group of sprawling western Canadian corporate ranches, most of which were located in the south-western **foothills** of Alberta. These included the Oxley, Waldrond, Quorn, and Cochrane ranches.

The Bar U had a longer history than most of the large ranches run by the cattle syndicates that first opened the Canadian west to **ranching.** Originally receiving financial backing from the Allen family of Montreal's Allen Steamship Company, the North West Cattle Company secured a lease on land along the Highwood River in the foothills south of Turner Valley. The Bar U's first manager was Fred Stimson.

During this initial period, lasting until 1902, Stimson focused on building up the size of the ranch's cattle herd. With no feedlots in existence, cattle were fattened on late spring to early fall open-range grazing, so they could survive the harsh temperatures and lack of graze available during the winter. The ranch headquarters remained small—most of the **cowboys** lived and worked out on the range.

In 1884, an American cowboy named George Lane started working on the ranch as a $35-a-month foreman. By 1902 he emerged as the chief owner of the Bar U, and figured among the "Big Four" of Canadian ranching—the other three men being Pat Burns, A. E. Cross, and Archie McLean. Lane built the ranch into what many considered the best run cattle operation in the world. The ranch also became the world's largest purebred Percheron stud farm, with as many as 300 brood mares yielding up to 100 foals in a breeding season. Heavy draft horses originating in the Perche region of France, the Bar U Percherons soon dominated show rings in Europe and North America.

Pat Burns succeeded Lane as principal owner of the Bar U in 1927, after selling his large meat-packing operation so he could focus on the ranches and the way of life he loved. Burns integrated the Bar U with his other Alberta ranch holdings. By this time most of the large ranching syndicates had already folded, their lands carved up into homesteads. But Burns piloted his ranches through the Great Depression and into the post-World War II era, before finally succumbing to the inevitable and closing the Bar U forever in 1950.

Because the ranch remained operational so much longer than the other large syndicates many of its buildings survived, including some constructed in the late 19th century. This legacy was preserved in 1995 when the ranch site and a fragment of adjacent range was opened as a national historic site. Under the protection of Parks Canada, the ranch today is being restored and interpretive programs chronicle the ranching history of southern Alberta.

Barr Colony. *See* **Lloydminster.**

Bears

Two of Canada's three bear species are found in Alberta—black bear and grizzly bear. The black bear is relatively common in the **Rocky Mountains** and their **foothills,** and throughout the **boreal forest** and **Canadian Shield** fragment. Where there are forests, black bears are usually present. The only exception to this is the woods of the **Cypress Hills** and **Elk Island National**

Park. Although all Alberta is historical range for black bears, they have been crowded out of the **prairie** and aspen **parklands** due to land clearing and hunting by humans.

Male black bears range in weight from 80 to 250 kilograms, with females being about 10 percent lighter. They range in colour from black, to brown, to cinnamon. During most of the year black bears are solitary, pairing up only briefly for mating. Cubs remain with the sow for about a year. Although most active at night, they do feed and travel during the day. Black bears maintain an average foraging range of about 200 square kilometres, but these can overlap with the ranges of others of their kind. Black bear density in Alberta forests is usually quite high, about one every 14 square kilometres.

Black bears have excellent senses of smell and hearing, so rely on these more than on their eyes. Their usual gait is a lumbering walk, which can quickly turn into a bounding gallop. Bears prefer vegetable matter to meat. They favour berries of virtually any variety over many other foods, but will also eat fresh sprouts of grasses and sedges, tree buds, roots, and tubers. Additionally they eat insects, small **mammals,** and **fish.**

Bears do not properly hibernate, rather they go into a deep sleep from about the end of October to mid-April—less in areas where winters are milder. By late summer they have packed themselves with a huge mattress of fat by gorging on everything possible. Around mid-autumn, they seek the heaviest snowbelt of their range and dig a shallow hole, usually under a tree, tall shrub, or overhanging bank. The heavier snow cover helps provide insulation so the hole need seldom be more than a metre or two deep. By the spring, the grossly overweight bear of the autumn will have become thin, possibly even emaciated. But it will have survived another winter.

The commonness of black bears and their relative boldness means they are the carnivore humans are most likely to come into contact with in Alberta. One of the reasons black bears are less afraid of humans than are most mammal species is that they have no real natural enemies other than the grizzly bear. Where a grizzly's territory and that of black bears overlap, the black bears are constantly on guard against sudden attacks.

Grizzly bears are much larger than black bears. Males weigh about 250 to 320 kilograms, females about 200 kilograms. They have prominent shoulder humps and long claws sticking out beyond the fur on their front feet. The name grizzly derives from the white tips commonly found on the hair of older males, which gives them a grizzled look. They can range in colour from black to light brown and individual bears usually have a variety of colour shades in their coat. There is little chance of confusing a grizzly with a black bear because of the distinctive shoulder hump, significantly larger size, and flatter, more dishlike shape of the face.

Although grizzlies are now confined to the Rocky Mountains, foothills, and northern reaches of the boreal forest, they once ranged throughout Alberta. Grizzly populations in the remaining range are quite small. Total grizzly population in Banff National Park, for example, is believed to be only about 80 to 100. The major problem grizzlies face is that they require large, unbroken ranges of wilderness for habitat. Outside of the Rocky Mountains such range is progressively harder to find.

Grizzlies have habits very similar to those of black bears, although they are more active during the day. They eat tubers and roots, and will dig marmots and ground squirrels out of their holes. Berries, of course, are the food that most packs on the fat required to make it through their winter sleep, so they devour all of these they can. Experts calculate that a grizzly bear can consume 200,000 buffaloberries a day. Grizzlies are also fairly good hunters and will kill weak cloven-hoofed animals, and sometimes cattle and horses. During spawning season, grizzlies are often seen at the edges of streams feeding on the fish.

Grizzly bears are extremely solitary, except when females have cubs. Their home ranges are large, at least 200 square kilometres. They travel vast distances that, over a lifetime, can add up to more than 4,000 square kilometres. Grizzly sows are highly protective of their young, in part because the boar will kill the cubs if possible. A sow will stay with her cubs for up to two years before leaving them to mate again. Grizzlies bed down for their winter sleep in a manner similar to that of black bears.

Contrary to some accounts, grizzly bears will almost always try to avoid confrontations with humans, taking flight if that option is possible and no cubs are threatened. People in the woods can usually avoid a meeting with either black bears or grizzly bears by making noise to warn of their approach. Most attacks in the wild occur at, or near, campsites, where food and cooking utensils have been improperly cached or cleaned up so that bears are attracted by the scent.

Bellevue Mine

With the completion of the transcontinental Canadian Pacific Railway line in 1885, steam locomotives were able to haul goods from one end of the nation to the other. They were powered by coal-burning boilers. This led to the immediate opening of mines throughout southern Alberta to provide coking coal for the railroad industry. In 1903, the French mining company West Canadian Collieries Ltd. opened the Bellevue mine in the **Crowsnest Pass.** Over 90 percent of the 13 million tons of coal mined here would be used to fuel steam locomotives.

Bellevue mine's operation was typical of most operating in the Crowsnest Pass. It used what was known as the room and pillar method, a mining technique designed for use in mountainous regions. This method entailed dividing the coal seam into large blocks by digging a series of tunnels, called rooms, about 15 to 18 metres apart.

The large blocks remaining between the rooms served as pillars and were left to support the overlying rock. When the mine had progressed to the limits of its coal seam or property, the miners started retreating, extracting as much coal as possible from the pillars while allowing the roof to collapse into the vacated stretch of tunnels before them.

In the early years, miners used picks and an explosive called coal powder to remove coal from the seam's face. This was a highly dangerous practice because of the gaseous and dusty underground conditions. Even a small spark could ignite a massive explosion. By the late 1920s, the pick and coal powder method was replaced by the use of compressed air picks, which operated more safely.

During the coal powder period, however, disaster struck on December 9, 1910. For the previous seven years the company had operated with a relatively good safety record. But at 8:00 p.m. an underground explosion rocked the mine. Forty-two men were working below ground that night; thirty of them died.

Tired and dirty at the end of another long and dangerous shift below ground, Crowsnest Pass coal miners pose for a photograph, circa 1919. (Glenbow Archives photo, NC-54-1665)

The post-accident investigation concluded that a rock fall caused some sparks to ignite methane gas present in the shafts. The burning gas set off a coal dust explosion, which demolished the mine's only ventilation fan. With the ventilation system destroyed, high concentrations of carbon dioxide and carbon monoxide—known as afterdamp—quickly developed, fatally poisoning most of the trapped men before rescuers could open the shaft.

A few weeks after the tragedy, Bellevue was back in operation. During the 1920s it achieved record production levels. On an average day a workforce of 500 miners was producing about 2,270 tonnes of coal.

With the beginning of the Great Depression, however, coal orders dwindled. By 1932 Bellevue and other mines in the Crowsnest Pass were embroiled in long and bitter strikes. In early May of that year, 75 Royal Canadian Mounted Police and a handful of strikebreakers smashed the Bellevue strike in a violent attack that soon turned into a riot. Labour unrest persisted in the coal mines of the Crowsnest Pass until the outbreak of World War II. Increased wartime need for coal led to higher production rates and a rise in salaries. In 1941, Bellevue mine produced 412,000 tonnes of coal—the largest annual production in its history.

With war's end, however, the demand for coal quickly decreased. Improved availability of electricity and natural gas as sources of power during the 1950s brought the coal-mining era in Crowsnest Pass almost to a close. In 1962, Bellevue ceased operation.

Today, part of the mine shaft has been preserved as the Bellevue Underground Mine Museum. A 300-metre shaft of the tunnel, featuring a room, coal chute, and original mine artifacts can be visited. To retain the historical sense of reality, the only light is provided by miners' lamps distributed to tour participants.

The mine museum is operated by Crowsnest Pass Ecomuseum Trust, which seeks to preserve and develop the historical and cultural diversity of the Crowsnest Pass.

(*See also* **Hillcrest Mine Disaster; Mining Industry; Nordegg.**)

Biodiversity

Alberta has six natural regions: **grasslands, parklands, foothills, Rocky Mountains, boreal forest,** and **Canadian Shield.** Within each of these broader regions is a series of 20 subregions. All of these regions and their subregions contain differing forms of geology, landforms, soils, hydrology, **climate,** vegetation, and wildlife. Alberta is the only place in North America where **prairie,** boreal forest, and mountain ecosystems meet.

This great variety of biogeoclimatic zones and ecosystems makes Alberta one of the most biologically diverse provinces or territories in Canada. With habitat ranging from alpine, to boreal forest, to prairie grasslands, to near desert, the province is home to many species of wildlife and vegetation. About 90 mammal, 340 bird, 10 amphibian, 8 reptile, 59 **fish,** and countless thousands of invertebrate animal species are present. At least 2,000 nonflowering, nonwoody plant species occur in Alberta. These are composed about equally of algae, fungi, lichens, and bryophytes. There are also about 17,000 flowering plants.

Many scientists believe there is currently a global "biodiversity crisis" underway. This crisis is the result of human action, either directly through pollution, forest clearing, tilling prairie, and draining wetlands or indirectly through the introduction of exotic species that subsequently crowd out native life forms. Scientists believe that between 1995 and 2020, humans will destroy more species than the entire process of natural selection culled in the past 3.5 billion years. Some experts predict that in the next 50 to 100 years, between 20 and 50 percent of all species known to exist in the world will disappear.

In Alberta, degradation or loss of habitat is by far the greatest cause of declines in wildlife populations and species diversity, as well as the loss of forms of vegetation.

(*See also* **Endangered Species; Special Places.**)

Birds

There are about 340 species of birds in Alberta. Approximately 250 of these nest in the province, while the remainder travel through during migration.

About 40 of Alberta's bird species are shorebirds, including plovers, sandpipers, turnstones, gulls, terns, herons, and dowitchers. Of these, the long-billed curlew, Eskimo curlew, mountain plover, piping plover, and upland sandpiper appear on the province's red and blue lists of animals considered at risk.

All species of grebes, avocets and stilts, cuckoos, kingfishers, swallows, cranes, mockingbirds and thrashers, waxwings, shrikes, and weaver finches found in Canada also dwell in Alberta. Most Canadian duck, loon, kite, hawk, eagle, osprey, grouse, ptarmigan, pigeon, dove, owl, hummingbird, woodpecker, jay, magpie, crow, pipit, wagtail, and falcon species are present in at least parts of the province.

Duck species are extremely well distributed. Green-winged teals, blue-winged teals, American wigeons, northern shovelers, mallards, northern pintails, lesser scaups, redheads, canvasbacks, and ruddy ducks are found throughout most of the province. Harlequins are generally only present in the **foothills** and **Rocky Mountains,** while buffleheads, common mergansers, and ring-necked ducks are seldom seen in southern Alberta.

Of the hawks, the northern harrier and red-tailed hunt throughout the province, but Swainson's hawk is restricted to Alberta's southern **grasslands.** The threatened ferruginous hawk is found only in the southern **prairie.** Only about 1,800 breeding pairs of ferruginous hawks are believed to remain in Alberta, limited to about 60 percent of their traditional range.

The American kestrel and merlin falcon are found Alberta-wide. The peregrine falcon is listed as an endangered animal under Alberta's Wildlife Act. In 1970 only one nesting pair of peregrines was known to be alive in Canada east of the Rocky Mountains and south of the Northwest Territories. This pair lived on the Bow River in southern Alberta. The following year a small population of peregrines was discovered in the Peace-Athabasca river delta in **Wood Buffalo National Park.** Since then a determined peregrine protection and reintroduction program has helped the population of peregrines in Alberta slowly grow, but it remains fragile.

Alberta's official bird, the great horned owl, and the short-eared owl inhabit the entire province, while the endangered burrowing owl is confined to Alberta's southeastern corner. Most woodpecker and flycatcher species are common everywhere in Alberta, as are swallows, except for the purple martin which is generally found only in the eastern central regions and along the **Peace River.**

In addition to the peregrine falcon, other birds listed as **endangered species** by Alberta's Wildlife Act are the American white pelican, whooping crane, **trumpeter swan,** ferruginous hawk, burrowing owl, piping plover, and mountain plover. Bird species account for 8 of the 12 animal species protected under the act.

One of the best places in Alberta for viewing birds is Beaverhill Natural Area, western Canada's only shorebird reserve, about 10 kilometres east of Tofield. Some 250 bird species have been identified here, including most of the province's shorebirds. Other good sites are the Inglewood Bird Sanctuary at **Calgary** (220 species listed), **Elk Island National Park** (230 species), **Waterton Lakes National Park** (230 species), **Jasper National Park** and **Banff National Park** (both listing 250 species), and **Cypress Hills** Provincial Park (more than 200 species listed). In addition to Inglewood Bird Sanctuary, other excellent urban bird viewing areas are Waskasoo Park and the Gaetz Lake Sanctuary at **Red Deer** (about 130 species listed) and

Capital City Recreation Park in **Edmonton,** where more than 120 species have been sighted, including bald and golden eagles.

Bison

There is no such thing as a North American buffalo. The name buffalo only applies to species found in Africa and Asia. The proper name for the largest land mammal in North America is bison. Its unique shoulder hump distinguishes it from buffalo, but early European observers first mistakenly thought the North American animal was related to African and Asian buffalo. The name was soon celebrated in song, folklore, and general North American and European terminology. Hunters who set about slaughtering the great animals for their hides, and to clear them from the land so the construction of railroads and agricultural settlement could proceed, were consequently called buffalo hunters.

Bison are actually distant relatives of domestic cattle. Fossilized evidence indicates that giant forms of these animals roamed North America 100,000 years ago. The two present North American subspecies, plains bison and wood bison, appeared in their current form about 6,000 years ago.

Plains bison occupied most of the central region of North America. Wood bison lived in lowland meadows and deltas of the Athabasca, Peace, and Slave rivers. Together, during prehistoric times, the range of these two subspecies extended from Alaska to Mexico and from the **Rocky Mountains** to the Allegheny Mountains.

It is estimated that by early 1800 about 60 million plains bison lived in the Great Plains region, which included southern Alberta. No accurate estimates exist on numbers of wood bison prior to the incursion of Europeans into their habitat.

By 1885, plains bison were virtually extinct, numbering barely 1,000, including a few captive individuals and a small herd protected inside the boundary of Yellowstone National Park. Wood bison came even closer to extinction, numbering fewer than 300 animals in the early 1900s.

In 1922, to help ensure the survival of the last known remaining herd of wild wood bison, **Wood Buffalo National Park** was created, extending over 45,000 square kilometres of Alberta and the Northwest Territories. Until 1925 it appeared the wood bison recovery was going well, but then a disease introduced into the population again reduced the wood bison to near extinction. In 1957, however, Canadian wildlife service officers discovered a remnant herd of about 200 animals, living deep in the woods of the park. In 1965, 27 of these were captured and transferred to **Elk Island National Park,** east of **Edmonton,** to serve as an insurance program in the event another disease devastated the growing Wood Buffalo National Park herds. Today about 3,500 wood bison are found in Wood Buffalo National Park and 350 in Elk Island. Small populations also live in other parks.

The plains bison has also made a comeback, thanks to careful preservation efforts by both U.S. and Canadian governments. More than 100,000 plains bison are now found in North America. In Canada, the largest herd of about 500 plains bison is at Elk Island National Park.

A typical plains bison bull weighs 730 kilograms, stands 1.75 metres tall, and measures over 3 metres from nose to tail. Both males and females have permanent horns and a characteristic growth of dark hair around the head, shoulders, and front legs. Females are usually distinguishable from males only because they are smaller and associate closely with the calves. Bison reach sexual maturity at three years of age and full maturity at six years of age. Their average lifespan is 15 years.

Wood bison have larger horn cores and denser fur than plains bison. They are longer from nose to tail, more elongated in front, and darker in colour. They weigh an average of 840 kilograms. Unlike plains bison, wood bison bulls do not assemble female harems. Instead, a bull will defend one female until she is ready to mate.

Both subspecies of bison are highly efficient grazers, far more so than domestic cattle. Before their confinement to parks, plains bison followed a pattern of annual movement that took them from open plains through the sheltered **foothills** and river valleys. This was not roaming, but rather the following of a calculated and predictable foraging pattern that ensured each new area entered was at its peak period of ripening forage. The predictability of the bison's migration enabled plains **First Nations peoples** to anticipate their movements and plan **bison hunting** activities accordingly.

Wood bison lived in smaller groups than the great herds of plains bison and were less prone to long migrations.

Adult healthy bison have no natural enemies other than humans. Calves, however, are vulnerable to predation by bears, wolves, and coyotes. Congregating in herds provides the adult bison with an ideal environment for protecting the young until they can fend for themselves. It also meets the need of these gregarious animals for the company of their own species.

Bison Hunting

For more than 10,000 years, **First Nations peoples** living in Alberta developed increasingly sophisticated techniques for hunting bison. For those peoples living on the plains, bison was almost the exclusive source for food and materials for clothing, bedding, shelter, fuel, tools, weapons, household utilities, and even symbols for worship. Although other animals were hunted, these merely provided a supplement to the primary diet of bison.

Across the Great Plains of North America an estimated 60 million bison roamed, but a land so vast also served to conceal this massive population from First Nations hunters. To ensure sufficient kill to meet their needs, the plains peoples developed an array of hunting techniques—the greatest level of sophistication displayed by development of communal jumps and pounds.

The most ancient method of hunting was stalking. Usually undertaken by one or two hunters, stalking required great patience and stealth. Bison have poor vision, so stalkers could approach from downwind through woods or on the plains in midday when the bison were usually lying down. Sometimes wolf or bison calf skins were worn to disguise the hunters and allay the great animals' fear. Stalking enabled hunters to get within easy range to kill a bison with arrows or spears. It was a technique, however, that was only useful for getting small amounts of meat, as seldom could more than one animal be killed.

Another method of bison hunting was called the surround. This entailed three or more hunters, either on foot or horseback, literally surrounding a small herd of bison and forcing it in upon itself until the animals became a milling, exhausted, easily killed group.

When substantial numbers of swift ponies became available, the surround was generally replaced by chasing. This involved riders slipping unobserved to within a close distance of the bison, charging, and singling out an animal for quick lethal arrow shots. Kills had to be achieved quickly because, although bison lack initial speed, they can soon outdistance horses.

Killing bison in full flight from the back of a galloping horse required great skill, courage, and a highly trained horse. To achieve a killing shot, the hunter had to place an arrow into a 27- to 40-centimetre circle immediately back of the foreleg. A good hunting horse was one of the plains hunter's most valued possessions. Injury or death among men and horses was common, but the chase also provided a way for warriors to establish prowess and status within the tribe.

Another way to hunt bison was to drive a herd into a natural terrain feature where they would be trapped and immobilized. This required the hunters to have an intimate knowledge of the land. In winter, bison could be driven into deep snow. The mired animals would then be approached by hunters wearing snowshoes who could easily kill them with spears and arrows. On ice, bison lacked traction and often skidded. This resulted in falls that broke legs or hips, making the injured animal easy prey. An animal who fell through the ice would drown and could be raised to the surface by the hunters. In summer, swamps or marshes served the same purpose, but retrieving carcasses was more difficult. The favoured summer trap terrain was steep coulees or box canyons into which the bison could be driven, contained, then killed at the hunters' leisure.

The most complex forms of bison hunting were communal kills known as jumps, such as the one found at **Head-Smashed-In Buffalo Jump,** and pounds. Both techniques involved meticulous planning, human construction, and the coordination of many people under the direction of experienced leaders.

Jumps utilized natural cliffs of sufficient height to kill or maim bison driven off the edge. Pounds used specially constructed corral-like structures built strongly enough to contain a group of bison. Both necessitated the building of drive lanes to force bison herds to flee to the cliff edge or into the corral. Drive lanes consisted of rows of rock cairns known as "deadmen." These cairns were arranged in a funnel shape that increasingly narrowed as the bison approached the killing zone.

Pound corrals were usually constructed in trees or below low hills for concealment. They were either square or circular in shape, built from logs and brush. The only entrance to the corral faced the narrow end of the drive lane and consisted of a low ramp, so once the bison raced up the ramp and bolted into the corral it was impossible for them to jump back out. Just before the entrance to the pound, the drive lane would usually be constructed of a solid wall of rock rather than separate cairns.

While pounds could be constructed almost anywhere the structure could be concealed, jumps were only utilized if they were near a major bison-grazing area. Sometimes the distances over which bison had to be driven to a jump were great. The drive lanes behind Head-Smashed-In, for example, stretch up to 15 kilometres.

It took several days to locate and collect bison in preparation for a kill. Young warriors dispersed over wide areas, using stalking and chasing techniques to gradually urge the herds toward the drive lanes. Once the bison were inside the lanes, a specially trained hunter would entice the animals toward the cliff by pretending he was a distressed, panicked calf. Other hunters pursued the bison, shouting and waving blankets to prevent their reversing and to panic them into galloping. More hunters positioned behind cairns would add to the animals' confusion and panic by shouting and waving blankets as well.

Many of the bison who went over the cliff edge would be killed or injured in the fall. The injured bison could be easily killed, often with spears or clubs. Animals trapped in a pound had to be killed by warriors standing safely outside the corral.

Both these methods of killing bison entailed enormous operations to process the huge quantities of meat and other bison parts. For this reason these two techniques were usually undertaken during mass gatherings of large numbers of a tribe, which at other times might be broken up into a dozen or more groups or clans.

The number of bison killed at a jump sometimes exceeded the needs of the people involved in the hunt. Archaeological evidence at the sites of some jumps indicates that occasionally more than 1,000 bison were killed. In these cases many of the carcasses were left to rot, but usually there was very little waste, with almost every part of the animals put to some use. Internal organs, for example, were sometimes transformed into food containers and the hooves could be made into ceremonial rattles.

With the European introduction of guns to the plains, bison hunting took a new turn as hunters could more easily kill the animals through chasing or even just standing at a distance and shooting the unwary animals down. By 1890, barely a hundred years after the introduction of firearms to the plains, First Nations and European hunters had reduced the huge population to slightly more than 1,000. For more than 10,000 years bison had seemed an inexhaustible resource, but it was a resource forever lost. The bison would survive, but only as an endangered, protected species.

Bobcats. *See* **Wild Cats.**

Boreal Forest

Alberta's largest natural region is the boreal forest. It consists of broad lowland plains and discontinuous hill systems. The bedrock is buried beneath deep glacial deposits. Outcrops occur only rarely along major river valleys. Extensive wetlands, including bogs, fens, swamps, and marshes, are common.

Six subregions have been identified by the Alberta **Special Places** initiative as making up the boreal forest. They are separated on the basis of vegetation, geology, and landforms.

- The dry mixed-wood subregion is characterized by level to undulating terrain. It is divided primarily into two large sections—one following the **Peace River** north to a point southeast of High Level, the other running in a wide swath along the northern shore of the North Saskatchewan River from the Saskatchewan border west to Edmonton and then extruding south in an ever-narrowing band west of Spruce Grove to a point west of Olds.

Vegetation in this subregion is transitional, a mix of central parkland (*see* **Parklands**) and central mixed-wood. Aspen and balsam poplar are the common trees. As the subregion begins to show more boreal forest features, white spruce and balsam fir replace aspen and balsam poplar stands. In areas where forest fires have failed to burn back mature stands, coniferous species are found.

Aspen forests have a diverse understorey, while coniferous forests have a greater cover of moss species. Dry, sandy uplands are usually occupied by jack pine forests. These may be quite open and have prominent lichen ground coverings. Peatlands are common, but not as prevalent as in other boreal forest subregions. Characteristic wildlife include the least flycatcher, Swainson's thrush, and pileated woodpecker.

- The central mixed-wood subregion is Alberta's largest subregion, encompassing most of the north-central to northeastern portion of the province along a line east of the Peace River and north of Lesser Slave Lake to the Saskatchewan border. With low relief and a level to undulating surface, its **climate** is moist and cool. Aspen, balsam poplar, and white birch are common, but replaced by white spruce and balsam fir in older growth stands untouched by forest fire. River flats have white spruce or white spruce/balsam poplar forest featuring large trees fed by the richer nutrient and moisture conditions.

  This subregion has the most diverse wildlife of the boreal forests. Red squirrel, dark-eyed junco, and boreal chickadee are common. In the swamp, pond, stream, and lake areas, beaver, moose, snowshoe hare, black bear, wolf, lynx, and ermine are prevalent. Fisher, wolverine, river otter, and **woodland caribou** are also found.

- The wetland mixed-wood subregion is concentrated in a wide band bordering Hay River and its tributaries. It features nearly level to gently rolling topography. The climate is colder than in the central mixed-wood, with snow cover lasting an average of 185 days per year—one of the longest in Alberta.

  Vegetation is similar to that of the central mixed-wood but there are more peatlands, willow-sedge wetlands, and upland black spruce forests. Drier sites typically feature pine or mixed aspen and white spruce.

Wildlife is sparse, both in species and numbers, because of the relative scarcity of deciduous and mixed-wood plant communities. Extensive wetlands, however, provide habitat for waterfowl, including sandhill cranes and the endangered whooping crane.

- On the sides and tops of plateaus and hill masses lies the boreal highlands subregion. It includes portions of the Cameron Hills, Caribou Mountains, Buffalo Head Hills, Birch Mountains, and Thickwood Hills, as well as the highlands south of **Fort McMurray** and around Graham and Peerless lakes. Climatic conditions are cooler and moister than in the central mixed-wood, so stands of balsam poplar and black spruce are more common on upland sites. There are extensive peat moss deposits and frequent areas of permafrost. Wildlife is similar to that of the central mixed-wood subregion, but woodland caribou are found only in the Birch and Caribou mountains.

- The Peace River lowlands subregion consists primarily of river-shaped landforms along the lower Peace, Birch, and Athabasca rivers, including the Peace-Athabasca delta—one of the largest freshwater deltas in the world. White spruce forests with large trees grow on terraces alongside the major rivers. Jack pine covers dry uplands, while mixed forests of aspen, balsam poplar, and white spruce favour the moister sites. A complex mosaic of aquatic, shoreline, meadow, shrub, and marsh vegetation occurs on lowlands. This diversity is caused by periodic flooding and resulting sediment deposits.

  The Peace-Athabasca delta supports a rich wildlife population and is a major nesting, moulting, staging, and migration area for waterfowl. **Bison** range over the extensive wet sedge meadows of the delta. American white pelicans nest along the Slave River and the most northerly populations of red-sided garter snake occur here.

  This subregion is also home to a variety of **fish,** including lake whitefish, northern pike, emerald shiner, longnose sucker, trout-perch, walleye, ninespine stickleback, flathead chub, burbot, spottail shiner, spoonhead sculpin, and longnose dace. Round whitefish and short-jawed cisco, occurring nowhere else in Alberta, are found here.

- The subarctic subregion occurs along the summits of the Birch Mountains, Caribou Mountains, and the Cameron Hills. These flat-topped hill systems are erosional remnants rising above the surrounding plain. Cool summer temperatures prevent organic soils warming above freezing, so permafrost is common. The most common forests here are black spruce with an understorey of Labrador tea and lichen growing on a surface of peat.

There is less wildlife diversity here because of the harsh environment and limited habitat variety. Species that are present include Arctic loon, surf scoter, American tree sparrow, snowshoe hare, and black bear. In the wetlands, moose, lesser yellowlegs, and rusty blackbird are found. Bistcho Lake is home to Alberta's largest concentration of nesting bald eagles.

Brooks Aqueduct

When completed in 1915, Brooks Aqueduct was the longest concrete structure of its type in the world. The 3.2-kilometre-long aqueduct was constructed by the Canadian Pacific Railway (CPR) as part of a canal system built to transport water from the company's dam, opened the previous year, on the Bow River at Bassano, west of the community of Brooks.

The aqueduct mimicked the grand irrigation systems of ancient Rome. Its pillars braced a concrete sling standing 20 metres above the ground to span a shallow valley separating the company's irrigation system from a dry expanse of **prairie.** Soon the overflowing concrete canal was bringing water to the land which previously had been considered agriculturally valueless.

The dam and canal system were part of an ambitious scheme by the CPR to irrigate more than 80,000 hectares of the 1.2 million hectares of land it owned between Brooks and **Calgary.** With water guaranteed, it could open the land to settlement and the development of farming.

Settlers from U.S. Dutch, German, Polish, Danish, Mennonite, and Swedish communities were lured to the region by the promise of cheap land and plentiful water for irrigation. The land prices were, however, far from cheap and the original plots of about 32 hectares were too small for profitable farming. Many of the farmers left, while those who remained formed associations to negotiate better terms with the railroad company.

For its part, in 1918, the CPR declared the irrigation system too costly to operate profitably. The farmers were urged to take the system over. Negotiations dragged until 1934 when they formed the Eastern Irrigation District and assumed control of the system.

The Brooks Aqueduct was abandoned in the 1970s in favour of an earthen canal. Today, the Eastern Irrigation District system includes two dams, more than 2,000 kilometres of canals, and 2,500 control structures serving one of the most agriculturally rich areas of the continent. About 600,000 square kilometres of land are now irrigated by this vast system.

The Brooks Aqueduct has been preserved as the Brooks Aqueduct National/Provincial Historic Site. Interpretive guides offer site tours and public programs from May 15 to Labour Day. The aqueduct is located eight kilometres southeast of Brooks, off the Trans-Canada Highway.

Buffalo. *See* **Bison.**

Bull Trout

Until the 1970s the bull trout was the most numerous homegrown Alberta sport **fish,** possessing the greatest natural range area throughout the province. Bull trout were common in the river and lake systems of the Rocky Mountains and their foothills, and extended from the headwaters of most major rivers—the Peace, Athabasca, North Saskatchewan, Red Deer, and the Bow and Oldman rivers to their confluence points with the South Saskatchewan—into the centre of the province. Today, no bull trout remain in most of this natural range.

The beginning of the bull trout's decline can be traced to the early 1900s when fish-stocking programs introduced new, non-native species of trout and char to streams previously dominated by bull trout. Brook trout were introduced into traditional bull habitat in the **Banff** area in 1910, and into Maligne Lake in **Jasper National Park** in 1928. Brown trout were first introduced at Raven River and Jasper National Park in 1924 and into the Bow River system the following year.

Introduction of these species gave anglers greater species variety, but it forced bull trout to compete with unnatural species for food and habitat. Anglers also viewed bull trout as unwanted predators feeding on the young of the more favoured, introduced trout and char species. From the 1930s to the 1950s, removal of large bull trout from streams was encouraged to increase survival odds for introduced species.

These species' introduction strategies precipitated a sharp decline in bull trout numbers and its disappearance from many streams and lakes. Permanent changes to water conditions, created by such factors as increased agricultural development, forestry, and damming operations, further threatened the bull trout.

While not in immediate danger of extinction in Alberta, unless managed wisely bull trout could continue to disappear from more rivers and lakes. Fish and Wildlife Services of the provincial government's Alberta Environmental Protection agency has taken steps to ensure that bull trout populations increase. A catch-and-release policy has been implemented throughout the province. Critical bull trout spawning areas are closed to all fishing on a seasonal or yearly basis. Stream habitat is also being improved through the removal of obstacles and other blockages that have interrupted bull trout migration routes.

Bull trout thrive in cold mountain lakes and streams. They can live more than 20 years, reaching lengths of 30 to 70 centimetres, and may weigh up to 10 kilograms. The largest bull ever caught in Alberta was taken from the Muskey River in 1947. It weighed 11.7 kilograms.

The bull trout is long and slender, but it gained the name "bull" because its head and jaw are large compared to the rest of its body. A typical bull can be correctly distinguished from other trout and char by the absence of black spots on its dorsal fin. This has inspired the Alberta Bull Trout Task Force slogan: "No black, put it back," as a means of helping anglers practise catch-and-release policies.

Bull trout are fierce predators, taking advantage of all available food sources. They feed primarily along the bottom and up to mid-water levels. Within this range, they will consume insects and other fish species. Mountain whitefish are a particular delicacy. Occasionally bulls will hunt on the surface and have been known to eat small **mammals,** such as mice, which accidentally fell into the water.

Cold groundwater-fed streams that are clean and free of sediment are required for spawning. Mountain headwaters are virtually the only suitable locations and in Alberta their number is limited. Spawning and nursery streams tend to be small and cold, so there is little in the way of food, space, or shelter. This naturally limits bull fingerling survival rates.

Increased erosion caused by nearby logging, road building, and other habitat changes has led to sediment buildup in such streams, rendering them unviable for bull trout spawning. Installation of culverts, dams, and reservoirs along bull trout migration routes further disrupts the natural reproduction chain.

Where populations of bull trout are in decline their recovery generally requires a period of 20 years. This is because bull trout grow slowly, taking five to six years before being old enough to participate in the spawning cycle. Where feeding conditions are poor, bull trout can require eight years to reach spawning age. Brook trout, by comparison, begin spawning at between two and four years old.

Despite the dangers facing the bull trout, its long-term outlook in Alberta is relatively good due to the recovery efforts undertaken by government, anglers, and industries whose practices near streams and lakes impact upon fish populations.

Calgary

On August 18, 1875, "F" Troop of the **North-West Mounted Police,** under the command of Inspector I. A. Brisebois, marched from **Fort Macleod** to the junction of the Bow and Elbow rivers. Upon arrival, the troops began construction of a police post and by Christmas Fort Calgary was operational. Calgary is an ancient Gaelic word, but its definition is uncertain. Some scholars believe it means "clear running water"; others hold that it is defined as "the haven by the wall."

In 1883, the Canadian Pacific Railway (CPR) reached Fort Calgary and the CPR subsequently laid out a townsite bordered to the southeast by the Elbow River and the north by the Bow River. The company named the town after the fort and in 1884 the small community became Alberta's first incorporated town. In 1893, Calgary became a city.

Cattle **ranching** was the predominant economic activity surrounding Calgary during the late 19th century. Until 1906, open-range cattle grazing policies adopted by the federal government discouraged farm-based homesteading. Calgary's pre-eminence as the capital of the Alberta territory's cattle industry led to its dominating the region socially, economically, and industrially. It is from this period that Calgary derives its nickname of "cow town."

Eventually cattle ranching was eclipsed by an influx of homesteaders taking up smaller land parcels for cash-crop farming. The population of the area grew rapidly in the early 1900s; between 1901 and 1911 Calgary's population jumped from 4,398 to 43,704. To the ever-lasting dismay of Calgarians the federal government opted to name **Edmonton** the capital of the newly declared province of Alberta in 1905 despite Calgary's being the larger, more economically important city.

In 1914, the first major oil strike occurred in the **Turner Valley,** southwest of Calgary. The opening of Alberta's first oil refinery in the city in 1923 secured its future as one of the world's major oil centres. Just before World War II the city was headquarters for more than 400 oil- and gas-related companies.

Between 1951 and 1971, Calgary more than tripled in size from 129,060 to 403,319. The early 1970s were plagued by a politically motivated world-wide oil crisis, causing North American oil prices to soar. During this period the city's downtown core was reconstructed into a metropolitan high-rise cluster. Calgary's per capita disposable income was the nation's highest and it had more Americans as residents than any other Canadian city.

Heavy dependence on the ups and downs of the **oil and gas industry,** however, haunted the city's fortunes in the mid-1980s as world prices collapsed. A deep recession settled on the city, depressing housing prices and causing record business bankruptcies. Throughout the 1990s, Calgary has slowly recovered from the mid-1980s economic blow, but it remains perilously dependent on an industry renowned for booms and busts.

Calgary's current population of about 727,000 makes it Alberta's largest city, with an impressive mosaic of museums, **post-secondary education** institutes, cultural facilities, and sporting venues. It is world famous for the **Calgary Exhibition and Stampede** held each summer. In 1988, Calgary hosted the **XVth Winter Olympics.**

Calgary Exhibition and Stampede

Billed as the "Greatest Outdoor Show on Earth," the Calgary Exhibition and Stampede is a ten-day **rodeo** and agricultural fair extravaganza that annually draws a crowd of more than one million.

At the core of the July Stampede's many events is the Half Million Dollar Rodeo—the richest purse ever offered in this sport. Hundreds of professional **cowboys** from around the world compete in elimination rounds, narrowing the field for the winner-take-all final day of rodeo on the closing Sunday. More than $250,000 is paid out in this grand finale infield competition, each major event's winner taking home $50,000.

Such a prize would have been inconceivable in 1884 when Calgary's local newspaper editor first proposed the community of 2,500 hold an annual agricultural fair. The first such fair was held on October 9, 1886. About $900 in prize money was given out and a crowd of 500 attended.

In 1889 the 38 hectares that still make up Stampede Park were purchased by the Calgary Agricultural Society from the Dominion government. The city took the property over in 1900 as part of a deal to eliminate the society's $7,000 deficit.

The fair went through a number of transformations and name changes but remained a small event until 1912 when trick roper Guy Weadick came to Calgary. A vaudeville and travelling rodeo show veteran, Weadick was long on vision and short on capital. He envisioned Calgary as the perfect venue for the biggest "frontier days show the world has ever seen…hundreds of cowboys and cowgirls, thousands of Indians. We'll have Mexican Ropers and Riders….We'll make Buffalo Bill's Wild West Extravaganza look like a side show."

Haunting the bar of the Alberta Hotel, Weadick finally impressed the right people and found himself bankrolled by four prominent Calgarians: George Lane, A. E. Cross, A. J. MacLean, and Patrick Burns. The "Big Four," as they were known, put up $100,000 and the Stampede was born.

Weadick delivered everything he promised. In September 1912, 14,000 spectators witnessed a spectacular show, which barely managed to break even. Weadick left town. But in early 1919 he was back, chatting up the Big Four, and managing to pull together the cash for a Victory Stampede that year which turned a profit.

By 1923 the stampede and exhibition societies merged into one entity — the Calgary Exhibition and Stampede. Weadick also brainstormed the creation of chuckwagon races and the Rangeland Derby was born. This event, which remains a stampede centrepiece, was first held in 1923. It was the first formal competitive chuckwagon race in history.

The merger secured the future of the Calgary Exhibition and Stampede. Since that time it has steadily grown and prospered.

At the core of its strength is the fact that it is a major show supported and organized at the community level. Run as a nonprofit organization, the Calgary Exhibition and Stampede has a core structure of about 1,700 volunteers serving on some 50 committees. It employs about 230 permanent staff and, primarily for the days of the event, another 1,330 part-time employees. Annual revenues routinely top $45 million.

Calgary Flames

On May 21, 1980, the Atlanta Flames of the National Hockey League (NHL) became the Calgary Flames.

The team's name is inspired by an event in the American Civil War. On September 2, 1864, General William T. Sherman's Union troops captured Atlanta and burned the city down. In 1972, when a contest was held to find a name for the new Atlanta hockey team, the Flames was suggested in tribute to this historic tragedy.

The Calgary Flames played their first game October 9, 1980 in the Stampede Corral, which held a maximum of only 7,242 spectators. The Flames' opponent was the Quebec Nordiques and the game finished in a

5–5 tie. Three years later the team moved into the Olympic Saddledome, which seats 20,000.

Prior to the Flames' move to **Calgary,** the team had never made the Stanley Cup finals. It would be five years after their first Calgary game before the Flames took a run at the cup. They played against the Montreal Canadiens and dropped the series one game to four. In 1988, the Flames were back in the Stanley Cup finals, again facing off against Montreal. This time they won four games to two, capturing their first, and to date only, Stanley Cup.

Calgary Stampeders

On October 22, 1945, the Canadian Football League (CFL) Calgary Stampeders kicked off their first game. They played the Regina Roughriders before 4,000 fans at Mewata Stadium. They won the game 12–0.

Their first Grey Cup win came on November 27, 1948 when they defeated the Ottawa Rough Riders in a game played in Toronto. They had ended the season with a perfect 12–0 game record. The next year they lost the Grey Cup final to the Montreal Alouettes.

Until 1960 the team enjoyed only moderate success, with no Grey Cup wins. They also became renowned for having the CFL's worst stadium facilities. In 1960, however, the McMahon Stadium was completed and suddenly the team boasted the best venue in the league. Despite this, it took another eight years for the Stampeders to make it to the Grey Cup final. On November 30, 1968, they lost to the Ottawa Rough Riders 24–21. In 1970 they were back for a Grey Cup final, but lost to the Montreal Alouettes.

The team's fortunes turned in 1971, when they took their second Grey Cup in a victory over the Toronto Argonauts.

In 1975, the Stampeders and **Calgary** hosted their first Grey Cup final, in which the **Edmonton Eskimos** played against the Montreal Alouettes. (Grey Cups are sometimes held in a franchise city other than those of the finalists.)

By 1986 the Stampeders had still not won another Grey Cup or even made the final. They were also teetering on the edge of bankruptcy. Fans launched a campaign known as Save Our Stamps, which took the acronym S.O.S. as its motto. The drive yielded season ticket sales of 22,400 and the team survived to play again, although with dismal results.

Not until 1989 did they manage a strong season, capturing second spot in the western division. By 1991, however, the community-owned team was again on the verge of financial collapse. Local businessman Larry Ryckman bought the team in October 1991. A few weeks later they captured a berth in the Grey Cup when Pee Wee Smith caught a legendary 66-yard bomb to make a winning touchdown in a game against Edmonton. They dropped the Grey Cup to Toronto.

In 1992, however, the Stampeders were back in the Grey Cup and achieved their first win in 21 years. The following year they won the Grey Cup again before a hometown crowd. But in 1994 they lost the western semi-final to the B.C. Lions, who pulled off a no-time-left-on-the-clock touchdown to win a 37–36 victory.

Again the community had to rally to keep the Stampeders from leaving Calgary, this time for another city. Faced with a January 1, 1995 deadline to either increase ticket sales or lose the team, the community came through with 16,000 season tickets sold. The 50th Anniversary of the Calgary Stampeders saw them still in the city of their birth.

In 1995, the Stampeders went to the Grey Cup as the winners of the northern division (the CFL having been restructured to allow American teams entry). They lost to the Baltimore Stallions 37–20. The Stallions became the first American-based team to win the Grey Cup.

For the often financially troubled Stampeders the 1995 season was marked less by their excellent performance and disappointing Grey Cup loss than by the loyal support of their fans. Average ticket sales throughout the season were 26,740 per game. The Labour Day classic saw the arena sold out to capacity—37,317.

Calgary Tower

This 190.8-metre needlelike tower has formed a distinctive part of the **Calgary** skyline since it opened on June 30, 1968. At that time the structure loomed over the city, but it has since been crowded by downtown-core skyscrapers. In recent years the 215-metre-high Petro-Canada Centre has surpassed the tower in height.

Originally built by the Husky Oil Company, the tower was known for several years as the Husky Tower.

Its observation deck is open to the public and can be accessed by a 48-second elevator ride. In the event of an emergency evacuation of the building, there are two staircases with 762 steps each, reaching from the ground to the observation tower.

The dining room on the observation deck rotates to provide a 360° panoramic view of the city and surrounding country. Each rotation takes one hour to complete.

Calgary Zoo

The second-largest zoo in Canada and ranked as one of the best in North America, the Calgary Zoo, Botanical Gardens, and Prehistoric Park was established in 1920. It has more than 1,100 animals representing some 300 species. There are also 27 life-sized dinosaur replicas in the prehistoric park section.

Every year about 850,000 visitors pass through the zoo, renowned for its efforts to faithfully re-create the natural habitat in which the various species of wildlife—especially **mammals** and **birds**—live. The zoo has also been active in helping to preserve some highly **endangered species,** such as whooping cranes and red pandas.

Canadian Shield

The Canadian Shield extends only peripherally into the far northeast corner of Alberta and includes two distinct subregions identified by Alberta's **Special Places** strategy.

- The Athabasca plain subregion is a low-lying area—encompassing the lowest points in Alberta where the Salt and Slave rivers cross into the Northwest Territories. Sand deposits are derived from the underlying Athabasca sandstones. Extensive stretches of sandy beach occur along **Lake Athabasca,** including a sand spit jutting three kilometres into the lake at Sand Point.

   Distinctive landscape features include kames, kettles, and active sand dunes. Kames are small hills or ridges formed by glacial deposits left when the ice retreated. Kettles are steep-sided hollows, created by glacial gouging and melting, in which water often pools because there is no surface route for drainage. At over 60 metres high, the Athabasca kames are among the biggest in the world. The active dune system is Alberta's largest. Stabilized paleodunes are unique in Alberta because they are aligned in opposite direction to the prevailing wind. Similar-sized dunes running longitudinally are found nowhere else in Alberta. The area is also dotted with lakes, but rivers are small and uncommon.

   Jack pine forests occur on sandy uplands. Peatlands range from relatively dry bogs dominated by jack pine, black spruce, Labrador tea, and reindeer lichen to wetter peatlands featuring black spruce, tamarack, Labrador tea, and sphagnum. A number of rare plant species occur in this subregion. The environment in the immediate vicinity of Lake Athabasca is different from the main uplands, with open white spruce forests running along the lake's shores.

Wildlife in this region has been little researched. Sandhill cranes and Caspian terns are known to breed here.

- The kazan upland subregion lying between the Slave River and Lake Athabasca and occupying the extreme northeastern corner of the province is characterized by extensive outcroppings of Precambrian granitic bedrock. The acidic content of bedrock outcrops directly influences vegetation. Glacial erosion has produced highly polished, striated, and grooved rock surfaces. Rock-basin lakes are common throughout this subregion. Rivers are again small, uncommon, and sluggish.

Exposed bedrock, some of which is 2.2 billion years old, is common throughout the subregion and soil has seldom developed on these surfaces. The vegetation is a mosaic of rock barrens, open forests of jack pine on sand plains and rocky hills, and black spruce forests in wet low-lying peatlands. Peatlands are mainly acidic, nutrient-poor bogs dominated by black spruce, tamarack, Labrador tea, reindeer lichen, and sphagnum. Permafrost is common.

Wildlife is relatively diverse and includes gray jay, snowshoe hare, lynx, and black bear in the jack pine forests. Wetland and open water species include common loon, bufflehead, moose, beaver, and mink. Bald eagle and osprey nest near lakes. Golden eagles nest on cliffs in the area, as does the rare and endangered peregrine falcon. The Arctic loon is a subarctic species known to nest here. Willow ptarmigan and, occasionally, barren ground caribou are found here during winter.

Cardston. *See* **Alberta Temple; Remington-Alberta Carriage Centre.**

Caribou. *See* **Woodland Caribou.**

Castle Mountain

This 2,862-metre summit in **Banff National Park** is a classic example of what geologists call castellate or layer-cake mountain formations. The term castellate derives from these mountains' resemblance to ancient castles.

A castellate mountain is formed from layers of resistant rock, such as limestone or quartz, alternating with less resistant rock, such as shale. Because the softer rock erodes more rapidly, the harder layers are undermined and tend to break off at right angles to form steep slopes and cliffs.

Castle Mountain was so named by James Hector of the **Palliser Expedition** in 1858. In 1946, however, it was renamed Mount Eisenhower to honour General Dwight D. Eisenhower, World War II supreme commander of the Allied Expeditionary Force which invaded France on June 6, 1944 at Normandy and undertook the liberation of western Europe. Years of protest by Albertans ensued and in 1979 it was renamed Castle Mountain.

Cave and Basin National Historic Site

In 1875, Peter Younge and Benjamin Pease—two American hunters and trappers—were guided by Stoney First Nations people to a **hot springs** on what would later be called Sulphur Mountain in the Bow Valley. They were the first non-First Nations people to visit the springs. One of the springs lay in an open basin, the other underground in a steamy cave accessible only through a small hole. Younge built a shack adjacent to what would eventually become the Cave and Basin National Historic Site, but lacked the money to register a claim to the land. The following year he abandoned the place.

Seven years later, in the fall of 1883, William McCardell, his brother Tom, and their partner Frank McCabe rediscovered the site. The three men were Canadian Pacific Railway (CPR) construction workers who spent their spare time prospecting. They noticed warm water and detected a strong smell of sulphur on the slope of a mountain on the south side of the Bow Valley. Soon they happened on the springs themselves and, after fashioning a rough ladder, descended into the cave. McCardell thought the inside of the cave looked "like some fantastic dream from a tale of the Arabian nights."

Hot springs at the time were considered a unique luxury and the mineral waters in them were believed to have great healing and restorative powers. The three men were well aware that they had happened onto something that could be mined more easily than gold.

Desperately seeking a means to lay claim to the land, they applied for a homesteading permit. As the land was unfarmable, it was denied. So, too, was a more logical application for a mineral lease. Despite these failures, and lacking any recognized legal claim to the land, they surrounded the springs with a log fence and put up a crude log shack they grandly called a hotel.

No sooner had word got out of the three men's discovery than various interlopers arrived to lay counterclaims of ownership to the hot springs. Legal actions followed. Finally the Canadian government interceded and decided to retain ownership of the springs in its own name. They paid the McCardells and McCabe a pittance of a few thousand dollars to get rid of their claim, which was the only one found to have even a dubious shred of legitimacy.

In 1885, William Pearce of the Department of the Interior visited the site and by November 25 succeeded in having a 25.9-square-kilometre tract of land surrounding the springs set aside as Canada's first park reserve. This was the core of what would eventually become **Banff National Park.**

Government workers blasted a tunnel into the hot springs cave in 1886. Bathhouses were built beside the two springs in 1887. Bathers paid 10 cents a swim.

In 1914, the present stone bathhouses were erected at a cost of about $200,000 and the pools were lined with concrete to create what at the time was Canada's largest swimming pool. Hordes of people came to the springs in the early 1900s, lured by the curative power they believed the waters held. Everything from gunshot wounds to mercury poisoning was supposedly healed by soaking in their waters.

Eventually, however, the minerals, combined with chlorine pumped in to render the water safe from human contamination, produced sediments that ate away the concrete lining. In 1975, the pools were declared unsafe and closed to the public.

A $12-million restoration project followed and in 1985 they reopened again in time for the centennial of Banff National Park and the Canadian Parks Service. Unfortunately the same problems reappeared in 1992 and the facility was once again closed to swimming. Today, the pools have a fountain in the middle in summer and are drained in the winter, but the bathhouses remain and a large exhibit centre tells the story of their past.

The only hot springs in Banff still open for public use is Upper Hot Springs, which was first developed in 1901 by the Canadian government. The Upper Hot Springs bathhouse was completed in 1935.

Caves

There are countless small caves in Alberta's **Rocky Mountains,** but major caverns are surprisingly rare. Most caves in the Rockies are really frost pockets, small openings created by the freezing and thawing of seeping water. These caves usually only extend a few metres into a rock face or fracture. Those caverns which do exist are all formed by the dissolving action of groundwater working on the region's vast limestone deposits.

Groundwater picks up carbon dioxide from soil, carbonic acid from the atmosphere, and sulphuric acid from pyrite and gypsum deposits through which it passes. When some, or all, of these acids are present in the groundwater and it comes into contact with limestone, a chemical reaction occurs that dissolves the limestone.

In other regions, such as British Columbia's northern Vancouver Island, the limestone deposits are, due to their configuration, more easily eroded by acidic groundwater so cavern creation is more extensive. Most limestone deposits in these regions are relatively flat lying, but the limestone in the Canadian Rockies is steeply sloped, rendering it less permeable.

Still, the groundwater in the Rockies has created some sizable caverns. The longest known cave system in Canada, for example, is Castleguard Cave in **Banff National Park,** which is also home to the largest known **hot springs** in the Canadian Rockies—Big Springs. Only about 20 kilometres of passages have been explored in this system, which extends several kilometres beneath the Columbia Icefield. Several of the passages here are blocked by glacial ice—a phenomenon unknown anywhere else in the world.

Although Castleguard is the longest known cave system, some spelunkers and scientists believe an unexplored cavern below the Maligne Valley in **Jasper National Park** may actually be Canada's longest single cavern. At Medicine Lake, Maligne River goes completely underground. Researchers have poured red rhodamine dye into sinks at Medicine Lake and have detected the dye emerging from the many springs found at Maligne Canyon, 15 kilometres away.

If only one passage were carrying all the water flow of Maligne River it would have to be 11 to 16 metres in diameter—a massive, naturally created tunnel. To date, however, spelunkers have been unable to find any access point to enter the system and begin its exploration.

One of Alberta's most accessible caverns, the Cadomin Caves, has an entrance point on a mountain face west of Hinton. The rare northern long-eared myotis bat is known to nest in this cave system.

Chinooks

A chinook is a warm, dry, gusty, westerly wind occurring along the eastern slopes of the mountains of western North America, which stretch from New Mexico to Alaska. This wind is most frequently experienced in the 400-kilometre-long line of **foothills** bordering the Canadian **Rocky Mountains'** easterly flank, especially in southern Alberta.

Although chinooks occur throughout the year, they are seldom noticed except during winter months. Chinooks blow about five to ten times a year in the southern part of the province. From **Calgary** to **Waterton Lakes**

National Park, an average of 30 out of every 120 days of winter will be influenced by chinooks.

The most noticeable effect of a chinook is rapid warming, with increases of over 25° Celsius in no more than an hour. Typically, a chinook occurs when the eastern slope is blanketed by a very cold Arctic air mass. From the west, a warmer Pacific low pressure system begins to flow across the Rockies, producing a massive standing wave as it pushes hard against the range's western flank. When the wave swells up and over the **continental divide** it strikes the dome of cold, dense Arctic air covering the prairies. Moisture contained in the Pacific system condenses, forming a cloud known as a chinook arch, which stretches in a long curve over the foothills. This arch will usually push outward from the foothills over the **prairie** as the chinook strengthens, eventually extending several hundred kilometres beyond the mountains.

The arch is the crest of the wave. Following behind it is a deep trough that rolls down across the surface of the land as winds that average 30 to 50 kilometres per hour but can blow up to 100 kilometres per hour. These winds can shove the cold air back from the mountains across the prairie for up to 200 kilometres. Snow melts quickly, in many cases simply evaporating. A chinook lasting several days will strip away all the snowpack from the lower mountain slopes, foothills, and valleys. The unseasonable heat wave usually ends with a powerful storm, followed by a return to clear, cold weather until the next chinook cycles in.

While chinooks are generally welcomed on the prairies and in the foothills, they create a negative weather pattern for those on the western flanks of the Rockies or in the mountains' main ranges. Here, the westerly flow of air at higher elevations causes turbulent air flow near the ground. At **Lake Louise,** for example, a chinook that is blessing Calgary with sunshine and warm temperatures will usually bring variable gusty winds and short, sharp blizzards broken by blue-sky patches. This phenomenon is called a foehn wall. The term foehn derives from the chinook-like foehn wind that blows in western Europe.

Chinooks are known to cause mood changes in the hours before they hit. Many people become irritable or restless. Studies show an increase in motor vehicle accidents, crimes, and suicides. Some scientists believe an approaching chinook raises the absorption rate of positive ions, resulting in changes to levels of serotonin, a hormone that affects mood and raises blood pressure.

The foothills and mountains affected by chinooks are home to most of the Rocky Mountains' elk and bighorn sheep population. This is because the warm temperatures melt away the snowpack sufficiently to provide good grazing conditions.

The term chinook is taken from the Chinook First Nations people of the Columbia River mouth region of Oregon state. Early Europeans and some **First Nations peoples** believed that chinooks originated here, blew down the Columbia Gorge, and then spread out to roll over the Rockies and onto the prairies.

Climate

Alberta enjoys some of the driest, bluest, and sunniest Canadian skies. Its air comes from two sources—the Arctic and the Pacific Ocean. Arctic air is usually dry and clear. The milder Pacific air comes to Alberta after a long traverse of British Columbia's multiple mountain ranges, finishing with a steep climb over the western flank of the **Rocky Mountains.** By the time the Pacific air starts flowing out from the **foothills** onto the plains, most of the moisture has been wrung from it, rendering it largely cloud-free.

The only province that competes with Alberta for status as the sunniest in the nation is Saskatchewan. The two toss the honour back and forth according to annual sunshine index figures. Most areas of Alberta average 2,000 hours of sunshine a year. The provincial high is usually experienced by Suffield and Coronation, both routinely clocking more than 2,500 hours annually. Summer is the sunniest season, in part because the northern portion of the province is experiencing up to 18 hours of daylight. Average summers bring skies that are bright with sunshine 60 percent of the time, and rarely do three days pass with no sunshine breaking through the cloud cover. In winter, about 40 percent of daylight hours are sunny. This is one of the highest "percentage-of-possible" totals experienced anywhere in southern Canada.

All this sunshine helps contribute to some of the nation's driest air. In July, average vapour pressure is 1.1 kilopascals, dramatically lower than southern Ontario's average of 1.6 to 1.8 kilopascals. At 6 percent, **Calgary** has experienced the lowest relative humidity ever recorded in Canada. This event happened on March 22, 1968, when the air temperature was 18° Celsius and the dewpoint −20° Celsius.

Alberta is also one of Canada's least foggy places. In southern or western Alberta, only 12 to 15 days a year see an hour or more of fog. The northwest experiences days of ice fog, which pushes the province-wide average of 20 days a year up to 30. Low-lying pollution in some areas adds a few extra days of fog each year.

The province's climate is continental. This means it has long, cold winters and short, cool summers, with a low yearly rainfall. Alberta shares the same belt of latitude as Labrador, the steppes of Eurasia, Mongolia's northern deserts, and the North China Plain. Latitude, however, is not the only determinant of climatic conditions. Altitude, distance from oceans, prevailing circulation of atmosphere, and local geographical features combine to influence an area's climate.

All of Alberta is protected to the west from the Pacific Ocean's maritime influences by the massive barrier of the Rocky Mountains. Although the Pacific air is quite dry by the time it reaches Alberta, it does contribute a significant degree of cloudiness, mildness of temperature, and increased windiness. In the foothills and **Peace River** country—where altitude decreases and rain-bearing air masses enter the province more freely from the west than elsewhere—precipitation can be relatively heavy. Nowhere, however, is precipitation in Alberta excessive. Montreal's yearly average, for example, is 1,070 millimetres, a figure which far exceeds that of even the wettest Alberta weather station.

Between the Arctic Ocean and the southern part of the American southwest no mountain ranges rise to break the flow of weather north and south. This means that cold, dry Arctic air clashes frequently with warm, dry air pushing up from the American southwest, often meeting over Alberta. Consequently, the province experiences wide variations in temperature, cloud cover, and precipitation between summer and winter and on a day-to-day basis.

Pacific Ocean air masses moderate conditions to ensure that Alberta's winter temperatures are neither as harsh nor as sustained as those of neighbouring Saskatchewan. Local geographical and topographical features also influence an area's climate. Hilltops are usually colder than adjacent slopes, but cold air drains downhill to the valley floor, bringing premature frost on clear, cold, still nights. Near lakes and rivers frost may not occur because the **water** adds heat to the surrounding landscape. Calgary, **Edmonton,** and other Albertan cities also affect local weather conditions by warming air temperatures and serving as wind shelters.

Nowhere in the Canadian prairies has a smaller annual temperature range than southwestern Alberta. A temperature range is the difference between the average coldest winter month temperature and warmest summer month temperature. In southern Alberta this range is only 26° Celsius, while in the northern portions of Alberta, Saskatchewan, and Manitoba the average range is 43° Celsius. But southwestern Alberta is also the **chinook** zone, where temperatures can rise by 25° Celsius in less than an hour.

The moderating influences of Alberta's Pacific air currents keep many southwestern Alberta temperatures in January at about −10° Celsius, about 8° Celsius higher than areas at the same latitude in Saskatchewan and Manitoba. Yet in the far north, all three provinces share average January temperatures of −25° Celsius.

Summers in Alberta see less temperature variation between north and south than at other times of the year. Temperatures along the province's northeastern border average a July mean temperature of about 15.7° Celsius, while on the **Milk River,** near the Montana border, it will only be about 3° Celsius warmer.

Spring and fall are Alberta's shortest seasons, most years lasting little more than a month. Surprise snowfalls can occur in May, usually immediately followed by a heat wave. In other years a snowstorm strikes southern Alberta in August, and when the melt is over the region experiences an Indian summer. The prolonged October autumn this brings will, however, normally end abruptly with the winter's first snowfall or a severe frost that destroys crops and kills livestock.

Alberta's winters defy regularity. Winter temperatures are extremely variable, both hourly and annually. Chinooks contribute to this variability, but so do the clashes of Arctic air with warm flows out of the American southwest and sudden forays of Pacific air currents.

Southern Alberta's coldest winter on record occurred in 1968–69 when average temperature between December and February was −16° Celsius, compared to the normal −7.2° Celsius. The winter of 1886–87 was Edmonton's coldest. Between December and February the average temperature was −20° Celsius, 7° lower than normal. Two years later, Edmonton enjoyed its mildest winter when temperatures ran 6° higher than normal. In some winters, when Arctic air flows dominate, cold spells of several weeks are common. In 1969, for example, Edmonton suffered 26 days of temperatures below −18° Celsius. The all-time provincial low was marked by Fort Vermilion on January 11, 1911, when the temperature bottomed out at −61.1° Celsius, the coldest reading ever recorded in Canada except the Yukon Territory.

Southeastern Alberta, near **Medicine Hat,** has the longest frost-free period outside a major urban centre of all the prairie provinces—125 days. Most grain-growing areas in Alberta have frost-free periods of about 100 to 120 days. The warming influence of cities upon a region is particularly evidenced by Edmonton's frost-free day rate. Edmonton proper experiences on average 140 frost-free days, while to the south at Edmonton International, which lies in a rural area, frost-free days number only 105.

Alberta's dry air gives it some of Canada's driest places. As little as 300 millimetres of precipitation falls annually in southeastern Alberta's dry belt, where rainfall is highly variable in intensity and droughts are prolonged. All of Alberta's **agriculture** occurs in areas receiving less than 500 millimetres annual precipitation. Most of the province's precipitation comes during the growing season from late May to early September. Precipitation totals for June average 75 to 100 millimetres and in the following two months the storm tracks shift northward, allowing the crops to slowly dry for harvesting. This trend is unreliable, however, so some growing seasons are overly wet and others plagued by drought. As a result, agriculture in Alberta is a relatively high-risk enterprise.

Even outside the agricultural zones, precipitation remains light. The north averages about 400 millimetres annually, while in the Rockies the average rarely exceeds 600 millimetres. About 60 percent of average precipitation in the mountains comes as snow.

Alberta experiences light accumulations of snowfall in most areas. Yearly totals throughout the province average about 150 centimetres. The **Lloydminster** area gets the least snow of all, less than 100 centimetres, while **Lake Louise** is the province's snowiest place with more than 400 centimetres annually. Across Alberta, snowfall accounts for about 30 to 35 percent of annual precipitation. In almost every weather station in the province, however, at least a trace of snow is recorded in every month of the year. Maximum snowcover usually occurs in southern Alberta in February, but remains less than 20 centimetres deep. Snow normally covers the ground throughout Alberta from mid-November to late March, with the last snow melting about the first of May.

Blizzards are common, and in the south are interspersed with chinooks. A blizzard is characterized by intense cold, strong winds, and snowfall. Visibility is reduced to below one kilometre due to blowing snow. The amount of snowfall is often light, but the driving force of the wind makes the blizzard capable of crippling transportation systems and endangering the lives of people unable to find shelter. Blizzards are most likely in February, but spring storms can occur (although many of these lack the full conditions of an official blizzard). On May 14, 1986, for example, knee-deep snow driven by 80-kilometre-per-hour winds swept across southern Alberta. More than one million people were affected by the storm. Thousands of motorists were stranded and dozens of communities lost all utility services.

The wind is almost an Albertan constant—there is nothing in the open prairie to impede its flow. In winter, southwesterly and westerly winds prevail, especially in the southern part of the province. During other seasons, west-northwesterly winds predominate. Average wind speed is strongest in the spring, exceeding the yearly average of 13 kilometres per hour by 10 to 15 percent.

Occasionally vicious **tornadoes** drop down from the thunderheads, causing serious property and crop damage and even loss of life. Smaller twisters, sometimes called wind devils, can occur almost any time during the summer. Often surviving for less than a minute, they are particularly noticeable in areas of freshly plowed farmland.

During summer afternoons, massive thunderheads often build up. Some yield only a small shower; others produce torrents of rain or unleash violent barrages of hailstones. **Hailstorms** can cause tremendous damage throughout the province, but central Alberta's "hailstorm alley" between Drumheller and **Red Deer** and Calgary experiences some of the world's most frequent and destructive hailstorms.

Below is a list of Alberta weather records.

- The highest recorded temperature in Alberta is 43.3° Celsius, recorded on July 18, 1941 at **Fort Macleod.**
- The lowest temperature is −61.1° Celsius, recorded at Fort Vermilion on January 11, 1911.
- Alberta's annual precipitation record was set at Cameron Falls in 1975 when 1,440 millimetres of moisture was measured.
- The most snowfall in one year was on the Columbia Icefields in the winter of 1973–74 when 1,066 centimetres accumulated.
- On June 29, 1964, Livingston Ranger Station was buried under the biggest summer snowfall recorded in Canada. In all, 111.8 centimetres fell.
- In 1972, Whitecourt experienced 65 days of fog and **Fort McMurray** residents splashed through 186 days of rain and snow to set respective Alberta fog and wetness records.
- During the winter of 1973–74, Coronation endured 33 days of blowing snow.
- In 1976, Manyberries, which averages 2,309 hours of sunshine per annum, recorded 2,785 hours of sunshine for a provincial record.
- The most powerful hourly maximum wind speed ever recorded in Alberta was at Bighorn Dam on January 15, 1972. Winds that day howled at 108 kilometres per hour.

- Edmonton has recorded the greatest number of frost-free days in Alberta—184 recorded at Edmonton Municipal Airport in 1980.

Cochrane Ranche Historic Site

By 1881, when Senator Matthew Cochrane established a vast 76,500-hectare ranch along the Bow River west of **Calgary** he already had a deserved reputation as a cattle breeder in the east. But the east lacked the land base required to field large herds like those fuelling the "beef bonanza" of the western United States. The North-West Territories, however, had land to spare and precious few settlers yet lured in by the Dominion Lands Act.

From 1880 to 1881, Cochrane used his political influence to broker an amendment to the act that permitted the leasing of large acreages for grazing. Previously, only smaller homestead operations had been permitted. The amendment granted leases to British subjects of up to 40,000 hectares for 21 years at a rate of $10 per 400 hectares (1,000 acres). Only the investors could homestead on the land.

The amendment sparked a land boom and the establishment of the large **ranching** syndicates that dominated southern Alberta's **economy** for most of the late 19th century. By the 1890s about 200 cattlemen controlled the region, forming a powerful economic, social, and political elite closely linked to the federal Conservative Party.

Cochrane struck quickly after the amendment was signed in Ottawa, creating an eastern-based syndicate that secured six leases encompassing 145,000 hectares. Although most of these leases were for the Cochrane Ranche on the Bow River, the syndicate's lands also included a large holding near **Fort Macleod** on the Oldman River. In 1881, he purchased 12,000 cattle in Montana and trailed them to the new grazing land on the Bow River.

The region seemed ideal cattle country. Blessed with **chinooks,** which regularly melted the winter

The larger-than-life Men of Vision *statue at Cochrane Ranche honours the ranching heritage of Alberta. (Mark Zuehlke photo)*

snow, excellent grazing was believed to be available year round. The Bow River and many nearby tributaries provided ample water for stock watering.

But Cochrane had underestimated the fickle nature of the winters in this area. No sooner had his trail-weary herds arrived from Montana than a severe winter struck in 1881–82. The following year was just as hard. By spring of 1883, only 4,000 head remained, the rest having starved or frozen to death.

The eastern shareholders overruled Cochrane and moved the surviving cattle to the Fort Macleod range, where winters were less harsh. Sheep and horses replaced cattle on Cochrane Ranche, but the land was too vast for either operation and the ranch became an endless money loser. By 1889, the ranch was abandoned, and the property eventually sold in 1906 after Cochrane's death.

Today the ranch site and surrounding 61 hectares of land are protected as the provincial Cochrane Ranche Historic Site. None of the ranch buildings remain, but an interpretive centre chronicles the ranch's experience. Nearby, the **Western Heritage Centre** also celebrates the province's ranching history.

Overlooking the ranch site stands the statue *Men of Vision*. Created by Cochrane artist Mac Mackenzie, the huge statue of a rancher looking out over the Bow Valley is one-and-a-third times larger than life size and weighs 1,633 kilograms. It was cast in England, shipped over in pieces, and installed in May 1979 as a tribute to the early pioneers and the dreams they held.

Cold Lake

This small eastern Alberta community of about 4,250 people is best known for its proximity to Canadian Forces Base (CFB) Cold Lake, the largest jet-fighter training base and testing range in Canada. The base's personnel of about 5,000 live to the south of Cold Lake, mostly in the vicinity of Medley.

Prior to the military base's establishment in World War II few people lived here, although it had been a traditional hunting area for the Chipewyan First Nations people for thousands of years and fur-trading posts had been opened on the lake's shores in the late 1700s. The first permanent settlement of the area by non–First Nations people was in 1910. That settlement grew somewhat after a branch line of the Canadian Pacific Railway reached Cold Lake in 1928.

The community of Cold Lake stands on the shores of Alberta's seventh-largest lake, from which the town derives its name. Cold Lake is a popular fishing, swimming, and boating recreational area. With 225 berths, Cold

Lake's boat marina is western Canada's largest inland marina. The lake is home to the most species of **fish** in Alberta—22—including walleye, pike, perch, and lake trout. It is also considered one of the top three birding sites in Alberta. More than 80 percent of all Alberta's bird species can be viewed here and the country surrounding the lake is home to 30 percent of Canada's warbler species.

Northwest of Cold Lake lie the Cold Lake Oil Sands. Although not as extensive as the **Athabasca Oil Sands** at **Fort McMurray,** they are the focus of a heavy-oil megaproject that started production in 1985. The sand here is buried about half a kilometre underground in a 50-metre thick band, making the surface mining techniques used at the Athabasca Oil Sands impractical. So Esso Resources Canada Ltd. devised a technique of pumping steam into the sand to thin the bitumen. Once thinned, the bitumen can be pumped to the surface for further refining. A very expensive process, the oil sands operation has suffered closures during periods of recession but has also become the primary force in Cold Lake's local **economy.**

In 1985, Cold Lake found itself in the world spotlight when U.S. and Canadian governments agreed to test Cruise missiles—self-guiding, long-range missiles capable of carrying nuclear warheads—at CFB Cold Lake's testing range. The Canadian government approved the testing at cabinet level, rather than through a vote in the House of Commons. A group of organizations tried to stop the testing by launching a court action. They argued the tests violated Section 7 of the Canadian Charter of Rights and Freedoms, which reads: "Everyone has the right to life, liberty and security of the person and the right not to be deprived thereof except in accordance with the principles of fundamental justice." The Supreme Court of Canada rejected the suit and the testing at Cold Lake proceeded, although peace activists maintained a vigil camp outside the base for the testing's duration.

Out of the Cruise Missile Case, as it is now known, evolved a Supreme Court decision of great import to the federal government's relationship with the Canadian court system. At first federal government lawyers attempted to derail the case by arguing the court had no jurisdiction to consider a challenge to a federal cabinet order. On May 9, 1985, the Supreme Court ruled against this argument, finding that federal cabinet decisions are subject to judicial review and control by virtue of Section 32(1) of the Charter of Rights. This has since opened the way for other legal challenges by citizens opposing a decision made by federal cabinet.

Columbia Icefield. *See* **Icefields; Icefields Parkway.**

Continental Divide

Often called the Great Divide, the Continental Divide runs north to south through North America down the centre spine of the main Rocky Mountain ranges. **Water** on its western slope drains to the Pacific; water on its eastern slope drains to the Arctic or Atlantic oceans.

Another less distinct continental divide runs across the breadth of Canada from the hydrological apex of the **Rocky Mountains** in the Columbia Icefield (*see* **Icefields**) through southern Alberta and east all the way to the Atlantic Ocean in Labrador. This gentle apex has sufficient slope on both sides—despite being virtually undetectable in most places without sophisticated measuring equipment—to direct the flow of water. North of this line, water flows to the Arctic Ocean, while water on its southern flank flows into the Missouri-Mississippi system. In Alberta, only the **Milk River** lies south of this divide.

Cottonwood Forests

One of the rarest and most endangered forests in Canada is southern Alberta's cottonwood forests. Native to the southern **grasslands** region, cottonwoods grow in the river valleys. The most extensive of these forests lie along the Oldman River and its tributaries west of **Lethbridge,** along the Bow River and its tributaries west of Cluny, along the Red Deer River below Finnegan, and along the lower **Milk River.** About 1,500 kilometres of river shore remains bordered by cottonwoods. This small remnant of a forest that once bordered almost all the shoreline of southern Alberta's rivers and streams and the bottomland of many **coulees** occupies a total area of only about 700 square kilometres.

This remnant cottonwood forest grows on a small island and along the western shore of the Red Deer River north of Drumheller. (Mark Zuehlke photo)

The cottonwood forests offer wildlife vital relief from the treeless **prairie.** In summer, their shade is vital to protect many species from temperatures that can reach 45° Celsius. The forests consequently have one of Canada's highest densities of breeding bird populations. The cottonwood grove at **Dinosaur Provincial Park,** for example, provides habitat to more than half of the 160 bird species found in the park. During breeding season and winter, deer also concentrate in the cottonwood forests. Several bat species, including the big brown bat, red bat, and long-legged bat, use the cottonwoods for roosting and breeding sites.

Beneath the cottonwood stands, the forest floor is blanketed by a rich diversity of vegetation. This understorey constitutes a vital part of the overall grasslands region ecosystem, as it provides protective cover for the cottonwoods' roots and reproductive process. Additionally the vegetation is important browse food for deer and other animals.

Four cottonwood species grow in southern Alberta: plains cottonwood, narrowleaf cottonwood, and the subspecies black cottonwood and balsam poplar. Plains cottonwood is found east of a line drawn between Lethbridge, Bassano, and Drumheller, and includes the cottonwoods of Dinosaur Provincial Park. Blackwood cottonwood and balsam poplar are found west of this line. Narrowleaf cottonwood is restricted in Canada to the Oldman River and its tributaries southwest of Lethbridge.

Cottonwoods begin life as small seeds with cottony tails or as suckers growing out of established cottonwood tree roots or buried branches. Both forms of new growth thrive best on freshly flooded sand or gravel bars alongside river channels. If moisture and sunlight are abundant, the young cottonwoods quickly establish roots to tap the water table and extend leafy stems 10 to 30 centimetres tall in the first year of growth. Provided the young seedling is not trampled, browsed, flooded, or desiccated by drought, it can grow to two metres height in a few years. At ten years of age, cottonwoods reach sexual maturity. They can live to be over 150 years old.

The danger to the cottonwood forests became acute shortly after the arrival of Europeans in southern Alberta. In the virtually treeless prairie environment, the cottonwoods were considered a prime source of lumber and firewood. Extensive stands were destroyed.

Soon the settlers began diverting the rivers and damming them for irrigation purposes. Some cottonwood stands were drowned beneath artificial lakes. Others were destroyed by drought created when a river was either diverted from its original course or sharply reduced in water flow by upstream damming. Due to flood control measures, many cottonwood forests no longer experienced the spring and storm flooding essential to foster seed and sucker growth. These forests stagnated, as the aging stands were unable to regenerate themselves—the cottonwood forest of Dinosaur Provincial Park is suffering this condition. Still other cottonwood forests were cleared for gravel pits, **agriculture,** and urban and recreational development, such as housing tracts and golf courses.

Damming and flood control development continue to jeopardize the survival of the remaining cottonwood forests. Their survival is further threatened by the fact that 48 percent of cottonwood stands are found on private land, where few restrictions can be imposed to prevent logging or other destruction. Only about 3 percent of cottonwood forests are protected by inclusion in parks.

Attempts are being made to aid cottonwood survival. Beginning in 1996, the Dinosaur Provincial Park cottonwood forest became the focal point of a major cottonwood regeneration study designed to encourage development of an understorey of young cottonwoods to ensure successional growth patterns. The initiative, expected to require at least five years, entails planting and nurturing cottonwood branch shoots directly under the mature cottonwood stands. Soil is aerated before planting to simulate the natural process created by area flooding during spring runoff and storms.

A University of Lethbridge study is examining how dam operations can be changed to permit the vital flooding for cottonwood forests. Land management measures are being introduced in some areas to restrict livestock grazing among cottonwood stands and to prevent further loss of cottonwood stands to land development projects.

Whether these initiatives will prove sufficient to ensure the survival of this critically endangered forest, however, is uncertain.

Cougars. *See* **Wild Cats.**

Coulees

Much of the Alberta **prairie** is cut by coulees, the common term for the distinctive valleys and ravines that break up the generally flat surface of the Canadian prairie. The term coulee derives from the French word *couler,* meaning "to flow." This refers to the fact that the coulees of the prairie were created by the force of rivers, many of which no longer exist except during heavy rain storms, spring melt, or as underground springs.

The sheltered slopes of the coulees and their usually moist bottom land create an environment that supports much of the prairie's **biodiversity.**

Prairie falcon and owls nest in the rock cliffs; endangered **northern leopard frogs** and striped coral-root orchids inhabit the coulee floor.

By linking different habitats, coulees act as natural corridors for plants and animals. This is especially important today as most of the non-coulee country of the prairie has been transformed from its natural state by agricultural development. The loss of natural spans of prairie makes it difficult or impossible for some native animals and plants to maintain the links between their remaining isolated pockets of habitat. Such links, however, are crucial to ensuring species diversity and the consequent ability to resist diseases and other threats to species survival.

Historically, coulees were important to **First Nations peoples.** They were favoured camping areas because the coulees provided shelter from storms and wind, and usually contained abundant water, game, and firewood. Raiding parties used them to avoid detection as they crept up on enemies. Early European hunters, traders, and explorers also found travelling through, or near, coulees made it easier to survive in the harsh prairie landscape.

Many coulees in southern Alberta run north-south, and were often used by whiskey smugglers slipping into Canada past the **North-West Mounted Police** outposts and forts. During U.S. prohibition from 1920 to 1933, Canadian smugglers returned the favour, running alcohol to the American border towns. (Prohibition in Alberta only lasted from 1920 to 1924.)

Some of the most natural coulee country remaining in Alberta is found on the southern shore of the **Milk River** in **Writing-On-Stone Provincial Park,** where several coulees running down to the river are separated by narrow shelves of native grassland prairie.

Cowboys

Alberta's first cowboys appeared in the 1880s, many drifting across the border from Montana and other American states. Their way of life dates back to the 16th century when Spanish conquistadors drafted First Nations men to serve as mounted herdsmen. They tended wild cattle left to roam on the vast open rangelands of South America, Mexico, and what is now southern California, east to the Louisiana River. Called *vaqueros*, these native cowboys established a tradition of dress that remains largely unchanged today. They wore buckskin clothes, wide-brimmed hats, tall boots fitted with spurs, *chaparejos* (protective skin or fur leggings), and carried *la reata* (lariat rope).

By the 1830s, American cowboys were working the ranges throughout the southwest. In the 1880s, cattle **ranching** emerged in southern Alberta—

centred around **Fort Macleod** and the Bow River Valley country west of **Calgary.**

Cowboys in Canada and elsewhere came from all walks of life. Prior to World War I, the majority of Alberta's cowboys were retired **North-West Mounted Police** troopers and officers, American cowboys, First Nations men, **Métis,** and British remittance men. Remittance men were "black sheep" sent to the colonies by disappointed upper-class British families. To ensure they remained in the colony rather than slinking back home, the family sent the young men a regular remittance or payment. After the war ended, the influx of immigrants from other parts of Europe further diversified the ethnic background of cowboys.

In late September 1882, one of Alberta's most legendary cowboys arrived, coming in as a drover on the North West Cattle Company drive of 3,000 head of Montana cattle. John Ware was a Black American who had been freed from slavery from a southern cotton plantation at the end of the American Civil War. He had drifted west, learning the cowboy trade at countless ranches along the way. By the late 1870s, he turned northward along the Western Cattle Trail from Texas to Wyoming and Montana, eventually ending up at the trail's furthest northern range—southern Alberta. There he discovered experienced cowboys were in short supply, so remained for the rest of his life. Ware died in the saddle at age 60, mortally injured in a riding accident near Brooks in 1905.

Another of Alberta's legendary cowboys was George Lane. Arriving at the **Bar U Ranch** in 1884 as a foreman, his knowledge of cattle and horse stock led to his gaining ownership of the Bar U. Along with Pat Burns, A. E. Cross, and Archie McLean, Lane was known as a member of the "Big Four" in Canadian ranching. These Calgary-based cattlemen gave Guy Weadick, a showman-cowboy, the financial backing needed to stage the first Calgary Stampede.

The cowboy life has been greatly romanticized in literature, film, and television. Reality was, and remains, less glamorous. Work was hard, often numbingly boring and repetitive. Living conditions closely parallelled those endured by enlisted soldiers and North-West Mounted Police troopers of the era. Cowboys lived in crude barracks-style bunkhouses and ate communally in a cookhouse. On the range, they slept in tents or line shacks. Free time was usually spent hunting, gambling, or drinking with fellow cowboys in the bars of the nearest community.

Pay was meagre. Before the outbreak of World War II wages remained relatively stagnant. A cowboy's average pay was $30 to $45 a month plus board. The cowboys were usually responsible for purchasing and maintaining their own saddles and other livery gear. In Canada, few cowboys carried guns when they were working and even fewer owned either a revolver or holster. Gunfights on the range or in saloons were largely unknown.

By the end of World War II the cowboy era in southern Alberta was closing. Most large ranches had long been broken up into small cash-crop farms. Cattle raising practice was increasingly less dependent on running cattle on the remaining rangeland.

Today a small number of Albertans still earn their living as cowboys, but they are as likely to ride an all-terrain vehicle as a horse. The cowboy tradition lives on, however, in Albertan culture. **Rodeos** are frequent, country music dominates the radio airwaves, and line dancing in country bars and clubs is an urban phenomenon. Cowboy hats and boots are common clothing for people who have never sat astride a horse, strung wire, or thrown a lariat. During today's **Calgary Exhibition and Stampede** sociologists have determined that as many as 65 percent of the city's residents don Stetsons and boots at least once.

Coyotes. *See* Wild Dogs.

Crowsnest Pass

With a maximum elevation of 1,396 metres, this pass through the **Rocky Mountains** runs from Coleman, Alberta to Sparwood, British Columbia. Only about 70 kilometres north of the U.S. border, the pass is traversed by Highway 3—the southernmost highway route crossing Alberta.

The Crowsnest Pass served for centuries as an easy travel route for **First Nations peoples.** The Kutenai used the pass to journey east to join the Crow people in **bison** hunts.

White explorers, including the eminent Canadian geologist George Mercer Dawson, found evidence of major coal deposits here. In 1898, the Canadian Pacific Railway (CPR) pushed a line through the pass to provide access to the mining operations developing in the region. The railway also served to raise the national flag over an area beginning to be encroached by American mining interests.

To raise funds for the rail construction the CPR negotiated an agreement with the federal government known as the Crow's Nest Pass Agreement. Under the agreement, the CPR was given a cash subsidy of $3.3 million and title to pass into B.C. in exchange for reducing, in perpetuity, eastbound shipping rates on grain and flour and westbound rates on specified products.

Although the agreement was fiddled with constantly as the federal government and the CPR tried to return rates to their real costs, Prairie farmers lobbied effectively for preservation of the lower rates, which enabled Canadian grain to reach world markets at competitive prices. Consequently, "Preserve the Crow" was an oft-rung battle cry heard in Prairie grain-farming communities far removed from, and little concerned, about the pass itself. In 1995, however, the agreement was finally scrapped by the federal government despite farmers' protests.

Until the late 1940s, the Alberta portion of the pass was particularly notorious for having some of the world's most dangerous mines. It was the site of Canada's worst mine disaster, the **Hillcrest Mine Disaster,** and Canada's worst natural disaster, the **Frank Slide.**

Today, it remains an important mining area and transportation route. Its spectacular mountain scenery and less-trafficked highway make the pass a popular tourist route through the Rockies.

Cypress Hills

The Cypress Hills of southeastern Alberta and Saskatchewan derive their shape and unique ecosystem from having once been an island—an island completely surrounded and in places cut through by glacial ice. These hills are actually more a flat-topped plateau covering a total of about 2,600 square kilometres, of which approximately one-third lies within Alberta. Their maximum elevation of 1,466 metres is found at the western extremity, about 35 kilometres northeast of Manyberries. This summit, known as "Head of the Mountain," is the highest Canadian elevation between Labrador and the **Rocky Mountains.** Steep, nearly vertical cliffs mark the north and west sides of the hills, but to the south they gently descend to merge gradually into the surrounding plains.

During the glaciation of the Pleistocene epoch about 35,000 years ago, the southward-flowing ice sheets thinned and split when they encountered the 1,400-metre level of the hills. Sixty-six metres of land totalling 200 square kilometres stood above the ice and was never glaciated. This area is now encompassed in Cypress Hills Provincial Park, Alberta's second-largest provincial park. Beginning about 12,000 years ago the last of the glaciers withdrew, exposing the scoured **prairie** landscape. Glacial meltwater etched deep channels along the north and west slopes. These depressions filled with water to form three lakes: Elkwater, Reesor, and Spruce Coulee.

The Cypress Hills' unique physiography creates an oasis effect. Here, in the midst of harsh, barely vegetated prairie, forests of lodgepole pine and aspen thickly cover the hills and wildlife is abundant. The hills' increased elevation brings cooler temperatures and additional rainfall (over 80 millimetres per year more than the surrounding prairie). The porous conglomerate and sandstone layers topping the hills capture the groundwater, releasing it slowly along the forested slopes. The movement of this underground water, however, weakens underlying clay layers, sometimes resulting in massive landslides.

Once the Cypress Hills were home to **bison,** prairie wolves, and grizzly **bears.** Even today the wildlife is diverse and abundant. Many species that live here are found nowhere else in Alberta but the Rocky Mountains. Scientists believe that in early post-glacial times a corridor of forest connected the hills and the Rockies. When that forest gave way to prairie the mountain wildlife found here was stranded. Lynx, wolves, and elk, as well as such Rocky Mountain bird species as dark-eyed juncos and yellow-rumped warblers remained behind. Some of the vegetation is also identical to that found in the Rockies.

Even more curiously, the drier southern slopes are home to species of wildlife and vegetation found nowhere else in Canada and more commonly occurring in the semi-arid deserts of the United States. These two anomalies have led some scientists to call the Cypress Hills a "geological practical joke" because fragile ferns and wild orchids (some 16 species) found only in high mountain areas of the Rockies thrive in moist shady nooks of the hills, while in the southern **foothills** horned toads and scorpions dwell among yucca grass.

Because of the small expanse of their habitat the native large **mammals** of the Cypress Hills were mostly extirpated by European hunters soon after their arrival in the region. The last large mammal—a wolf—was shot in 1926. In 1938, elk were reintroduced to the park. Moose, never before present here, were introduced in the 1950s, as were red squirrels and wild turkeys. Today, 37 mammal species and more than 200 species of **birds** live here.

The Cypress Hills were so named by French-Canadian explorers who mistook the prevalent lodgepole pine for the jack pine of eastern Canada, which they called *cyprès.* They named the area *Montagne de Cyprès,* which later English commentators translated as the Cypress Hills. Perhaps the first person to call the area an oasis was John Palliser, when the **Palliser Expedition** passed through the area in 1858. He wrote of the hills, "These hills are a perfect oasis in the desert we have travelled."

First Nations peoples often referred to the hills as the "Thunder

Breeding Hills." For them the Cypress Hills were a place of mystery, where they came to worship and perform Sun Dances.

Cypress Hills Massacre

On April 29, 1873, a band of American wolfers was pursuing a raiding party of Blackfoot warriors who had stolen about 40 of their horses a few days earlier. They came upon a small Assiniboine camp in the Cypress Hills. The people in the camp knew nothing of the stolen horses and had played no role in the theft. That mattered little to the wolfers. The men unslung their repeating rifles and opened fire on the helpless group of men, women, and children. Minutes later most everyone in the camp lay dead.

The wolfers were never brought to justice, as their identity was never discovered.

When news of the massacre reached Ottawa, it provided the impetus necessary to rush passage of a bill presented only the day before by Prime Minister John A. Macdonald which called for the formation of the **North-West Mounted Police.** The new paramilitary force would be sent west the following year to establish the rule of Canadian law upon the American whiskey traders and wolfers who had been operating for several years with impunity in southern Alberta.

Wolfers were a particularly vile group. They poisoned **bison** carcasses by saturating them with strychnine. Returning to the dead animals days later they would often find a hundred or more wolves who had died from eating the poisoned meat. The wolves were then skinned for their fur. The **First Nations peoples,** European bison hunters, fur traders, and even the whiskey traders all despised the wolfers.

Devil's Coulee Dinosaur Eggs

On May 24, 1987, Wendy Sloboda was exploring the **coulees** along the **Milk River** ridge near her family's ranch when she found some small fossil fragments. The 19-year-old amateur palaeontologist suspected they might be dinosaur eggshells, so she sent them to Dr. Len Hills at the University of Calgary. Hills examined the shells and confirmed Sloboda's guess. He notified Dr. Philip Currie at the **Royal Tyrrell Museum of Palaeontology** of the discovery.

The museum was already planning a survey expedition in southern Alberta to look for dinosaur eggs, so the crew started its expedition at the coulee where the shells had been found. Wendy Sloboda joined in the search, which lasted for three weeks and encompassed hundreds of kilometres. As the weeks drew on the hunt continued to prove fruitless. On the expedition's second last day, the crew arrived at a favourite picnic spot of the residents of nearby Warner, called Devil's Coulee. At this site bedrock poked up from soft clay-based soil.

Technician Kevin Aulenback sat down for a moment's rest on a hillside in the coulee. Looking down, he noticed a small bone protruding from the ground. Gazing up the slope, Aulenback saw bits of eggshell and part of an egg with vertebrae sticking out of it. Minutes later, the crew gathered on the slope to start examining Canada's first discovered dinosaur nesting site. The eggs averaged 20 centimetres in diameter. Many contained perfectly formed embryonic bones of unborn **dinosaurs.**

The dinosaur eggs discovered at Devil's Coulee are those of the duck-billed hypacrosaur and are about 75 million years old. Hypacrosaurs were herbivores capable of bipedal movement. A mature hypacrosaur had a long tail, a sharply defined finlike backbone, and stood two to three metres high, about the size of a present-day elephant. Yet young hatchlings were so small they could fit inside two human hands. The parents cared for their young— averaging four to six per clutch—until they were old and large enough to fend for themselves against the constant threat of predators.

Devil's Coulee's geology indicates that during the Cretaceous Period, 140 million to 65 million years ago, the southwestern part of **ancient Alberta** was cut by shallow, seasonal rivers that flowed eastward across a forested plain. Regular floods often swamped large parts of this land, but with the water's withdrawal the forest quickly returned to the floodplain. It was on the floodplains that hypacrosaurs gathered to mate, nest, and hatch their eggs. Since the first egg discovery at Devil's Coulee, researchers have found numerous egg clusters, fragments of embryonic bone, and thousands of pieces of eggshell—suggesting the coulee was once a regularly used hypacrosaur rookery.

Today, the site is protected by the provincial government. There is an interpretive centre on site, which has public displays and also serves as a research and bone preparation and examination facility. Tours of the bone beds and egg site can be arranged through the centre. It is possible for visitors to spend a day digging alongside palaeontologists for bones in the coulee. Devil's Coulee is located west of Warner, off Highway 506.

Dinosaur Provincial Park

Covering 6,622 hectares of **badlands** in the Red Deer River Valley, Dinosaur Provincial Park contains the world's richest dinosaur fields—the Judith River Group. Dinosaur skeletons discovered here date back 75 million years to the Cretaceous Period of **ancient Alberta.**

Fossil remains of what are believed to tally 36 different species of **dinosaurs** have been unearthed, almost 17 percent of all the world's known dinosaurs. The **fossils** of another 84 animal species found here include crocodiles, lizards, turtles, and giant flying reptiles. Remains of clams, snails, and plants are also common, reminders that this area was once a tropical forest periodically submerged by a sea. More than 300 museum-quality specimens have been removed from the palaeontological excavation sites in this park.

Between 1979 and 1991, researchers focused on a large dinosaur graveyard about the size of a football field, identified as Quarry 143. This bone bed contained the fossilized remains of more than 220 dinosaurs of the same species—the horned dinosaur *Centrosaurus*—including about 50 males and a larger number of females and babies. Researchers initially concluded that the centrosaurs died en masse, probably drowned in a sudden flood. The presence of so many dinosaurs, all of the same species, in such a concentrated space suggests the centrosaurs gathered together in great herds as they searched for new feeding and breeding grounds.

In 1992, researchers discovered several other *Centrosaurus* bone beds and realized they lay at the same level as Quarry 143. In 1995, two of these bone beds were opened. The specimens found were in better condition than those previously discovered. Preliminary results of this investigation suggest links among the deaths of centrosaurs in the various sites, but that at least two mass death events are represented. This makes the cause of the mass deaths more mysterious than first thought, as it seems unlikely separate floods would result in so many centrosaur deaths.

The **Royal Tyrrell Museum of Palaeontology** operates a satellite field station in the park. Here many fossils exhumed in the park are studied, stored, and displayed. Each summer researchers (the greatest concentration of palaeontologists known to occur in any place at one time) descend on the park for an intense period of digging that starts in late June and usually lasts no more than ten weeks. Most of the areas in which digging takes place are barred from public access, although tours are offered.

Because of the park's rich fossil beds, unique badlands, and endangered **cottonwood forests,** Dinosaur Provincial Park was declared a

UNESCO World Heritage Site in 1979. It is one of the most popular of Alberta's **provincial parks.**

Dinosaurs

The oldest identifiable dinosaur bones and teeth discovered in Alberta were found in a **Milk River Formation** at Verdigris Coulee, near **Writing-On-Stone Provincial Park.** A small collection of **fossils** reflects an 80-million-year-old dinosaur community. The creatures were duck-billed hadrosaurs, ceratopsians, small and large carnivores, and armoured ankylosaurs. For 15 million years these dinosaurs all roamed Alberta.

Nowhere on earth has yielded more individual dinosaur skeletons than the Judith River Group of **Dinosaur Provincial Park.** Another vast quarry of dinosaur bones was first unearthed by Joseph Burr Tyrrell in 1884 where the Kneehills Creek joins the Red Deer River. In 1985, the **Royal Tyrrell Museum of Palaeontology** opened near this site. Throughout Alberta, evidence of dinosaurs and their fossilized remains are uncovered regularly by trained researchers and amateurs alike.

The term dinosaur was first coined by Richard Owen, a London surgeon and bone collector. He defined it as meaning "terrible lizard." Palaeontologists now look for specific characteristics before classifying any creature as a dinosaur. It must have long bones in the palate, three or more vertebrae where the hips attach to the backbone, a backward-facing shoulder joint, and an index "finger" with three or fewer joints. Complicating this definition is the fact that **birds** fulfill all the necessary criteria to be considered

Albertosaurus *was eight metres of fierce carnivore. Its hind legs ended in sharp claws used for raking prey, while its powerful jaws enabled it to rip apart a carcass with razor-sharp teeth. (Frances Backhouse photo)*

dinosaurs. It is possible that modern birds are the only surviving descendants of the long-extinct dinosaurs.

Dinosaurs moved with their legs tucked under their bodies, distinguishing them from lizards and crocodiles, whose legs protrude from the side. They walked on their toes just like modern birds. Dinosaurs lived on land and neither swam nor flew. They laid eggs and lived only during the Mesozoic Era, which lasted from 210 million years ago to 65 million years ago. All are now extinct.

It is believed that dinosaurs evolved from a type of reptile known as thecodonts during the middle of the Triassic Period. Why this evolution took place is unknown, but it is clear that thecodonts evolved the ability to walk on two legs. Probably they only used this form of movement for short, violent dashes after prey or to themselves evade predators.

Early dinosaurs refined this method of movement, becoming able walkers and runners capable of speeds exceeding 10 kilometres per hour. Some could hit speeds of 20 to 50 kilometres per hour—making them the fastest creatures then alive. Their jointed limbs and free-moving front limbs gave the dinosaurs distinct advantages over other Triassic Period species.

At the end of the Triassic a mass extinction occurred, but the dinosaurs recovered quickly and dominated all other land-based species for the next 145 million years. As the Triassic gave way to the Jurassic Period dinosaurs became more diverse, some returning to a four-legged stance. Ten-metre tall, 2.3-tonne allosaurs, among the period's most efficient meat eaters, harried 90-tonne sauropods or the heavily armoured stegosaur (both moving on four legs). Like modern-day wolves, it is believed allosaurs often improved their chances of bringing down gigantic prey by hunting in packs. Scurrying around beneath these leviathans' feet was the chicken-sized compsognathid.

The habitat covering much of the world at the time, including Alberta, was ideal for dinosaurs—swamps, thick forests, giant inland seas, large rivers and lakes. During the Cretaceous Period beginning 140 million years ago, flowering plants became the dominant form of vegetation in areas such as Alberta. This development coincided with the emergence of many new species of dinosaurs, which pushed the majority of Jurassic species into decline and eventual extinction. Among those pushed aside were the massive, long-necked sauropods. In their place emerged duck-billed hadrosaurs, horned ceratopsians, solidly armoured ankylosaurs, and dome-headed pachycephalosaurs. All of these had shorter necks, more suitable for grazing on the lower flowering growth that was now common herbivore forage. From 140 million to 65 million years ago these dinosaurs formed part of the richest period of dinosaur species proliferation.

The herbivores needed armour, speed, agility, or a combination of these features to survive. For this was also the period during which the greatest dinosaur meat eaters prowled the earth—the 14-metre-long, 8-tonne *Tyrannosaurus Rex*, the 25 percent smaller *Albertosaurus*, and other killing machines. Some carnivores were about the size of a human and lacked teeth. These were *Struthiomimus*, which was ostrichlike, and *Ornithomimus*, which was somewhat birdlike in shape. It is believed these creatures probably served as scavengers, cleaning up the carcasses left by well-fed larger meat eaters. Another small carnivore, velociraptors, had large brains, forward-looking eyes, long ostrichlike legs, vicious claws, and grasping hands. All this, combined with their ability to use stealth, made them one of the period's most formidable hunters.

By the end of the Cretaceous Period, however, dinosaurs were in decline, as evidenced by fossil finds. Compared to the 75-million-year-old bone beds at Dinosaur Provincial Park, fossil beds from 67 million to 65 million years ago contain only about 25 percent as many species of meat eaters and 50 percent as many species of herbivores. This indicates a dangerous loss of diversity, one of the leading causes of eventual species extinction.

About 65 million years ago the age of the dinosaurs ended quite suddenly. Most geologists and palaeontologists support a theory that earth was struck by one or more asteroids (an event that precipitated earlier mass extinctions), creating conditions unsuitable for dinosaur survival. It is thought to be unlikely that dinosaurs perished everywhere in one instant mass extinction. Rather, it is probable that in parts of the world close to the asteroid strike or strikes they perished almost immediately, while in areas more remote from impact points the decline was more gradual—possibly taking thousands of years. However the extinctions occurred, scientists agree that about 60 to 80 percent of all living species became extinct at the end of the Cretaceous, including all dinosaurs.

Dunvegan. *See* Fort Dunvegan.

Dunvegan Suspension Bridge

The Dunvegan Suspension Bridge crossing the **Peace River** on Highway 2 is Alberta's longest clear-span bridge and the fourth-longest suspension bridge in Canada. The 550-metre bridge was completed in 1960, replacing a ferry service.

Easter Egg. *See* **Pysanka.**

Economy

With an annual gross domestic product (GDP) of about $100 billion, Alberta has Canada's fourth-largest economy, after Ontario, Quebec, and British Columbia. In real terms this economy has doubled in size since 1974, while the **population** has increased by only 63 percent during the same period.

It is an economy firmly based on natural resources. Petroleum extraction, mining, and forestry account directly for slightly more than half of total GDP. In addition, many of the province's other economic sectors involve secondary processing of natural resources. Refined petroleum products, for example, generate about $3.8 billion annually and the production of petrochemicals and plastics contributes another $3.8 billion.

The other major economic factor is the **agriculture** industry, generating annual farm cash receipts of about $5.4 billion.

With a small population compared to its natural resource and agricultural production, Alberta is heavily dependent on exporting to other provinces and countries. Only 47.8 percent of its goods and services are consumed within the province. Of the remainder, 21.6 percent goes to other provinces and 30.6 percent to the international marketplace.

Alberta companies export goods and services to more than 150 countries, but the vast majority of exports goes to the United States. In most years between 77 and 80 percent of all exports are to America. Japan, Alberta's next biggest international trading partner, receives only about 5.5 to 7 percent of total exports.

Most exportation is of raw or minimally processed natural resources and agricultural products. Primary agricultural products average 10.5 percent of total exports, while manufactured goods constitute 36.8 percent. About half of all exports are of mined natural resources—including oil, gas, coal, and sulphur. The majority of manufactured goods exported from Alberta also derive directly from mined or logged natural resources. All three major manufacturing sector exports—chemicals, paper, and refined petroleum and coal—are principally derived from natural resource exploitation. Together these three account for nearly 23 percent of all manufactured goods exports.

Dependence on a natural resource economy that must export products means the province's economic health is particularly vulnerable to developments in world markets and fluctuations in internationally determined commodity prices. Swings in world commodity prices subject the provincial economy to periods of rapid growth followed by slowdowns, recessions, and occasional depressions. Heavy dependence on the United States makes the province's economy particularly vulnerable to economic developments south of the border.

Like other Canadian provinces dominated by a natural resource-based economy, Alberta's provincial government is constantly striving to diversify the economy by encouraging the development of stronger manufacturing and advanced technology industries. These attempts have met with moderate success in the manufacturing sector, which has tripled its size since 1970 and now ships approximately $24 to $25 billion in goods annually. The majority of this manufacturing activity, however, remains focused around value-added uses of natural resource products, which can be as susceptible to world price fluctuations as the natural resource sector.

Although advanced technology industries remain modest, this is a rapidly expanding sector that holds much promise for diversifying the province's economy in the next century. More than 50,000 Albertans are directly employed in approximately 1,200 types of advanced technology enterprise. Electronics and telecommunications companies in Alberta, for example, number about 225 and in 1994 shipped products valued at $2.2 billion—a 50 percent increase over the previous year.

An ever-growing sector of Alberta's economy is **tourism,** which employs approximately 100,000 people and generates about $3 billion in annual revenues.

Despite the province's economic base resting on natural resources, agriculture, manufacturing, and advanced technologies, most Albertans do not work directly in these sectors. Two-thirds of all Albertans in the **labour force** are employed in the service sector, which includes business and financial services, transportation, tourism, retail trade, and health and **education** services.

Albertans are Canada's most avid consumers—routinely leading the way in the nation's per capita consumer spending. Retail sales in past years have routinely topped $20 billion, creating a strong retail sales industry that employs about 183,000 people. It also encourages the growth of mega-malls, of which the **West Edmonton Mall** is both the penultimate expression and the world's largest.

Helping to fuel the retail sector is the fact that Alberta is the only province to have no provincial retail sales tax—a fact which makes shopping one of the province's significant tourist attractions.

With a government that has historically been one of Canada's most pro-business, Alberta has created the nation's most favourable tax climate for business investment. Overall, the province enjoys the lowest taxes in Canada. In addition to there being no retail sales tax, Alberta has the country's lowest gasoline taxes, lowest personal income tax rates, and no provincial payroll or capital taxes.

(*See also* **Forest Industry; Mining Industry; Oil and Gas Industry.**)

Edmonton

With a population of 627,000 people, Edmonton is the second-largest city in Alberta after **Calgary.** The provincial capital, it is also one of the world's largest northerly cities.

The city takes its name from Edmonton House, a fur-trading fort opened by the Hudson's Bay Company (HBC) in 1795 at the junction of the North Saskatchewan River and its smaller tributary, the Sturgeon River. It was named after the English home of the chief factor's clerk, John Peter Pruden. Between 1795 and 1830 Edmonton House was renamed Fort Edmonton and relocated several times before being moved to higher ground near the present-day Alberta **Legislative Building.** The fort remained at this location until it was demolished in 1915, but was abandoned in 1870 when the HBC ceded Rupert's Land to the Canadian Dominion government.

Edmonton's growth was slow in the 1800s, due to the harsh **climate** and its isolation—a branch railway was not extended from Calgary until 1891. Even this branch line terminated at Strathcona on the opposite bank of the North Saskatchewan River. In 1905, the Canadian Northern Railway provided the city with a transcontinental link. By then, Edmonton was experiencing some prosperity and development due to agricultural settlement throughout the surrounding region and the aftereffects of having served as a staging area for gold seekers heading to the **Klondike Gold Rush.** The same year, it was designated by the Liberal Party–controlled federal government as the provincial capital, possibly because it was a Liberal bastion and rival Calgary solidly supported the Conservative Party.

In 1912, Strathcona and Edmonton amalgamated. The two cities had a joint population of about 40,000. When World War I broke out in 1914 Edmonton's population had grown to about 50,000. Until 1940 its fortunes were intrinsically linked with those of the vast **agriculture** industry it supported. Its growth was slow, but steady. In 1941, it was Canada's ninth-largest city with a population of about 92,000.

World War II sowed the seeds of an economic diversification that continues today. Edmonton thrived economically because of its designation as a strategic centre for northern military operations, including the construction of the Alaska Highway. Increased need for reliable sources of petrochemical supplies resulted in several oil refineries being built in the city. Following the war, construction of more refineries and gas processing plants cemented Edmonton's national and international importance as a major oil and gas centre.

In the post-war period, Edmonton also underwent a major population boom to support its increased industrial base. Between 1941 and 1981 its population increased more than sixfold and the city extended its boundaries numerous times.

Although much of Edmonton's growth has been fuelled by development in the oil and gas exploration and processing industry, this sector provides surprisingly little of the city's employment. Rather, its presence generated development of a large service-based sector that accounts for almost 40 percent of the workforce. This service emphasis is best reflected by the presence of major shopping malls and retail and wholesale operations — with the **West Edmonton Mall** their ultimate expression. Edmonton's status as the provincial capital has also ensured that it has a large government sector workforce.

Edmonton has developed a rich cultural and sports community, which includes three of the largest performing-arts organizations in Canada — the Edmonton Symphony Society, the Edmonton Opera Association, and the Citadel Theatre. (*See also* **Performing Arts.**)

Edmonton Eskimos

The Edmonton Eskimos trace their lineage back to a rugby football club formed in 1892. The game played was a hybrid of English rugby that incorporated some of the techniques of soccer, but involved carrying and throwing the ball instead of kicking it. This variation originated at McGill University in Montreal, so modern-day football is truly a Canadian, not American, invention.

The Eskimos were first known as the Esquimaux, changing their name in 1910 to its modern form. In 1921, they became the first western Canadian team to play in a Grey Cup game, a national football championship established in 1909 and named after the donator of the trophy, then Governor General Earl Grey. They were shut out by the Toronto Argonauts 23–0. Back the following year, the Eskimos lost to Queen's University 13–1. In 1923, they dropped the western championship to the Regina Roughriders. Losing again the following year to **Calgary,** the team folded, only to be resurrected again in 1928.

Football as a game was still evolving toward its present form. In 1929, the team played its first game featuring the forward pass when quarterback Joe Cook connected with Pal Power for a touchdown pass.

The following year the team moved to Clarke Stadium and played there, with some lost seasons, until the end of World War II. In 1948, a reorganized Edmonton Eskimo Rugby Football Club emerged as a publicly owned team. Shares were $1 each, with 20,000 offered. It was not until 1952 that the team again reached a Grey Cup, losing to the Toronto Argonauts 21–11.

In 1954, the Eskimos introduced the twin-fullback formation and electrified the nation with some outstanding football. During the Grey Cup, Jackie Parker scooped up a last-minute fumble to score a touchdown and lead the team to a victory over the Montreal Alouettes. They took the cup again in 1955 and 1956, but lost the western final to the Winnipeg Blue Bombers in 1957.

Back in the Grey Cup in 1960, they were defeated by the Ottawa Rough Riders 16–6. They would not return to the Grey Cup field until 1973, losing to Ottawa, then losing to Montreal the following year. But in 1975 Edmonton captured its fourth Grey Cup in a 9–8 squeaker over Montreal.

In 1978, the Eskimos started a remarkable run, capturing five consecutive Grey Cups to set a Canadian Football League (CFL) record. **Edmonton** hosted its first Grey Cup in 1984, but the Eskimos were not among the teams playing. They returned to the Grey Cup final in 1986, but lost to the Hamilton Tiger-Cats. In 1987 they were back and captured their tenth Grey Cup by defeating Toronto 38–36. They lost to Winnipeg in 1990, but emerged victorious in 1993 to take their 11th Grey Cup. In 1995 the team set a CFL record by making the playoffs for a record 24 straight seasons. On November 24, 1996 in Hamilton, Edmonton lost the Grey Cup to Toronto in a closely fought 43–37 scoring free-for-all, the second-highest points per Grey Cup game recorded.

Edmonton Oilers

In 1972 the Edmonton Oilers were born as one of the founding franchises of the World Hockey Association (WHA). The first season they wore jerseys bearing the name Alberta Oilers, with their home ice at the Edmonton Gardens. The team's talent was lacklustre at best and to nobody's surprise they failed to make the playoffs. Renamed the Edmonton Oilers for the 1973–74 season, the rebuilt team made the playoffs but was knocked out in the first round.

On November 4, 1974, the Oilers moved to the new Northlands Coliseum. That night 15,326 people—the largest crowd in WHA history—packed into the arena. Despite the loyal crowd of fans, the team failed again to make the playoffs. The following year they earned a spot in the playoffs, but were eliminated in the first round.

The Oilers continued to languish until March 2, 1977, when Peter Pocklington became sole owner. Pocklington had his sights on switching the team from the WHA to the National Hockey League (NHL). To do that he had to build a team that could win.

On November 1, 1978, Pocklington acquired three players for the team, among them a spidery, thin 17-year-old named Wayne Gretzky from Brantford, Ontario. Two months later, on January 26, 1979, Pocklington signed Gretzky to a 21-year contract. That summer the team was accepted into the NHL. Pocklington predicted they would win the Stanley Cup in five years at the outside.

In the 1979–80 season they made it to the playoffs. Despite establishing many season records throughout the next few years, the Oilers kept getting knocked out of the playoffs. In 1982–83 they reached the Stanley Cup finals but lost to the New York Islanders. The following year they were back, once more facing off against the Islanders. On May 19, 1984, the team captured the Stanley Cup, realizing Pocklington's five-year prediction. The next year they again captured the cup. Throughout this time the team's fame was furthered by Gretzky's record-breaking prowess. By the 1986–87 season, Gretzky held 44 individual records and was being hailed as probably the greatest hockey player in world history.

The Oilers, however, experienced a slump in their fortunes after 1985, failing to win another Stanley Cup until the 1989–90 season. This was their second season without Gretzky, who was traded by Pocklington to the Los Angeles Kings in 1988—a deal allowed under the terms of the contract he had signed with Gretzky nine years earlier.

Between 1990 and 1996 the team had some dramatic seasons, but failed to achieve another Stanley Cup win. The Oilers, however, remain one of the strongest contenders in the NHL and local support for the team is such that the arena is generally sold out during home games.

Edmonton Space and Science Centre

Since its opening in 1984 more than 5 million people have visited the Edmonton Space and Science Centre in Coronation Park. The centre contains an IMAX theatre, the Margaret Zeidler Theatre, an observatory, a simulated space station and mission control complex called Challenger Centre, and a science shop.

The science displays are contained in three galleries. The lower gallery examines the human body and medical technology, the middle gallery focuses on future communications technology and also features a piece of the moon, while the upper gallery houses the Challenger Centre. In this centre participants crew a simulated mission into space. Laser light shows are a daily feature in the Margaret Zeidler Theatre, the largest planetarium dome in Canada. Its laser and planetarium shows use more than 200 computer-controlled projectors, special effect projectors, and a two-watt krypton laser system combined with 23,000 watts of audio power.

Science demonstrations are offered throughout the day at the NOVA Science Carnival, and an observatory next to the complex provides the opportunity to view the sun, moon, planets, stars, and galaxies through powerful telescopes.

Its facilities make this science centre one of the top-ranked such venues in North America.

Education

Each year about 540,000 students fill Alberta's early-childhood to grade 12 classrooms. Of these about 123,000 attend high school, 120,000 junior high school, 257,000 elementary school, and about 40,000 are enrolled in early childhood services (ECS). The provincial department of education oversees the schooling of these students and provides annual funding of about $3 billion (about $1.5 billion coming from direct provincial government grants, the rest from local residential and nonresidential property taxes).

In Canada, provinces are responsible for providing education to their citizens. The province sets the curriculum, designs province-wide tests to ensure conformity of standards, and provides grants to enable school boards to fund operations.

The Alberta School Act of 1905 governs the education system. This act established two publicly funded school systems, one public, and a separate school system known as the Roman Catholic School system. Parents have the right under the act to choose what type of education their children will receive.

In addition to these two systems, home schooling and schooling in other private institutions are allowed. Accredited private schools that follow government-approved curricula and hire certified teachers receive 75 percent of the provincial grant that would be payable to schools operating within the public or Roman Catholic system.

The right of **francophone Albertans** to receive their education in French is upheld by the Canadian Charter of Rights and Freedoms. In addition to English- and French-language programs, Alberta's schools also offer language courses and programs at select schools in Arabic, Chinese, Cree, German, Hebrew, Japanese, Latin, Spanish, and Ukrainian (*see* **Ukrainian-Canadian Albertans**).

There are approximately 2,150 schools operating in Alberta. Of these more than three-quarters are public schools, about 250 are Roman Catholic schools, and 200 are private schools. Approximately 185 ECS private operators receive funding to provide care for children aged four to six years.

(*See also* **Post-Secondary Education.**)

Elk Island National Park

Located 45 kilometres east of Edmonton and divided by the Yellowhead Highway, Elk Island National Park is a small island of nature surrounded by agricultural and urban areas. Its 194 square kilometres are part of the Beaver Hills, a unique region rising 60 metres above the plain to form a matrix of knob and kettle (respectively glacial mounds and depressions) country, along with wetlands and mixed (but predominantly aspen) forest.

Prior to the coming of Europeans, the Beaver Hills had been home to a rich diversity of wildlife. By 1815, the fur trade had nearly extirpated beaver from the area. By the late 1860s, the **bison** were gone and most other large mammal populations were virtually eliminated.

In 1906 only 24 elk, 2 to 3 moose, and about 35 mule deer were known to still live in the Elk Island area. A group of five Fort Saskatchewan residents lobbied the federal government to create a wildlife sanctuary in hopes of saving this meagre population. Their effort was successful and Elk Park, a 42-square-kilometre area, was protected—the first wildlife preserve for large **mammals** in Canada.

The park's land surrounds a lake known locally as Island Lake (now named Astotin Lake). Numerous small islands dot the lake, including one called Elk Island because local elk swam out each year to use the island as a birthing site.

In 1907, about 400 plains bison were shipped to the park from the

Pablo-Allard herd in Montana. The intention was to keep the bison at the park only until completion of a fencing project at Wainwright Buffalo National Park. The following year, Elk Park was renamed Elk Island Park. In 1909, the fencing at Wainwright Buffalo National Park was completed and 325 plains bison were shipped there, but some 50 to 70 animals evaded capture and formed the foundation of the park's plains bison herd. Widespread disease among the Wainwright herd led to that park's eventual closure and abandonment. The few surviving bison would be moved to **Wood Buffalo National Park.** Twenty-three wood bison were added to Elk Island's plains bison population in 1965.

Today, Elk Island is home to a healthy population of mammals that had nearly been eliminated in the early 1900s. About 730 plains bison, 335 wood bison, 1,700 elk, 330 moose, 475 deer, 100 coyotes, and 500 beaver live inside the park boundaries. To help keep this population safe from human threat, Elk Island is the only national park in Canada to have a completely fenced boundary.

The park contains 250 lakes and ponds, one of the main attractions for the 240 species of Alberta's 340 bird species that frequent Elk Island. Of this number, 170 species use the area for breeding. Since motorboats were banned from Astotin Lake in 1978 some species, including grebes and loons, have returned.

In 1987 a trumpeter swan transplant program was initiated at Elk Island, a historic summering and breeding range for the world's largest waterfowl. Today, two pairs of **trumpeter swans** nest in the park and efforts are underway to increase this small population to about ten pairs.

The park is also an important sanctuary for Alberta flora species. More than 25 percent of all vascular plants known in Alberta grow within its boundaries, including eight rare species and over 300 flowering plants.

The park has about a dozen hiking and cross-country ski trails ranging from 3.5 kilometres to 18.5 kilometres in length, camping, and access to lakes for water sports.

Endangered Species

There are currently 12 animal species considered endangered under Alberta's Wildlife Act. These are the swift fox, **woodland caribou,** barren ground caribou, wood **bison,** American white pelican, whooping crane, trumpeter swan, ferruginous hawk, peregrine falcon, burrowing owl, piping plover, and mountain plover.

All officially endangered species in Alberta are either **mammals** or

birds. There are, however, several reptile, amphibian, and invertebrate species also at risk. To date, these species are limited in protection to inclusion on the province's Status of Alberta Wildlife red, blue, yellow, green, and status undetermined lists (with levels of endangerment running from red as the highest to green as the lowest). Although the provincial government terms wildlife as including plants, no plants are included in the Wildlife Act's Endangered Species list or figure on the more critical provincial red and blue lists despite the fact that some plant habitats, such as **cottonwood forests,** and individual species such as the yucca plant, are considered threatened. Critics contest that this absence of extended protection for vegetation has created "a no man's land for plants."

Other than the **Special Places** strategy, there has been no concentrated effort to protect sufficient habitat areas to ensure **biodiversity** within Alberta's many ecosystems. Environmentalists say that the Special Places strategy has been increasingly compromised through opening of protected places to logging, mining, oil and gas exploration, and other economic development. Many scientists, naturalists, and others involved in endangered species recovery work argue that protection of a species is only possible if the entire biodiversity of its habitat is adequately protected. Species require sufficient, usually unbroken, range to sustain genetic diversity through breeding among population groups.

Fines of up to $100,000 and six-month jail sentences can be imposed for killing or trafficking in body parts of endangered species. It is also illegal to disturb their dens or nests. Critics of the Wildlife Act point out that habitat protection is neither sufficiently required nor enforced by the Act. Habitat loss or damage accounts for up to 80 percent of species decline worldwide.

Those animals on the Status of Alberta Wildlife lists have no legislated protection, although their presence on the list is publicly promoted to decrease thoughtless killing and habitat damage. In many cases management plans exist to enhance the survival odds of particular species.

An interesting aspect of the Wildlife Act's endangered species list is that one of the species is not in danger of either extinction or extirpation (where a species no longer exists in Alberta or in Canada, but is present elsewhere). The barren ground caribou is listed because of its close resemblance to the truly endangered woodland caribou. Look-alike species are increasingly added to endangered species legislation and lists around the world. This ensures that poachers, hunters, and others cannot use the defence that their killing of an endangered species was accidental, due to confusion with a similar species. (*See also* **Trumpeter Swans.**)

Environmental Concerns. *See* **Biodiversity; Cottonwood Forests; Endangered Species; Northern Leopard Frog.**

Erratics

Erratics, of which the Okotoks erratic is Alberta's largest, are glacier-transported rock fragments that differ from the bedrock in the area where they were deposited when the glacial ice melted away. Erratics have been carried from one kilometre to as far as 800 kilometres. Those transported long distances generally consist of rock resistant to the shattering and grinding effects of being trapped inside or on top of the massive ice sheets. An erratic can often be analysed by rock type and tracked back to its original mountain.

The erratics of Alberta were scoured off the slopes of the **Rocky Mountains** or deposited on top of glaciers by rock slides caused when ice undermined the supporting bedrock. This debris was then carried eastward onto the Alberta plains by a vast glacier that eventually plowed into the immovable Laurentide ice sheet. The glacier, which was up to one kilometre thick, was deflected southeast, parallelling the Rockies.

The Okotoks erratic is believed to have been carried from Mount Edith Cavell in Jasper National Park to its current location in the midst of the southern Alberta prairie. (Mark Zuehlke photo)

When the ice melted some 14,000 years ago, a string of erratics remained behind in a narrow belt extending from **Jasper National Park** along the **foothills** to northern Montana. This group is known as the Foothills Erratics Train.

The Okotoks erratic is composed of hard quartzite. Some researchers believe it tumbled off the side of **Mount Edith Cavell** in Jasper National Park during a rock slide about 18,000 years ago, coming to rest on the glacier's surface. The rock weighs about 16,500 tonnes and is 41 metres wide by 18 metres long by 9 metres high.

Ethnicity

Most Albertans can trace their roots back to European extraction. The predominant ethnic origin is British, accounting for about 493,000 people. This is followed by 185,600 Albertans of German ethnicity.

Alberta is home to the nation's second-highest concentration of Ukrainians. About 104,350 people of Ukrainian descent call the province home, just below Ontario, which has about 105,000 Ukrainian Canadians.

Albertans of French origin number 74,600, only slightly higher than the growing **population** of Chinese, which tallies about 71,650. Chinese-Canadian Albertans will probably soon outnumber those of French ancestry, as Chinese immigration is outpacing French-Canadian birth rates. The Chinese community in Alberta dwarfs those of other peoples of eastern or southern Asian extraction. Including Chinese Canadians, this grouping numbers only 114,900.

First Nations peoples total 68,450, of whom approximately 20,500 are **Métis**. Both Métis and First Nations populations have declined slightly since the 1980s.

Albertans of Dutch extraction number about 54,750. The ethnic groups mentioned are the province's most numerous. The rest of Alberta's 2.77 million people come from a wide range of ethnic origins, some numbering only in the low hundreds.

It is interesting to also note that the majority of Albertans are of mixed heritage. About 1,068,000 claim descent from parents of combined ethnicity. Of these, 105,800 are of mixed British and French extraction. A further 56,800 have a French parent and a parent of different ethnicity. Intermarriage is clearly a major cause of the decline in the number of **Francophone Albertans.**

Feral Horses. *See* Wild Horses.

Ferries

In 1919, 77 ferries provided motor-vehicle links across many of the province's waterways. Today, only 7 remain but these provide valuable links in Alberta's highway system where the cost of constructing bridges is unwarranted by traffic flow.

The Shaftesbury Ferry (Secondary Highway 740) on the Peace River is pushed by a tug boat and the LaCrete Ferry (Secondary Highway 697), further north on the **Peace River,** is self-propelled.

The remaining five ferries run on a cable and winch system. The Klondyke (Vega) Ferry provides a crossing on the Athabasca River for Secondary Highway 661. The Rosevear Ferry on Secondary Highway 748 crosses the McLeod River, northwest of Edson. Crowfoot Ferry on Secondary Highway 956 crosses the Bow River west of Bassano. Two ferries provide crossings of the Red Deer River—Finnegan Ferry on Secondary Highway 862, and Bleriot Ferry on Secondary Highway 838.

Because of its proximity to Drumheller and the **Royal Tyrrell Museum of Palaeontology,** the Bleriot Ferry is Alberta's busiest. In 1913, it carried 1,230 vehicles, mostly horse-drawn, across the river. Today, it handles more than 28,000 vehicles a year with an average annual passenger load of about 84,000.

Bleriot Ferry is named after Andrew Bleriot, one of the region's early settlers. In 1909, Bleriot's brother Louis, also an area pioneer, became the first person to fly the English Channel.

XVth Winter Olympic Games

In 1988, **Calgary** hosted what is still known internationally as the most successful winter Olympic games in history. More notable than the games themselves, however, has been the legacy they left behind of world-class sports complexes and a fund that continues to support provincial athletic and sports events.

The games generated a $150-million profit, $90 million of which was channelled into an endowment fund administered by the Calgary Olympic Development Association (CODA). This fund oversees the operation of

Olympic facilities in and around Calgary. The other $60 million financed the Canadian Olympic Association's national athlete and coaches programs.

Through investments, CODA's fund has grown from $90 million to about $130 million. Each year, 5 percent, or about $6.5 million, is withdrawn and used to improve facilities at Canada Olympic Park, to support other Olympic facilities, and encourage Calgary's hosting of World Cup and World Championship events.

Between 1988 and 1996 the Olympic facilities hosted 26 World Cup and World Championship meets. Most were held at Canada Olympic Park, a 95-hectare facility containing ski jumps, and bobsled and luge runs. This site also houses the Olympic Hall of Fame, the largest museum in the world devoted to the Olympic Games. Three floors, containing 1,500 displays, trace the history of the Winter Olympics. Other sporting events are regularly held at the Olympic Speed Skating Oval.

Another legacy of the games is the Olympic Saddledome, home to the **Calgary Flames** of the National Hockey League. This arena can seat about 20,000 people. The roof of this unique structure is shaped to replicate a cowboy's saddle and is the largest free-span concrete roof in the world.

Olympic Plaza, a downtown park, hosted the nightly medal-presentation ceremonies. Today, it is used in summer for regular outdoor concerts and, in winter, the large wading pool becomes a public ice-skating rink.

First Nations Land Claims

When the area known as Rupert's Land became part of Canada in 1870, the federal government negotiated treaties with the **First Nations peoples** living there. In what is present-day Alberta three major treaties—Treaty Six, Treaty Seven, and Treaty Eight—were all concluded by 1899.

All three treaties involved First Nations people exchanging title to their land for specific benefits, including the provision of Indian Reserves. (See **First Nations Peoples** for more on treaty details.) Although most First Nations received some reserve land, not all did and many received less than their treaty entitlement. This failure to fulfill treaty obligations has led to the present-day land-claim negotiations and settlements between the federal government and Alberta's First Nations.

The province is obligated to resolve outstanding treaty land entitlements. In 1930, Crown lands and resources were transferred from the federal government to the province. The Natural Resources Transfer Agreement (now called the Constitution Act, 1930) contained specific provisions regarding treaty entitlements. Those terms required the province to transfer back to federal control unoccupied Crown lands required to fulfill federal government treaty responsibilities.

Until the late 1970s First Nations in Alberta had little success in getting either the federal or provincial governments to enter into negotiations to resolve outstanding treaty issues. By 1980, growing frustration among First Nations led to demonstrations and direct action intended to force the governments to negotiate. In 1980 the Blood nation at Cardston blockaded access to some local businesses and boycotted schools and other facilities.

In northern Alberta, the Cree people of Lubicon Lake had been entirely excluded from Treaty Eight (as were some six other northern First Nations). Although recognized as a distinct band in the 1930s, the federal and provincial governments refused countless attempts by the Lubicons to initiate negotiations aimed at resolving outstanding land claims. Meanwhile, following World War II, the provincial government issued oil and gas exploration leases throughout the area. By the 1980s more than 400 wells had been drilled within a 16-kilometre radius of the Lubicon settlement.

To draw attention to their claim, the Lubicons organized a boycott by First Nations of the 1988 **XVth Winter Olympics** in Calgary. Although the

By 1893, when this picture was taken, the Blood people had surrendered much of their land as part of Treaty Seven. The great bison herds upon which their culture had thrived had been slaughtered. The inequities of this treaty and others signed by First Nations peoples in Alberta during the mid- to late 1800s would result in the many land-claim negotiations currently underway across the province. (Glenbow Archives photo, ND-34-20)

boycott drew national and international attention to their cause, it took an autumn blockade of the disputed land to win provincial government agreement regarding the size of the land claim to be negotiated. However, federal government involvement over jurisdictional matters relating to the negotiations led to a stalemate.

Several significant treaty land claim settlements have been reached. These usually entail the federal government contributing cash and the provincial government putting up a blend of cash and land to resolve the claim. In 1986, for example, the Mikisew Cree First Nation at Fort Chipewyan received 4,970 hectares of land and $17.6 million from the province, with the federal government adding another $9 million. This $26.6 million (plus land) settlement is one of Alberta's richest.

In addition to treaty land entitlement claims, there are two other types of First Nation land claims: Aboriginal or Comprehensive Land Claims, and Specific Land Claims. The former arises when a First Nation's title to lands is considered unextinguished by any treaty mechanism (as in the Lubicon claim). Specific Land Claims occur when a First Nation believes the federal government has neglected its duties and responsibilities as outlined in the Indian Act in managing the First Nation's lands or monies. Both types of claim are generally the sole responsibility of the federal government, with the provincial government involved rarely as a third party.

First Nations Peoples

Human habitation of the western hemisphere appears to have occurred no earlier than 30,000 years ago. Humans are believed to have come to this hemisphere from other continents about the time glacial-age ice began to recede from vast portions of North America. There is no evidence of humankind evolving independently anywhere in the hemisphere.

Archaeologists generally agree that humans migrated from present-day Siberia via a land bridge crossing the Bering Sea into Alaska. These migratory populations were the ancestors of the First Nations peoples who eventually settled throughout North and South America.

They did not come to North America in a steady stream or even a constant trickle; rather it appears they came in a series of pulses across the narrow Bering Strait bridge. Having entered North America, they drifted east and south along ice-free corridors, especially, at first, by an ice-free route stretching through Alaska and Yukon valleys to a gap between the two great glacial ice masses existing to the east of the **Rocky Mountains** in present-day Alberta.

This corridor was usually ice-free from about 30,000 years ago to the end of the last great glacial surge known as the Wisconsian, ending about 10,000 years ago. Four thousand kilometres long, the corridor extended from the Richardson Mountains in the Yukon to the **Lethbridge**-Waterton Lakes region. It is thought to have passed through such modern-day townsites as Edson, **Nordegg, Rocky Mountain House,** and **Calgary.** This gap encouraged the oldest migrating groups to continue moving southward, deeper into North America and on to South America, searching for warmer climates.

Migration from Asia to North America is believed to have ceased abruptly 6,000 to 8,000 years ago. The reason has not been determined, but geological evidence indicates land-fold changes may have broken the Bering Strait bridge, making it hazardous for non-seagoing peoples to cross. Evidence also indicates that many glacial-age animal species in parts of Alaska suddenly perished in some kind of mass destruction. Perhaps this unknown cataclysm made conditions in the region untenable for human passage.

An archaeological site in Calgary (*see* **Archaeology**) indicates that prehistoric people may have passed through Alberta about 20,000 years ago. An ancient campsite at Vermilion Lakes in what is now **Banff National Park** suggests the presence of prehistoric humans 10,000 years ago.

The earliest Albertans were nomadic, living as hunters and gatherers. About 9,000 years ago people specializing in communal hunting of **bison** lived in Alberta's southern plains. Prehistoric Albertans hunted elk, antelope, deer, muskrat, beaver, badger, fox, and other game. It was, however, **bison** that provided the greatest food supply and encouraged development of larger tribal groupings capable of pooling resources and working together to develop efficient **bison hunting** techniques.

By the time the first Europeans appeared in Alberta, the southern part of the province was occupied by the Blackfoot people, composed of three tribes: Blackfoot proper (Siksiki), the Bloods (Kainai), and Peigan (Pekuni), as well as the Gros Ventre tribe (which by the early 1800s had migrated south into the U.S.). The Ktunaxa (formerly Kutenai or Kootenay) inhabited the southwestern mountains and foothills of Alberta, although they ventured often into the plains to hunt bison. The Sarsi were concentrated in the Bow Valley, sustaining strong links with the Blackfoot.

North of the North Saskatchewan River the Athapaskan-speaking tribes of the Beaver, Slavey, and Chipewyan were found. In east-central Alberta the vast Algonquian-speaking Cree nation, extending from Hudson

Bay to the eastern base of the Rocky Mountains, was concentrated. Albertan Crees were divided into two subgroups, plains Cree and woodland Cree.

Horses appeared in southern Alberta about 1730—originally introduced to North America during Spanish conquistador Hernando Cortez's invasion of Mexico in 1519, but taking a couple of hundred years to be traded so far north. Prior to the horse's introduction, Alberta's First Nations people had used dogs as pack animals.

During the prehorse period, plains peoples generally lived in small, mobile bands rarely exceeding 50 people. Belongings were transported by dog-pulled travois—poles joined by a frame harnessed to the dog, with the other end dragging along the ground. The amount of supplies a dog could drag was much smaller than a horse could pull.

Once horses became common, plains peoples could suddenly transport more supplies, range farther afield, and hunt bison more effectively. Larger bands were possible because hunters could cover an extended range and still be within easy distance of camp. The size of **tipis** increased, because horses could manage greater weights.

Further changes in First Nations' culture and distribution came with the introduction of guns. In Alberta, the Cree were first to obtain guns through their long trade lines extending to Hudson Bay. This enabled them to push the Beaver nation out of the Athabasca Valley by 1760. The Beaver moved west, forcing the Sekani north and west to the Rocky Mountains in British Columbia's northeastern corner.

In 1754, fur trader Anthony Henday came to Alberta to determine if the people there could be induced to hunt and trap for the Hudson's Bay Company. Trading posts followed, with Fort Chipewyan opening at the confluence of the Peace and

With the coming of Europeans to the prairies, First Nations peoples blended traditional methods of making clothing with forms of beaded decoration. This picture, circa 1910–15, shows Blackfoot Daisy Norris wearing a beaded rawhide dress with a heavily beaded cradle board on her back. (Glenbow Archives photo, NA-5217-3)

Athabasca rivers in 1788 and Fort-of-the-Forks opening the same year further south on the Athabasca River.

Soon after European arrival smallpox epidemics devastated Alberta's First Nations. The 1837 epidemic, for example, killed two-thirds of the Blackfoot nation.

Christian missionaries also came, with the first, Rev. Robert Rundle, arriving at Fort Edmonton in 1840. Soon Methodist, Anglican, and Roman Catholic missionaries had spread throughout the province, concentrated on locations at or near the fur-trade forts. The effect of European-introduced diseases, undermining of traditional religions by teachings of Christianity, increasing slaughter of the bison, and growing dependency on the fur-trade economy combined to destroy the fabric of First Nations' culture and society.

When the western territories became part of Canada in 1870, the federal government set about negotiating treaties with the, by this time, largely demoralized nations. Treaty Six, signed by the Cree in 1876, provided for the Crees' surrender of the central part of Alberta. However, Big Bear, the leader of 65 Cree lodges, refused to sign the treaty. He did so only on December 8, 1882 when his people were faced with starvation due to the near-extinction of the bison.

The southern limit of Treaty Six was marked by a line from the Rocky Mountains along the Red Deer River trail to Tail Creek, then due east for 32 kilometres and southeast in a straight line to the confluence of the Red Deer River with the South Saskatchewan River. The northern boundary was from the source of the Red Deer River, north to Jasper House, down the Athabasca River to the town of Athabasca, due east to Lac La Biche and continuing east along a line parallelling the Beaver River.

The following year, 1877, the Blackfoot, Blood, Peigan, Sarsi, and Stoney nations signed Treaty Seven. They surrendered all land south of Treaty Six. The northern part of Alberta was largely signed away by the Beaver, Cree, Slavey, and Chipewyan under Treaty Eight in 1899.

Most of the treaties shared common conditions. Reserve lands were set aside based on a size calculation of five people per square mile. Tools, farm implements, nets for fishing, and livestock were provided. Treaty money of $5 a year was given each person, with chiefs receiving $25 a year and councillors or minor chiefs receiving $15. Health services, education, and hunting rights were promised.

With the bison all but exterminated by 1880, the plains peoples could no longer sustain their traditional way of life. As land became overhunted in the north, or cleared for **agriculture,** northern peoples too found it impossible to live the old way. Most reluctantly turned to the reserves as their only option for a home.

Despite years of oppression, the First Nations in Alberta endured and today are undergoing a renaissance evidenced by economic gains based on self-sufficiency, and a rediscovery of traditional cultures and traditions.

(*See also* **Medicine Wheels; Petroglyphs and Pictographs.**)

Fish

There are 51 native fish species in Alberta and 8 that have been introduced. All are capable of reproducing in Alberta's freshwater bodies. Seventeen species are sought by anglers.

Alberta's native fish species come from 13 families, ranging from the primitive jawless lamprey to the advanced, spiny-rayed members of the perch family. Species from two other families have been introduced to some of the province's **hot springs.**

All Alberta's fish are freshwater species, spending their entire lives in the province's rivers, creeks, lakes, and ponds. (Alberta has just one **water** system with a clear, undammed run to an ocean—the Slave River.) They are also all opportunistic feeders, taking whatever they can kill or digest.

Alberta's total water coverage is 16,796 square kilometres of the province's total area of 661,188 square kilometres—only 2.5 percent. This is less than Canada's other provinces except Nova Scotia, New Brunswick, and Prince Edward Island.

The province's lakes are relatively shallow, the deepest being Waterton Lake with a maximum depth of 135 metres. Water temperature, flow rates, bottom composition, and surrounding habitat all influence which fish species thrive or subsist in a body of water.

Alberta has one lamprey species, the Arctic lamprey. This is the province's only representative of the class known as higher jawless fishes.

All other Alberta fish, native or introduced, are of the bony class. The province is home to one species of sturgeon, the lake sturgeon. It has two mooneye species—goldeye and mooneye. There are 14 minnow species, including lake chub, pearl dace, northern redbelly dace, northern squawfish, and redside shiner. Seven sucker species occur naturally in Alberta— quillback, longnose sucker, white sucker, largescale sucker, mountain sucker, silver redhorse, and shorthead redhorse. The only bullhead catfish is the stonecat, and the only pike the northern pike. There are 15 species of trout, including two ciscos, four whitefish, the Arctic grayling, and the more common trout species, such as cutthroat, rainbow, bull, and lake. Four trout (more correctly char) species have been introduced—golden, brown, Dolly Varden, and brook. Trout-perch are also found. The only cod is the burbot. Two livebearers have been introduced, the western mosquitofish and sailfin molly. Two sticklebacks are native to Alberta, the brook and ninespine, while the threespine stickleback has been introduced. Alberta's four sculpins are the slimy sculpin, shorthead sculpin, spoonhead sculpin, and deepwater sculpin. There are five perch species—Iowa darter, logperch, yellow perch, sauger, and walleye. The African jewelfish has been introduced.

No fish species are considered endangered in Alberta, nor do any figure on the province's red and blue lists of species considered threatened. The **bull trout,** however, is considered by the province to be somewhat at risk, as it has disappeared from much of its traditional range.

Foothills

Extending north from Turner Valley along the eastern edge of the **Rocky Mountains** in a gradually widening belt is the foothills natural region. It also encompasses several outlying hill masses, including the Swan Hills, Porcupine Hills, Pelican Mountains, and Clear Hills. The formation of these hills was similar to that of the Rocky Mountains, which most of the region borders, but because of their sandstone composition they were more easily eroded.

The foothills have been divided into two subregions by the Alberta **Special Places** natural areas preservation strategy—the lower and upper foothills.

Bighorn sheep graze in the foothills country of the Sheep River west of Turner Valley. (Frances Backhouse photo)

- The lower foothills include rolling topography created by deformed sandstone and shale along the edge of the Rocky Mountains, as well as erosional remnants with flat-lying bedrock, such as the Swan Hills, Pelican Mountains, and Clear Hills (see **Mount Columbia** for further explanation of flat-lying bedrock).

  The foothills' geological top covering is primarily moraine left during the glacial retreat with extensive organic deposits found in valleys and wet depressions. Shales and sandstones occur as outcrops along the mountains. Although cooler in summer than the adjacent, lower elevation, **boreal forest** regions, the lower foothills are warmer in winter because they are somewhat sheltered from cold Arctic air masses.

  The forests reflect the transitional nature of this subregion, presenting a mixture of white spruce, black spruce, lodgepole pine, balsam fir, white birch, and balsam poplar. Lodgepole pine forests occupy extensive portions of the upland regions. Black spruce concentrates on moist upland sites in the north and on poorly drained muskegs.

  Wildlife is abundant, encompassing a great diversity of species found also in the boreal forest and Rocky Mountain regions. Black-tailed deer, red squirrel, and spruce grouse are common. Deciduous forests support ruffed grouse, warbling vireo, black-capped chickadee, and Tennessee warbler. Closer to boreal forest regions, moose, yellow-bellied sapsucker, and purple finch become more common.

- The upper foothills subregion occurs on strongly rolling topography along the eastern edge of the Rocky Mountains. Bedrock outcrops of shales and sandstone are frequent. Alberta's highest summer precipitation occurs here, averaging about 340 millimetres, with a mean annual precipitation of about 540 millimetres. Winters are colder than in the lower foothills. Forests are almost exclusively coniferous, dominated by white spruce, black spruce, lodgepole pine, and subalpine fir.

  Characteristic wildlife species are elk, black and grizzly **bears,** pine siskin, and yellow-rumped warbler. Animal species diversity is less than in the lower foothills because of reduced plant diversity.

Forest Industry

More than half of Alberta—about 360,000 square kilometres—remains covered by forests. The majority is found in the vast **boreal forest** of northern Alberta with a smaller wedge of forest hugging the **Rocky Mountains** along an ever-narrowing front that extends south from the boreal forest to the U.S.-Alberta border. About two-thirds of this forested land contains commercially productive timber stands.

Until recently the forest industry in Alberta was relatively small. In 1985, for example, forest products accounted for only $66 million of the province's gross domestic product of $56.5 billion. As of 1994 this figure had risen to $2.9 billion of a total GDP of about $83.5 billion. Forestry is now the province's fourth largest industry, after energy, **agriculture,** and **tourism.**

Total industry shipments (including value-added products) totalled $3.5 billion in 1994. About 20,000 people are directly employed in forestry, with another 30,000 indirectly dependent on the industry.

White spruce is generally considered Alberta's most commercially valuable timber. Its light wood is easily worked and holds paint and glue well. White spruce also makes good pulpwood. Lodgepole pine is the second most commercially utilized wood in Alberta, used for pulpwood, plywood, and sawn lumber. Balsam poplar and trembling aspen are used primarily for plywood.

Rapid forest industry growth has resulted in equally rapid expansion of logging into regions of old-growth boreal forest. This has led to several environmental conflicts and fears that the industry is insufficiently regulated by government to ensure sustainable logging and preservation of natural wildlife habitats. There is also a serious problem with the sale of timber from less-regulated private landholdings, which has caused environmental damage in some parts of the province.

Much of the increasing growth of Alberta's forest industry results from the fact that neighbouring provinces and states, such as British Columbia and Montana, formerly possessing greater timber stocks and more commercially valuable species, are experiencing timber shortfalls because of overlogging and poor forest-management practices.

The challenge facing Albertans is to ensure that the long-term potential of provincial forests is not sacrificed for short-term profit and job creation.

Fort Calgary. *See* **Calgary.**

Fort Chipewyan. *See* **Historical Overview; Lake Athabasca.**

Fort Dunvegan

In 1805 traders with the North West Company (NWC) established a post along the **Peace River** on a narrow fertile valley plain flanked on both sides by high banks. The post factor was Archibald Norman McLeod. He named the post Dunvegan, after the McLeods' ancestral castle on the Island of Skye.

Fort Dunvegan's traders were uniquely blessed by the post's setting. Although this post was far enough north that winters were harsh, the fertile soil proved ideal for gardening. Soon the traders were cultivating potatoes, various other vegetables, and grain. The local crops allowed them to have a diet seldom enjoyed at the trading posts. In 1821, NWC merged with the Hudson's Bay Company. The original fort was replaced in 1877, the new one adjacent to the old structure.

In 1869 a Roman Catholic missionary, Father Christophe Tisier, arrived to work among the Beaver, Cree, Iroquois, and Sekani **First Nations peoples** living in the surrounding territory. A church, named St. Charles Mission, was erected in 1885, with a rectory added in 1889 to house a growing number of Oblate Roman Catholic priests and lay brothers.

Across the river from the fort and Catholic mission, an Anglican mission was begun in 1879 by Thomas Bunn, a school teacher, and continued by Reverend John Brick. The succeeding minister, Reverend Alfred Garrioch, planted Manitoba maple seeds in the 1880s and the mission soon became known as "The Maples."

Both missions encouraged local First Nations people to settle in the valley and abandon traditional ways of life to practise farming. Only moderately successful, neither mission attracted a significant permanent population.

By 1914, stopping houses for travellers sailing on the steamships plying the Peace River stood on both sides of the river. A **North-West Mounted Police** post and telegraph office sat on a hill overlooking Dunvegan. The small community was promoted optimistically as a future city. In 1915, however, the Edmonton, Dunvegan and BC Railway bypassed Dunvegan in favour of a route

St. Charles Mission, constructed in 1885, was an integral part of the Fort Dunvegan trading post and Roman Catholic Oblate mission. (Mark Zuehlke photo)

via Peace River and Spirit River. With the closure of its trading post soon after, Dunvegan declined and the two missions also closed.

The fertile valley encouraged some settlers to remain, though, and today Dunvegan survives as a rich market gardening area.

The Alberta government has restored the factor's house and the St. Charles Mission church and rectory as a provincial historic site.

Fort Macleod

In October 1874, a contingent of **North-West Mounted Police** (NWMP) under the command of Major James F. Macleod reached **Fort Whoop-Up** at the junction of the Oldman and St. Mary rivers. The whiskey-trading post was captured without a shot fired, but the NWMP decided the fort would not suffice as a base for establishing a Canadian paramilitary presence in the Alberta territory. On the advice of their **Métis** guide, Jerry Potts, Macleod chose to build a fort on an island in the Oldman River, where there were **cottonwood forests** for building materials and good graze for horses. The site was named Fort Macleod. Its location astride the major north-south transportation route from the North-West Territories to Fort Benton in Montana State resulted in Fort Macleod becoming the focal point for the rapidly expanding cattle **ranching** industry.

Until 1882, the fort also remained the main base for NWMP operations in present-day southern Alberta. In 1884, the flooding problems that had plagued the island fort every spring prompted its relocation to the Oldman River's south shore. Fort Macleod was by this time already waning in importance, because the previous year the Canadian Pacific Railway had passed through Fort Calgary, ensuring that community's future as the cattle kingdom capital of southern Alberta.

In 1892, Fort Macleod was incorporated and by 1910 its population had reached 2,500. Optimism among the local chamber of commerce that the town could successfully outpace rivals **Calgary** and **Lethbridge** continued to run high despite the many indications to the contrary. The community was promoted as "the Winnipeg of the West." By 1914, however, it was evident Fort Macleod would remain a small, local distribution centre.

Today its population stands little changed from the early part of the century—about 3,200.

A fire destroyed most of the downtown's wooden buildings in 1906. This calamity led to the passing of a bylaw requiring all new structures to be built of brick or stone. The legacy of this bylaw remains in the 30 heritage buildings forming the downtown core. On the edge of downtown, a replica of the NWMP's Fort Macleod stands. Together, the fort and historic downtown prove a major tourist attraction, annually drawing some 60,000 visitors.

Fort McMurray

With a population of about 35,000, Fort McMurray is located in the heart of the **Athabasca Oil Sands,** one of the world's largest oil reserves. Although today the city is heavily dependent on the oil sands for its existence, it was originally founded in the 1790s as a North West Company fur-trading post. That post was abandoned in 1821, but in 1870 the Hudson's Bay Company rebuilt the fort, naming it McMurray after the chief factor of Fort Chipewyan.

Fort McMurray's factor, Henry Moberly, had ambitions for the region, but knew this section of the Athabasca country would remain virtually undeveloped unless transportation problems were solved. He studied the possibility of using steamboats on the Athabasca and Slave rivers, but rapids made it difficult to provide an unbroken waterway system, which could then be linked to **Edmonton** by a short wagon trail. As a result the fort, eventually a small community, barely survived until 1922 when a railroad was pushed up from Edmonton to Draper, 12.8 kilometres south of Fort McMurray. Beyond Fort McMurray, the Athabasca River was navigable for its entire 4,800-kilometre length to the Arctic Ocean. With a railroad link between Fort McMurray and Edmonton, ships could now continue the northward journey, making the development of Arctic regions simpler than ever before.

The railroad was also constructed to provide access to the oil sands, known since the late 1700s to contain oil. Edmonton commercial interests and the federal government both wanted to develop this obvious treasure trove. The technology to extract the oil from the sand, however, did not exist. Various attempts to tap the oil through conventional drilling all failed. During World War II the community briefly flourished when wartime oil demand led to the implementation of an experimental extraction process for tar-sand oil but war's end led to the abandonment of this government-funded operation.

Fort McMurray languished as a transportation stop, which also had a few **fish** plants and a salt-extraction factory. In World War II it enjoyed brief prominence as a military base.

But interest in the oil sands never disappeared and scientists continued to study the problem of how to extract the oil. In 1964, federal and provincial governments approved the Great Canadian Oil Sands project and modern Fort McMurray was born. At the time only 1,200 people lived in the town, but as construction began the community boomed, growing to more than 10,000 by the mid-1970s and more than tripling again by 1987.

It has survived downturns in oil prices and grown into a thriving, modern, and vibrant city with college facilities. A small cultural and artistic community has helped Fort McMurray shed its boomtown image of the 1970s and early 1980s. The Oil Sands Interpretive Centre offers detailed and interactive displays explaining the operation and development of the Athabasca Oil Sands project.

Fort Whoop-Up

In 1869, John J. Healy and Alfred B. Hamilton of Montana state came to the junction of the Oldman and St. Mary rivers to establish a trading fort. Its primary commodity was whiskey, which the unscrupulous pair sold to **First Nations peoples** living in the then unpoliced southern **prairie** of the Canadian west. Initially they named the fort after Hamilton, but after one trading season the Blackfoot burned the place to the ground—hoping the traders would stay away.

The following year, however, they returned and built a second, larger fort, appropriately named Fort Whoop-Up. The name is said to be a mocking salute to Fort Benton, Montana merchant I. G. Baker, who warned his nephew, Hamilton: "Don't let the Indians whoop you up." Hamilton and his partner had every intention of ensuring the First Nations peoples whooped it up on their rotgut whiskey. Their fort soon became the most notorious and formidable of the American whiskey-trading posts built in southern Alberta during this period. The country around the fort quickly became known as Whoop-Up Country in its honour.

Hamilton and Healy's fort had been constructed to ensure it would not meet the fate of the first stockade. Its walls stood four metres tall and were topped by sharpened stakes; two bastions were stocked with brass cannon; iron bars covered all the exterior doors, windows, and even the openings of the chimneys. Any attacker would suffer heavy losses.

The booze sold was vile. It was often made by bringing tobacco, old tea leaves, and molasses to a full rolling boil, cooling the liquid produced, then seasoning it with Perry's Painkillers and a bit of real alcohol. To achieve a dubious pink colour, red ink was mixed in. The liquor burned and was sometimes deadly to consume.

Their whiskey produced a quick profit and the violence and social disruption left in the traders' wake were of little concern. Many traders were hardened veterans of the American Civil War, men who could find no work in their homeland or had no interest in returning to the drudgery of the farms or factories from which they had gone to the most terrible war the world had yet witnessed.

The Blackfoot nation was particularly vulnerable to their trade. Smallpox and other European-introduced diseases had killed thousands and devastated the tribes' political and social structures. The **bison** were fast disappearing from the Great Plains. Traditional Blackfoot society was falling apart in the wake of the loss of the animal upon which it was founded. Despair was rife; for many, liquor provided a welcome relief from the horror of day-to-day existence.

Reports soon reached Ottawa of the damage caused by the whiskey trade and the lawlessness following it into Canada's west, as increasing numbers of unscrupulous Americans flowed across the border in search of easy profit. In 1872, Colonel P. Robertson-Ross was sent west to investigate. What he saw left him appalled enough to urge the federal government to create a military force and deploy it immediately to the Canadian west.

Prime Minister John A. Macdonald agreed, spurred also by the **Cypress Hills Massacre,** and the **North-West Mounted Police** (NWMP) marched west from Fort Dufferin, Manitoba in July 1874. On October 9, the red-coated paramilitary force arrived at Fort Whoop-Up. The troops took up positions overlooking the fort, arrayed their cannon and mortars, and prepared to do battle with the traders. From the fort came neither gunfire nor any sign of movement. Finally, Major J. F. Macleod and his **Métis** scout, Jerry Potts, rode down to the fort and knocked on the gates. A few minutes later, a fort employee, Dave Akers, appeared and invited the bemused Macleod to lunch. Over the meal, the American informed the major that the traders were gone, having fled at the first sight of the approaching troops.

Healy went on to become first a Montana newspaper editor, a sheriff, and later hotel owner, before reappearing in Canada during the **Klondike Gold Rush** in the late 1890s as a miner and manager of a trading and transportation company. Hamilton also became a sheriff and then a member of the Montana state legislature.

Fort Whoop-Up was closed and soon most of the other whiskey forts were also abandoned—the traders escaping back across the border with their profits. Whiskey smuggling from the United States into southern Alberta continued. The NWMP, and later its descendent force the Royal

Canadian Mounted Police, would patrol the border against liquor smugglers until the end of World War I.

Today nothing but a cairn marks the spot where the fort stood. Nearby, at Indian Battle Park in **Lethbridge,** a replica of the fort features many original artifacts, including one of the cannon, and audiovisual displays relating the fort's history.

Fossils

Virtually the entire record of life on earth is captured in Alberta's innumerable fossil beds. Few other places in the world have such concentrated and diverse fossilized specimens of plants and animals.

The bone beds at **Dinosaur Provincial Park,** near the **Royal Tyrrell Museum of Palaeontology,** and the **Devil's Coulee dinosaur eggs** site have all greatly increased palaeontological knowledge of the evolution, life, and eventual extinction of **dinosaurs.** So, too, do the approximately 20 dinosaur trackway sites that have been discovered in Alberta. These sites contain fossilized footprints of dinosaurs trapped in shales and other rock. From these footprints, scientists are able to develop understanding of how dinosaurs interacted with their habitat and mixed with other life forms.

While fossils of dinosaurs are common throughout Alberta and are especially frequent along the Red Deer River, **Milk River,** and in other parts of the **badlands** country of southern Alberta, some of Alberta's richest sites contain fossils of plants and animals that lived before, during, and after the time of the dinosaurs. Dinosaur Provincial Park, for example, contains thousands of non-dinosaur fossils.

In the Windermere Supergroup rocks exposed near **Lake Louise** and Jasper, stromatolite mounds are found—colonies of proalgae, the first form of life on earth (*see* **Ancient Alberta**). The Windermere rock dates back 760 million years and is composed of a mixture of pebbles, sandstones, shales, and limestones. Originally deposited on the floor of the Pacific Ocean, this rock was later upthrust as part of the bedrock of the **Rocky Mountains.**

No fossilized record of the Cambrian Period (from 600 to 500 million years ago) in Alberta begins to rival the vast Burgess Shale find near Field, British Columbia, where thousands of fossils denoting more than 120 different species have been discovered. But there are many lesser sites in the Alberta Rockies where such common Cambrian fare as trilobites can be found. Fossil hunting, however, is prohibited in the national parks of the Rocky Mountains.

In the northeast corner of **Banff National Park,** off the **Icefields**

Parkway, stands a spectacular cliff known as Weeping Wall. In its drab grey Devonian and Carboniferous limestone deposits, a vast coral reef full of ancient life can be examined. Calcareous algae, stromatoporoids, and count-less other creatures are trapped in Weeping Wall's rock, dating from 425 to 345 million years ago.

South of the village of Cadomin, near **Jasper National Park,** a small deposit of Spray River Group rock contains piles of belemnite remains. These common creatures of the Triassic Period had rod-shaped internal skeletons and were related to modern squid. In the sandstone rock bor-dering many Alberta rivers, coiled, flat ammonite fossils are plentiful. Ammonites are a type of mollusc from the Mesozoic Era.

In Verdigris Coulee in **Writing-On-Stone Provincial Park** fossilized teeth of **mammals** from the Cretaceous Period have been found. These mammals, which shared the earth with dinosaurs 75 million years ago, were generally about the size of small rodents today.

From **Medicine Hat** to **Lethbridge,** the ancient Bearpaw Sea once cov-ered southern Alberta. The fossil beds at Horsethief Canyon, near the Royal Tyrrell Museum, contain oysters and clams. In various bone beds once cov-ered by the Bearpaw Sea and its estuaries, fossils of prehistoric sharks, marine turtles, giant lizardlike mesosaurs, and plesiosaurs have been dis-covered. Plesiosaurs were either short-necked pliosaurs or long-necked elasmosaurs. Both forms were capable of using paddlelike limbs to virtual-ly fly along the surface of the water in lightning-fast spurts, making them highly ferocious and effective carnivores.

About 65 million years ago, dinosaurs and many other species sud-denly became extinct. Scientists theorize that these creatures of the Mesozoic Era suffered extinction at least partly as the result of a massive asteroid colliding with earth. *T. rex* Ranch north of Tolman Bridge on the Red Deer River is most famed for the partial skeleton discovered there in 1981, but it also contains a vast wealth of geological evidence supporting this theory.

Fossils from the **Cypress Hills** in southeastern Alberta contain signif-icant representations of life from the Tertiary Period, that date from 42 mil-lion to 35 million years ago. In these fossil beds, skeletal remains of **birds,** snakes, **amphibians,** turtles, and **fish** are present. Most interestingly, the beds contain several hundred forms of mammals, ranging from small to very large animals. Mice, bats, rabbits, flying lemurs, primitive dog-sized horses, and rhinoceroses have all been found here. There are also fossils of two bizarre, giant piglike mammals, known as entelodonts and brontotheres.

The former had bony cheek and jaw protuberances used for display and fighting. The latter had a pair of bony growths where rhinoceroses carry a horn.

About two million years ago the period of ice ages began, continuing in Alberta until the final retreat about 12,000 to 15,000 years ago. Fossil beds near Medicine Hat contain remains of animals from this time, including woolly mammoths, modern-sized horses, and llamas (which originally evolved in North America but later disappeared from this continent, surviving only in South America). Less ancient fossils here include those of reindeer and camels.

Fossilized evidence, such as a find along the banks of the Bow River in **Calgary** (*see* **Archaeology**), suggest the presence of human beings in Alberta as early as 20,000 years ago. But most archaeological sites indicate that humans had little significant presence until about 12,000 years ago.

Foxes. *See* **Wild Dogs.**

Francophone Albertans

The French and French Canadians have the longest history of any non– **First Nations people** in Alberta. That history has three distinct phases—the fur trade, the development of a series of viable French-speaking communities during the late 1800s, and the post-province formation period stretching from 1905 to the present.

French was the first European language spoken on the Canadian plains. French and French-Canadian explorers, fur traders, and *voyageurs* began entering the Canadian west in the early 18th century. By the 1740s French-Canadian fur traders were using both the North and South Saskatchewan River as transportation routes. On the eve of the British conquest of Canada in 1760, about 200 French-Canadian traders were established in semi-permanent trading posts located west of Lake Superior.

Following the British victory, French-Canadian *voyageurs* went to work for the Scottish, British, and American traders who formed the North West Company (NWC) and the Hudson's Bay Company (HBC). The NWC had French-Canadian employees from nearly every parish between Montreal and Quebec City. Every exploration venture into western Canada following the British conquest was composed primarily of French-Canadian *voyageurs*.

Until the middle of the 1800s Fort Edmonton, for example, had so many French Canadian and **Métis** stationed there that French was the fort's most commonly spoken language. When the HBC and NWC united in 1821, further recruitment of *voyageurs* from Quebec was curtailed. Many existing employees—both French Canadian and Métis—were released as the two companies consolidated operations.

Some of the French Canadians and Métis who lost their fur-trade jobs moved westward from the Red River in Manitoba into present-day Alberta, often working as buffalo hunters. Their numbers were further strengthened by the arrival of French-speaking missionaries at forts between 1818 and 1842.

In 1843 Father Thibault opened a mission at Devil's Lake (later called Lac Sainte Anne) 72 kilometres west of Fort Edmonton. Here 40 Métis families settled and took up farming.

Father Albert Lacombe joined this mission in 1852. He eventually recognized that Lac Sainte Anne's land was too swampy and the frosts came too early for it to prove viable as an agricultural settlement. Accordingly, he set about establishing a new mission in 1861 called Saint Albert (after Lacombe's patron saint), west of Fort Edmonton. Saint Albert became the first Roman Catholic bishopric in Alberta ten years later.

Along the banks of the Sturgeon River at Saint Albert Métis settlers marked off long narrow lots fronting sections of the river banks. This pattern of development, where each farm was footed on the river, was modelled on original settlement patterns adopted by French Canadians along the banks of the St. Lawrence River as early as 1640. As in the St. Lawrence model, houses were set about 250 to 350 metres apart. A grist mill was soon constructed by the church, which also imported agricultural implements for the settlers. French-speaking nuns arrived to teach the children and to care for the sick.

By the late 1880s Saint Albert had a population of about 1,000 and was thriving as an agricultural settlement. The development of Saint Albert coincided with a trickle of French-Canadian farmers from Quebec to the Fort Edmonton region. By 1885 the majority of non–First Nation residents in the area were of French origin.

Canada's federal government had formally recognized the French-Canadian presence in the west in the North-West Territories Act of 1875. The Act permitted the use of French in the courts and legislative council, the formation of Roman Catholic Schools, and the use of French as the language of instruction within those schools.

This tolerance of cultural diversity, however, was overturned in 1892, by which time English-speaking settlement in the North-West Territories, of which Alberta was a part, outpaced French. Following the example set by

Manitoba two years earlier, the North-West Territories assembly made English the chamber's sole language. It also ordered Roman Catholic Church schools to use English as their language of instruction. French instruction was only allowed in primary school to children who spoke no other language.

French-speaking westerners resisted these efforts to destroy their culture. So too did the Roman Catholic Church. Priests such as L'Abbé Morin and Father Lacombe encouraged French Canadians in eastern Canada to settle in Alberta, hoping to regain a majority population in the region so that the anti-French language policies could be repealed by a francophone-controlled territorial assembly.

Thousands of emigrants responded to the Church's call. The majority were not from Quebec, however, but from Ontario or the Atlantic provinces. Many others were from the New England area of the United States.

French-Canadian settlement initially centred on the **Edmonton** area. As the fertile land in this region was taken up, new settlers went to other parts of Alberta. Settlements were established on the Métis reserve at Saint Paul, at Bonnyville, and in the Lac La Biche area.

Shortly before World War I, French Canadians homesteaded in the **Peace River** region at Falher. The settlement expanded rapidly with the construction of a railway through the area. After 1926 the Peace River area became one of the largest French-Canadian settlements in Alberta.

Although Alberta's French-Canadian **population** was growing, it was still being outpaced by the growth of the English-speaking population. The attempt to secure the future of the French language in Alberta through increased French-Canadian settlement was failing.

As early as 1916 the census illustrated how rapidly the province's French-speaking population was being overwhelmed by an influx of English-speaking settlers. The census showed only about 25,000 people of French origin out of an approximate population of 500,000, most of whom spoke English as their mother tongue.

Not all French Canadians in Alberta lived in agricultural settlements. Francophones also established a significant presence in the emerging urban centres of **Calgary** and Edmonton. Edmonton was Alberta's centre of French-speaking life. Until 1916, francophones accounted for 2,600 of the city's population of 53,850, making them the second-largest linguistic community in Edmonton. However, this small percentage of the city's population continued to decrease.

With the growth of the English-Canadian population in Alberta came changes to the structure of the province's Roman Catholic Church. By 1913, only 30 percent of Roman Catholics in the Canadian Prairies were francophones. Soon English-speaking bishops were being appointed, leading to the Church abandoning its francophone colonization efforts.

The French-speaking community in Alberta was facing ethnic dissolution by 1926. Politically it was so divided it exerted little influence in provincial or municipal politics. Francophone children received as little as one hour's instruction a day in French and many could no longer adequately write or speak their mother tongue.

The Association canadienne-française de l'Alberta (ACFA) was formed that same year. Its objective was "to destroy the inferiority complex that exists too often among the French Canadians of Alberta."

Education was seen as a cornerstone in preserving the community. French-language schools were privately financed. The Jesuit-operated classical college in Edmonton (which granted baccalaureate degrees in the arts from Laval University in Quebec City) was attended yearly by as many as 200 students, most francophone Albertans. The graduates of this and other schools emerged as the new elite of the Alberta francophone population.

ACFA also organized the francophone community politically and culturally. It published a French-language newspaper called *La Survivance* and promoted the development of parish-based credit unions and cooperatives. In the face of open hostility from the English Canadian majority in Alberta, ACFA lobbied for many years for establishment of a French-language radio station in the province. Finally, in 1949, CHFA opened in Edmonton.

Growing assertiveness on the part of Albertan francophones and the rise of political unrest in Quebec combined in the early 1960s to enable reforms at the provincial level that would help the community's survival. In 1964 the provincial School Act was varied to allow any school district to introduce French as well as English as the language of instruction in grades one to nine. In 1968 this was extended to grade 12. French immersion schools were permitted in 1976. By 1979, 40 percent of Alberta children with French as their mother tongue were receiving bilingual or French immersion educations.

Despite the advances Albertan francophones have secured in such areas as education, their community remains threatened. Increased urbanization is defusing the concentration of the francophone community and reducing its influence in traditional francophone enclaves, including the Peace River area. Young francophones settling in Edmonton, **Red Deer,** or Calgary are less likely to vigorously sustain their francophone identity.

Intermarriage is a further cause of the decline of French heritage in the province.

In terms of percentage the francophone community's population in Alberta continues to decline—reducing further its influence politically and socially. Today, approximately 74,600 Albertans (or 2.7 percent) consider themselves of French **ethnicity.**

Frank Slide

At 4:10 a.m. on April 29, 1903, an enormous 30-million-cubic-metre wedge of limestone cascaded down the east face of Turtle Mountain, crushed the entrance to the Frank Mine, obliterated the eastern end of the town of Frank, and engulfed a section of the main **Crowsnest Pass** road and Canadian Pacific Railway (CPR) line. In 90 seconds, three square kilometres were buried beneath a 14-metre layer of rock. An accurate death toll has never been determined, but at least 70 of Frank's approximate population of 600 were killed. The official death toll was set at 76. Only 12 bodies were recovered. In terms of lives lost, the Frank Slide remains the worst natural disaster in Canadian history.

In the slide's wake, a thick pall of dust settled over the valley. Underground, in the Canadian American Coal and Coke Company's Frank mine shafts, 20 miners working the night shift watched in horror as the tunnels heaved and rocked. When the entranceway collapsed, three men who had been eating their lunch in the opening were crushed to death. The survivors found the passage clogged with debris and believed the mine had suffered damage from some bizarre explosion. They started digging. Thirteen hours later the men dug their way to safety by following a coal seam to the surface. A month after the slide, a horse named Charlie was rescued when a mine shaft was reopened. The animal had survived by eating bark from the timbers supporting the shaft ceiling and drinking rainwater that had leaked into the tunnel.

Within minutes of the slide, CPR brakeman Sid Choquette scrambled desperately across the rocks of the slide to the main line. He arrived in time to flag down an approaching passenger train, the Spokane Flyer, before it collided with the massive wall of rock burying the railroad line.

The house of Sam and Lucy Ennis lay directly in the path of the slide. Inside were the Ennises, their four children, and James Warrington. Rescuers dug frantically into the pile of debris and pulled all seven people safely from the wreckage of the home. Also found inside the debris of the Ennises' home was Mrs. John Watkins. She had somehow been flung into her neighbours' home. Although suffering from shock, internal injuries, and multiple cuts caused by rock splinters, the woman survived. So did her three children, found in their own home. Eighteen-month-old Marion Leitch was discovered lying unharmed in her cradle on top of a stack of hay next to her family's demolished house. She and the cradle had been thrown out of the top storey of the home. Her two sisters, Jessie and Rosemary, were rescued from inside the house. Both their parents and four brothers were killed. In all, 23 people were rescued from the rubble.

In the aftermath, many theories were advanced to explain the slide's cause. Early newspaper reports blamed a volcanic eruption, an earthquake, a mine explosion, and even a meteorite strike. Most scientists now believe that the slide resulted from the geologic nature of Turtle Mountain. The twin-peaked mountain's maximum elevation was 2,200 metres. The limestone formations on the mountain's face lay in sharply inclined layers poised above the valley floor. Each year, as winter ice melted, the space between these layers enlarged and the mountain's face became increasingly unstable. Mining activity, especially blasting and poor engineering practices, below the face further weakened the rock formation.

In 1911, a government commission declared the north peak of Turtle Mountain unstable. The residents of Frank were ordered to evacuate their homes and businesses. The government paid 50 percent of their moving costs to new homes in nearby Blairmore and Coleman. For those residents who refused to abandon the community, the government financed moving the remaining buildings across the railway line to a supposed safer location. The mine continued operation. Reopened only three weeks after the slide, it closed in 1917 following an explosion and fire that caused extensive damage.

Today about 100 people live in the relocated community. On a rise overlooking the slide debris, the Frank Slide Interpretive Centre profiles the history of the Crowsnest Pass area and provides a detailed examination of the events surrounding the slide and its probable cause. The provincial government has monitored rock movement at Turtle Mountain since 1933 and has determined there is significant risk that the mountain may again experience a major rock slide.

Giant Easter Egg. *See* **Pysanka.**

Glaciation. *See* **Ancient Alberta; Icefields.**

Glenbow Museum

The Glenbow Museum in **Calgary** is the largest museum in western Canada, providing a comprehensive chronicle of western Canadian history. A variety of exhibits and artifacts chronicles the culture of pre-contact **First Nations peoples** through the arrival of European explorers, fur traders, **North-West Mounted Police,** settlers, and railway builders.

The museum's second floor houses a collection of more than 24,000 works of contemporary and Inuit art, as well as historical works by many of Canada's noted early artists. On the fourth floor is a large military collection, mineralogy displays, and exhibits relating the role of the warrior in society, plus a large West African collection.

Glenbow's eclectic collection reflects the interests and tastes of its main benefactor—oilman, lawyer, and philanthropist Eric L. Harvie. In 1954, ten years after he became a multimillionaire following the discovery of oil at Leduc—where he owned the surrounding mineral rights for 200,000 square kilometres—Harvie founded Glenbow Museum. The museum was intended to house the many Canadian and international artifacts and art works he had gathered during two decades of collecting.

In 1966, Harvie donated his personal collection to the people of Alberta. The Glenbow-Alberta Institute was formed to administer the huge collections of artifacts, paintings, books, and documents already housed in the museum. The original building was replaced in 1976 when the provincial government erected an eight-storey building providing 8,361 square metres of display space. In 1979, the Harvie family donated an additional $20 million in art and collectibles to the museum.

Several expansions of the facility have occurred since then. The ongoing addition of books, manuscripts, and photographs to the museum's archives and library has resulted in Glenbow becoming the largest non-government archival collection in western Canada. This collection is a vital resource to researchers working in virtually any field of western Canadian studies.

Grande Cache

In 1966 the McIntyre Porcupine Coal Mine was opened to supply coking coal for export to Japan. The mine lay about 450 kilometres west of **Edmonton** and 185 kilometres south of **Grande Prairie** in an isolated corner of the province on the edge of the **Rocky Mountains.**

Over the next three years the company undertook construction of a carefully planned community to accommodate its miners and their families. Situated on the side of Grande Mountain overlooking the Smoky River, the town was built 20 kilometres south of the mine to ensure a scenic environment.

Grande Cache today has a population of about 4,000 people and is developing a small tourist trade to supplement the mining **economy.** To the town's south spreads Willmore Wilderness Park, which protects a remote part of the Rocky Mountains accessible by about 750 kilometres of hiking trails.

The name Grande Cache derives not from the mine, but from the fur-trade era. In 1821 a Hudson's Bay Company trader, Ignace Giasson, was caught in deep snow while bringing a large number of furs down the Smoky River. He was forced to abandon the furs in a large cache, whereafter a nearby lake, ford, and the valley in which the furs were left became known as Grande Cache. The town took its name from these features.

Grande Prairie

In 1881 a Hudson's Bay Company trading post was erected on the site of what would eventually become the city of Grande Prairie. The region's future as a grain-growing capital was presaged shortly thereafter when Louie Callihou, a part-Iroquois farmer, sowed some grain and put up a barn and a corral. Fur traders called the area Buffalo Plains, but when Father Grouard, a Roman Catholic missionary, came to the area he declared the gently undulating expanse of wilderness "la grande prairie" and the name stuck.

By 1900 a trickle of homesteaders was settling into the area. The arrival of the railroad in 1916 spurred the rate of settlement. But it was the end of World War I and a veteran land settlement agreement that brought a massive influx of homesteaders into the region. By the 1930s, the community of Grande Prairie served as a wholesale centre for a vast farming region. With a population of only 1,450, it was generating annual retail sales in excess of $2 million.

Grand Prairie's economic future was secured with diversification in the 1970s through development of petrochemical plants and oil refineries—

a result of the city's proximity to the province's largest gas reserve. In 1973, an $80-million pulp mill was also opened. The present population of Grande Prairie is about 29,000.

The city contains a beautiful expanse of parkland extending from a large artificial reservoir in the north along Bear Creek south of the city boundary. Near the community are wetlands that provide vital nesting areas for **trumpeter swans.**

Grizzly Bears. *See* Bears.

Grasslands

The grasslands are a flat to gently rolling plain broken by several major hill systems. One of six natural regions in the province, it encompasses the majority of southern Alberta east of the **foothills.**

Most of the bedrock in the grasslands is covered with glacial till deposits. Some areas are blanketed by glacial lake sediments, sand dune fields, and outwash plains. **Badlands** have developed where river valleys and associated **coulees** and ravines are carved deeply into the bedrock. They are found most often along the Red Deer, South Saskatchewan, and Milk rivers. The **Milk River** drainage system contains the only exposures of igneous bedrock in the grasslands of western Canada. All other bedrock exposures are of sedimentary rocks.

Four subregions occur in the grasslands. Each is distinguished by differences in **climate,** soils, and vegetation.

- The dry mixed-grass subregion, as identified by the Alberta government **Special Places** initiative, encompasses a landscape with generally low physical relief. Elevations range from 600 metres above sea level near Empress to more than 1,300 metres on the lower slopes of the **Cypress Hills,** Sweetgrass Hills of Montana, and Milk River Ridge. This subregion is the warmest and driest in Alberta.

    The name mixed-grass comes from the predominance of both short and mid-height grasses. The most widespread grasses are the mid-height grasses, which include spear grass, western wheat grass, and June grass. Short grasses include blue grama.

    Of the four grassland subregions, dry mixed-grass contains the highest diversity of animal species. Many species, especially those of the sand dune areas and of the province's extreme southeast corner, occur nowhere else in Alberta.

    Much of this subregion has been heavily grazed by cattle, resulting in a particular distribution of species in these areas. In heavily grazed areas, **birds** such as the horned lark, McCown's longspur, and chestnut-collared longspur, and Richardson's ground squirrels are common. Less heavily grazed areas more genuinely reflect the original natural habitat, with Baird's sparrow, Sprague's pipit, sharp-tailed grouse, and upland sandpiper common. Sage grouse, lark bunting, Brewer's sparrow, and pronghorn antelope prefer sagebrush areas.

The sandy areas support some rare species, including Ord's kangaroo rat and western hognose snake. Riparian shrubland and forest support a diverse animal community, including brown thrasher, gray catbird, mourning dove, and white-tailed deer. The rock outcrops and badlands provide ideal nesting habitat for golden eagle, ferruginous hawk, and mountain bluebird. Several bird species are found in the region's wetlands, as well as the boreal chorus frog, **northern leopard frog,** and plains spadefoot toad.

- The mixed-grass subregion differs from the dry mixed-grass subregion in that it encompasses gently undulating to rolling morainal and glacial lake deposits, with small areas of steeper terrain along the lower and middle slopes of Milk River Ridge, and the Sweetgrass and Cypress hills. Because of its higher elevation and closer proximity to the Rocky Mountain foothills it is a cooler and moister environment than the dry mixed-grass subregion, which generally lies to the east of the mixed-grass subregion.

  Native grasslands are primarily needle grasses and wheat grasses. Tall shrubs and trees, particularly those constituting **cottonwood forests,** grow in moist draws and river valleys. Wildlife is similar to that of the dry mixed-grass subregion.

- The northern fescue subregion is characterized by gently rolling ground moraine and hummocky moraine. Sand plains, dune fields, and glacial lake deposits also occur here. **Rough fescue** is the dominant grassland. Wildlife is again similar to that found in the dry mixed-grass. This region extends from just south of Drumheller in a narrow-arcing band through Coronation and continuing to the Saskatchewan border.

- The final subregion in the grasslands is the foothills fescue subregion. It is located on the flanks of the Rocky Mountain foothills as well as the upper elevations of the Porcupine Hills, Sweetgrass Hills, and parts of the Cypress Hills plateau. Elevations are overall much higher than in the other grassland subregions—averaging 1,000 metres or more and ranging up to 1,400 metres in the Cypress Hills. **Chinooks** are frequent and winters are milder, with more spring snowfall than in the lower grassland subregions.

Grasslands in this subregion are dominated by rough fescue, blue-bunch fescue, Parry oat grass, and intermediate oat grass. In the Cypress Hills, Parry oat grass is rare and bearded wheat common. Extensive narrowleaf cottonwood stands, found nowhere else in Canada, occur along the Oldman, Belly, Waterton, and St. Mary rivers. The foothills fescue subregion is unusual in that despite its moister climate fewer animal species make their home here than in the other grassland subregions.

Hailstorms

Alberta has some of the world's most severe hailstorms. The region of central Alberta between Drumheller, **Red Deer,** and **Calgary,** shaped somewhat like a right-angled triangle with Red Deer at its apex and Drumheller and Calgary forming opposite points of its base, experiences more hailstorms than any other in Alberta and is one of the most hailstorm-prone areas in the world. This region is known as "hailstorm alley," with its average of four to six hailstorms per year, compared to the rest of the province's annual rate of three hailstorms.

Hail normally occurs during localized thunderstorm showers. A hailstone begins as a frozen rain droplet or snow pellet, falling through a cloud with an internal temperature below 0° Celsius. As it falls, it picks up more moisture by colliding with unfrozen droplets. The stone's descent through the cloud is slowed by vertical air currents averaging 10 to 50 metres per second rushing up through the cloud. The extent to which a hailstone's descent is slowed contributes greatly to its growth, as does the cloud's humidity level. By the time the hailstone escapes the cloud and falls to earth it can vary in average diameter from five millimetres to ten centimetres and weigh from 0.1 kilograms to 1 kilogram.

Most hail in Alberta falls during late afternoon thunderstorms. Severe hailstorms may last several hours and leave a hail swath up to 50 kilometres wide and hundreds of kilometres long. Average Alberta hailstorms, however, last only ten minutes. July is the province's leading hail month, with storms occurring somewhere in the province 21 out of 31 days. By

September, thunderstorms occur on an average of only one day a month and hailstorms seldom develop.

The worst hailstorm in Canadian history, and in terms of property damage the worst Canadian storm recorded, took place on September 7, 1991 at Calgary. In 30 minutes, more than $400 million damage was incurred when stones the size of baseballs tore holes in the roofs of buildings, dented automobiles and, in some cases, collapsed car roofs and shattered their windows, as well as pulverizing surrounding croplands. Calgary's previous worst recorded hailstorm had been on July 28, 1981, when $100 million damage was caused during a 15-minute barrage.

Hail also figured in Canada's worst natural disaster, which killed 27 people, injured 300 more, caused $300 million in damage, and left thousands homeless. On July 31, 1987, hailstones accompanying the **tornadoes** that caused most of the damage hammered the city. Some of the stones weighed 2.64 kilograms, the heaviest ever recorded in Alberta.

Hailstorms can pose severe danger to wildlife and domestic livestock. On July 14, 1953, a hailstorm raging down hailstorm alley left 36,000 ducks and thousands of other **birds** lying dead in its wake. Four days later, another 27,000 ducks were killed in the same area by hailstones.

Head-Smashed-In Buffalo Jump

Located in the Porcupine Hills of southern Alberta, Head-Smashed-In Buffalo Jump is one of North America's oldest, largest, and best preserved **bison hunting** jump sites. This vast site, 18 kilometres west of **Fort Macleod,** sprawls over 595 hectares. From the wealth of archaeological information contained within its boundaries, scientists have been able to trace the evolution of communal hunting using jumps from the technique's earliest beginnings to the site's eventual abandonment in the early 19th century.

Declared a World Heritage Site in 1981 by the United Nations Educational, Service, and Cultural Organization (UNESCO), Head-Smashed-In was first used as a bison-killing site at least 5,700 years ago and perhaps as early as 8,000 B.C.

The site did not come to possess its unusual name until about 150 years ago. According to local First Nations' legend, a young brave wanted to witness a vast herd of **bison** being driven off the cliff to their deaths. He hid in the shelter of a ledge cut into the sandstone cliffs, watching the animals cascade past him like water rushing over a waterfall. It was, however, an unusually large kill. The animals piled up, finally rising so high the brave was pinned against the cliff wall by bison corpses. When his people came to do the butchering, they found the young man's body. His skull had been crushed by the bisons' weight. They consequently named the place Head-Smashed-In.

Below the various jumps, massive bone deposits range up to ten metres in depth—proof that the site was used for hundreds of kills. Mixed with the bones is an archaeological record of successive ages of tools and weapons.

The system of drive lanes at Head-Smashed-In is the largest and most elaborate in existence. Cairns numbering in the thousands mark out dozens of lanes. Some stretch back from the cliffs over 15 kilometres of **prairie.** At sites above the cliff several **petroglyphs and pictographs** are found. One site was used for vision quests and other ceremonies involving communication with the spirits.

In 1982, the provincial government approved the opening of a major interpretive centre at Head-Smashed-In. Construction was started in September 1984 and completed in October 1986 at a cost of $9.82 million. This remarkable centre is a seven-tiered building buried discreetly within a 300-metre-long, 11-metre-high cliff to the immediate south of the bison-killing cliffs. To avoid disturbing fragile archaeological deposits, builders removed a section of the cliff, built a massive concrete box inside, then pulled the earth and grass back on top of the structure.

The resulting impression is that the building is a natural product of erosion. Its exterior closely resembles the colour and texture of the surrounding rock outcrops. Inside, subdued sandstone hues are sustained and integrated into dioramas documenting the bison-hunting culture of the plains **First Nations peoples** from ancient times to the arrival of Europeans.

Interpretive trails provide access to the bison gathering basin, the drive lanes, various kill sites, and a campsite and processing area at the base of the cliffs.

High Level Bridge

The longest and highest trestle-construction bridge in the world, High Level Bridge spans 1.6 kilometres at a height 94 metres above the floor of the Oldman River valley. Built in 1909 by the Canadian Pacific Railway at the then astronomical cost of $1.3 million, the bridge dramatically reduced the length of line running between **Fort Macleod** and **Lethbridge** by replacing a network of 22 wooden bridges.

Its construction required the use of more than two million kilograms of steel, 13,000 cubic metres of concrete, and 34,500 litres of paint. The bridge crosses the valley on the western edge of Lethbridge, near 3rd Avenue.

Highways

More than 20,000 kilometres of paved roads and highways provide an extensive transportation grid throughout the province. Highway 1 and Highway 16 are multi-lane, divided highways running across the province from east to west. Both are part of Canada's coast-to-coast highway system. Highway 1, the Trans-Canada, runs from the Saskatchewan border through **Medicine Hat** to **Calgary** and via **Banff** to the British Columbia border. Highway 16, the Yellowhead, enters Alberta from Saskatchewan at **Lloydminster** and passes through **Edmonton.** Just west of Hinton this road narrows to a two-lane highway to pass through **Jasper National Park** and cross the B.C. border. Southern Alberta is traversed east to west by Highway 3 (the **Crowsnest Pass** Highway), which extends from Medicine Hat through **Lethbridge** to the B.C. border inside the Crowsnest Pass.

The major north-south route through Alberta is Highway 2, linking Calgary and Edmonton via **Red Deer.** To the north, this highway connects with the Alaska-Dempster Highway. In the south, the most rapid route from Calgary to major highway connections at the U.S. border follows Highway 2 to **Fort Macleod,** where it runs briefly east on Highway 3 before turning at Lethbridge to follow Highway 4 linking into Interstate Highway I-15 at Sweetgrass, Montana.

(*See also* **Icefields Parkway.**)

Highwood Pass

Highway 40, running through **Kananaskis Country,** crosses the Highwood Pass, which, with a 2,206-metre summit, is Canada's highest drivable pass.

This is the least developed zone in the Kananaskis area. Dominated by the Highwood Mountains to the west, it is a land of high alpine meadows and subalpine forest. Wildflowers blanket the meadows in late spring and early summer.

The region is home to elk, bighorn sheep, black and grizzly **bears,** as well as smaller **mammals,** such as Rocky Mountain pikas. (Pikas are guinea pig–sized members of the order Lagomorpha, which includes rabbits and hares. Although there are 18 species of pika worldwide, only 2 are found in Canada—the Rocky Mountain pika and the collared pika.)

In winter, the Highwood region is a critical wintering habitat for much alpine wildlife, particularly herds of elk. Primarily to protect these herds from disturbance by motorized traffic and humans, most of Highway 40 is closed to traffic from December 1 to June 15.

Just prior to the highway's opening, snowplows push a one-lane track through the winter's snow accumulation. In the days before the highway is officially opened to motorized traffic, cyclists from all over Alberta and the world come to enjoy the motor-free opportunity to traverse the pass.

Hillcrest Mine Disaster

On June 19, 1914, at 9:30 a.m., a series of powerful explosions tore through the tunnels of the Hillcrest coal mine in the **Crowsnest Pass.** When the explosions stopped, rescue teams began the gruesome work of digging out survivors and bringing the bodies of the dead to the surface. Of the 235 men who had gone underground that morning, 189 were dead. The Hillcrest Mine Disaster remains the worst mining accident in Canadian history.

Some of the miners were killed outright by the explosions. Far more died breathing in afterdamp—a poisonous mixture of carbon dioxide and carbon monoxide left in a mine shaft following consumption of available oxygen by an explosion. Those asphyxiated by the afterdamp were often found face down in puddles of water, rags wrapped across their mouths in a vain effort to create a protective gas mask.

Eighteen men and adolescent boys managed to find their own way safely to the surface. One of these survivors was David Murray. When he discovered that his sons, Robert, William, and David Jr. were still in the mine shaft, Murray went back inside. He was killed by the afterdamp, as were his three sons.

Most of the dead were buried in three mass graves in the Hillcrest Cemetery. The miners killed that morning left behind 130 widows and nearly 400 children.

The cause of the explosions remains uncertain. Most experts believe a rockfall probably generated sparks that ignited methane gas present in the tunnels.

Before and after the Hillcrest Mine Disaster, the many coal mines of the Crowsnest Pass region were plagued with disasters and accidents. Explosions were common, as were tunnel collapses and various forms of atmosphere poisoning from coal dust and afterdamp. Safety procedures in Alberta mines were among the poorest in the world.

A U.S.-sponsored survey in 1910 identified the mines of Alberta and British Columbia—especially those in the Crowsnest Pass—as having the world's worst safety record. In 1924, Alberta's provincial archivist reported "that every 100,000 tons of coal produced in the last 15 years has cost a human life."

The dangerous conditions in the mines, low pay, and the often violent union-smashing tactics of the provincial government and mine owners served to rally miners and their families around pro-union and Socialist or Communist political parties. Until the late 1940s, when many of the mines closed for good (Hillcrest closed in 1939), the province's coal miners formed the backbone for a vibrant and strong left-wing political movement in an otherwise conservative-leaning Alberta.

(*See also* **Bellevue Mine; Mining Industry; Nordegg.**)

Historical Overview

The first European entered present-day Alberta on September 11, 1754 near the modern village of Chauvin, on the Saskatchewan border east of Wainwright. Prior to Anthony Henday's arrival, **First Nations peoples** had been the sole human occupants of the region for at least 15,000 years. Henday was a Hudson's Bay Company (HBC) fur trader seeking a trading relationship with the Blackfoot nation.

For the next hundred years the fur trade dominated the province's history. The first European settlements were fur-trading forts. Peter Pond, a trader with the rival North West Company (NWC), established Alberta's first European settlement in 1778—a trading post on the Athabasca River. The NWC intended to have the first opportunity to purchase furs being shipped east by First Nations and **Métis** trappers. In 1788 Fort Chipewyan opened at the confluence of the Athabasca and Peace rivers, effectively interdicting the flow of furs east along this major east-flowing waterway.

To increase the NWC's knowledge about this largely unknown region, so it could develop fur-trade routes more efficiently, Alexander Mackenzie departed Fort Chipewyan in 1789 to trace the Mackenzie River (named in his honour) nearly to the Arctic Ocean. He then explored the **Peace River** in 1792, hoping to find a route to the Pacific Ocean. In 1793, aided by First Nations guides, he reached the Pacific at present-day Bella Coola in British Columbia.

The HBC countered Mackenzie's push into Canada's most westerly regions by sending David Thompson and Peter Fidler to explore and map the Athabasca and Saskatchewan rivers in 1790 and the early 1800s. Both companies followed up their explorations by building an ever-lengthening network of trading forts reaching westward to the Pacific. At Fort Chipewyan, Fort Vermilion, Fort George, Fort Assiniboine, **Lesser Slave Lake,** Fort Edmonton, and **Rocky Mountain House** the two companies established forts competing directly with each other for furs. Often these forts glared across the river at each other.

With costs escalating and the competition threatening to ruin both companies, the NWC merged with the HBC in 1821. The newly constituted HBC built its last Alberta fort in 1870 at Fort Smith on today's Northwest Territories–Alberta border. By that time the fur trade was already in decline. On June 23, 1870, the Canadian government assumed possession of all HBC territory known as Rupert's Land, including the future province of Alberta.

Prior to the cession of HBC lands to the Canadian government the only significant European presence in the region was that of fur traders and missionaries bent on converting First Nations peoples to Christianity. The first resident cleric was Methodist Robert Rundle, who arrived in 1840 and worked out of fur-trading forts in the Athabasca and Assiniboine river region. Two years later Roman Catholic Father Jean-Baptiste Thibault arrived. Soon Anglican, Roman Catholic, and Methodist missionaries were vying for the souls of Alberta's First Nations peoples. Initially they based their operations out of trading posts. But the missionaries soon sought to guide First Nations away from dependency on the fur trade and toward farming and the establishment of permanent settlements. To this end, a number of small farming settlements were built, although these were usually located close to the trading posts.

When the Canadian government took over control of the HBC lands it sought a development strategy from the pages of the reports of the **Palliser Expedition** of 1857–58. John Palliser and his team of experts in fields ranging from geology to astronomy had identified large tracts of arable land in present-day Alberta, discovered many coal deposits, and found passes through the **Rocky Mountains** suitable for a railroad to connect the new nation from coast to coast.

In 1871 the region between the new province of Manitoba and the Rockies was organized as the North-West Territories. The Dominion Lands Act of 1872, modelled on American homestead legislation, provided legal authority for lands to be given to intending settlers. Settlers paid a $10 fee and had to complete specified developments according to a set schedule. A survey system divided arable **prairie** into square townships. Each township comprised 36 sections of 260 hectares (640 acres), with the basic homestead made up of one 65-hectare (160-acre) quarter-section. Two sections in each township were reserved for public use.

The government also decided it was imperative that a trans-Canada railway be constructed. Funding of the Canadian Pacific Railway (CPR) was made possible by providing the CPR with vast land grants across the prairies and raising cash by selling large land tracts to colonization companies.

Despite the arrival of the CPR in **Calgary** by 1883, and the resolution of legal claim to the land through the settlement of treaties with the First Nations peoples, European settlement largely failed to materialize throughout the late 1800s. Most colonization companies consequently went broke.

In 1881, only about 1,000 non–First Nations settlers lived in present-day Alberta. Ten years later that number had risen to only about 17,500, most involved in **ranching** or running businesses in the few small communities.

A critical problem remained that, although the land was arable, its **climate** was harsh and crops fared poorly. Near the end of the century, however, varieties of fast-maturing hard spring wheat were developed that did well on the Canadian prairies. At the same time the arable land in the American west had been largely taken, so potential settlers had to look to more northerly climes.

The federal cabinet minister in charge of immigration, Clifford Sifton, found further fuel for settlement by opening Canada's doors to central and eastern European settlers (*see* **Ukrainian-Canadian Albertans**). As agricultural settlement accelerated, others were lured to the region to work in the coal mines developing throughout southern Alberta, particularly in the emerging mining communities of the **Crowsnest Pass.** Immigration boomed and the province was assured a multicultural face that continues today.

By 1901, Alberta's **population** was about 73,000 and on September 1, 1905 the territorial district became a province. Provincial status resulted from public demands for increased local autonomy. Four major controversies initially occupied the Alberta political landscape. Three of these became long-festering wounds Albertans still regard as classic examples of federal meddling in provincial affairs. The federal government imposed the following on Alberta: an assurance that the predominantly francophone Roman Catholic population would be entitled to government-funded separate schools; the boundary between Saskatchewan and Alberta would be drawn on 110° west longitude rather than Alberta's hoped for 107° west longitude; and **Edmonton** received provincial capital status instead of Calgary, which at the time most Albertans preferred as the site of the capital seat. Even more vexing than these perceived slights, however, was the very real paternalistic decision by the federal government to retain control of Crown lands and natural resources. These controls were not ceded to the provincial government until 1930.

Through the early 1900s the province prospered, but discontent grew among farmers and coal miners over the conditions under which they laboured. Farmers felt they were being squeezed into poverty by the triad of the **railways,** grain-elevator companies, and the banks. In answer they created their own political movement, the United Farmers of Alberta (UFA) and in 1921 the Liberal party was swept aside as the UFA formed the provincial government. It would retain control until 1935, when another made-in-Alberta party, William Aberhart's Social Credit League, came to power.

By that time the UFA had proved incapable of coping with the economic devastation of the Great Depression, which blanketed the Prairie provinces more deeply than many other parts of the nation. The new party drew upon a mixture of Aberhart's religious fundamentalism and Major C. H. Douglas's curious monetary theory, known as social credit. Douglas believed "poverty in the midst of plenty" arose when the **economy** became concentrated in the hands of a few, such as the banks. If capitalism was allowed to operate free of such concentration, then all people naturally prospered. Following from this line of thought, it was the government's responsibility to create social dividends to ensure capital could not be concentrated by the banks and other powerful interests. By combining this theory with the Protestant work ethic, Aberhart captured the imagination of many Albertans and the Social Credit Party was born.

In 1903, Homer H. Houghton built this cabin east of Claresholm in order to settle on his new homestead. (Glenbow Archives photo, NA-1306-4)

Farmers rallied to Social Credit's platform, but the miners embraced socialism and communism. In doing so they won the ire of the government, which actively helped mine owners to break strikes and did little to improve below-ground working conditions. Mining disasters in Alberta were common: the **Hillcrest Mine disaster** of 1914 was the worst in Canada's history. Until the end of World War II **the mining industry** remained an important part of Alberta's economy, but with war's end and a shift away from coal as a primary source of energy many mines closed. With their closure the left-wing influence of the mine workers was broken. Today, Alberta has the nation's lowest unionization levels and leftist movements exert little influence.

Although oil and gas were discovered earlier in the Turner Valley, it was the discovery of the **Leduc Oilfield** in February 1947 that began the process of transforming Alberta's economy from one based on **agriculture** to one based on petroleum products. The province's economy is now extremely dependent upon the health of the **oil and gas industry** despite ongoing attempts to create a more diversified economic base.

Politically, the province remains staunchly conservative and the Conservative Party has formed the government without interruption since defeating the Social Credit in 1971. But it is a made-in-Alberta conservatism with firm roots reaching back to the philosophies of the now largely forgotten Social Credit Party. Premiers of recent years have drawn on the populist traditions of the past to advocate and win overwhelming support for dismantling supposed big government, balancing the provincial budget, and slashing the provincial deficit despite dramatic reductions to the quality of health care and the overall deterioration of the province's social safety net. They have also tapped the historical animosity toward the federal government by blaming most of the province's woes on politicians in Ottawa.

Albertans have shown an inclination to stick with a premier until he either retires or dies in office. Aberhart was premier for eight years until his death in 1943. His successor Ernest Charles Manning was premier from 1943 to 1968, an amazing 25 years. Conservative premier Peter Lougheed held office from 1971 until his retirement in 1986.

Hoodoos

Assuming often fantastical shapes, hoodoos are naturally carved rock or earth pedestals, pillars, or columns. They range from a few centimetres in height to several metres. Hoodoos are produced by the combined erosional

As a hoodoo is worn away by erosion, its hat will eventually shrink and ultimately topple away. (Regan Paynter photo)

action of wind, rain, and running water, which sculpt the formations into various shapes.

The term hoodoos is largely restricted to western North America. It is, however, an African word describing a form of witchcraft, in which humans are turned into pillars of earth. **First Nations peoples** believed the largely sandstone pillars in Alberta were either petrified giants or **tipis** housing evil spirits.

There are significant hoodoos southeast of **Lethbridge,** at **Writing-On-Stone Provincial Park,** hatless hoodoos at **Tunnel Mountain** near **Banff,** and developing hoodoos along Cavell Road in **Jasper National Park.**

The presence of hats is integral to the development of hoodoos because they are formed by a hard layer of resistant material capping a softer substance. The harder material stands upon the ever-eroding softer base and forms a cap that protects the base from erosion by water, wind, and slashing rain.

Eventually the material supporting the cap will become so eroded that the cap topples down. This is probably what has happened to the hoodoos at Tunnel Mountain.

Hot Springs

The number of hot springs in Alberta's **Rocky Mountains** is unknown. Throughout the mountains, however, there are numerous hot springs—large and small.

Undoubtedly the most famous are at the **Cave and Basin National Historic Site** near **Banff,** which has been a tourist attraction since 1887. But in other more isolated areas, undeveloped hot springs may be found.

The hottest of the larger known springs in Alberta is Miette Hot Springs, 41 kilometres east of **Jasper.** Its average temperature is 53.9° Celsius. Cave and Basin at Banff are 32.8° and 34.5° Celsius respectively.

The water in hot springs starts as rain and snow, becomes surface water, then slowly moves below ground. During a long descent the water dissolves minerals from the permeable or fractured rock through which it passes. The water also warms by 1° Celsius for every 30 metres of descent. Once the water reaches a depth of three kilometres it exceeds the boiling point, attaining temperatures of more than 100° Celsius.

In Alberta's Rockies many fault planes extend from the surface to great depths. When the superheated water below the three-kilometre-depth point reaches one of these fault planes it rises rapidly, like steam hissing up the spout of a kettle. As it rises, replacement water is sucked in from the surrounding rock. This keeps hot water rushing up the fault plane in a continuous flow. During its ascent the water cools, often mixing with groundwater near the surface, but enough heat is retained to create natural warmwater bathing areas.

Because gypsum and pyrite are both present in much of the bedrock through which the water passes, the water boiling up into the surface springs usually has a strong rotten-egg odour caused by hydrogen sulphide gas. The gas, dissolved by the water during its contact with gypsum and pyrite, also causes the milky colour common to Rocky Mountain hot springs.

Various types of algae and bacteria live in Rocky Mountain hot springs. In marshes and springs feeding Cave and Basin hot springs, tropical **fish** may also be found. Western mosquitofish were introduced here by the National Parks service in 1924 to feed on mosquito larvae. Other people have illegally introduced various species of tropical fish over the years. Most common among these is sailfin molly and African jewelfish.

Hutterites

Scattered throughout Alberta are 147 Hutterite colonies, constituting the majority of Hutterite communities in North America. Alberta is home to about 12,000 of the continent's total estimated Hutterite population of 30,000. An average of about 80 people live in each colony. When a colony's population reaches 125 to 150 it is usually divided, and a new colony founded.

Hutterite history dates back to Europe's Protestant Reformation period. In the late 1520s various sectarian groups, especially in Germany, emerged under the banner of Anabaptists. The Anabaptists rejected Roman Catholic

Church authority. They sought a Christian relationship between man and God that was both simpler and arrived at through an individual decision made at adulthood. This latter aspect led to the practice of adult baptism, or rebaptism, which is the literal meaning of Anabaptism. The Anabaptists also believed in pacifism and in most cases refused to pledge allegiance to any worldly authority—either church or state.

The Anabaptists were relentlessly persecuted by both Roman Catholic and Protestant rulers. Most were killed or forced to renounce their faith. Small fragments of the movement scattered as refugees to other parts of Europe. Among this latter group were the Mennonite, Amish, and Hutterite sects, which all eventually sought refuge in the United States to escape the never-ending persecution that followed them wherever they took refuge in Europe.

The Hutterites take their name from Jakob Huter. Huter organized disparate groups of Anabaptists who had fled to Moravia—now part of the Czech Republic—in 1528. He preached that life could be patterned on Acts 2:44: "And all that believed were together, and had all things in common." From this precept the Hutterites developed a strictly communal way of life and a rejection of the material world. Huter was arrested and burnt at the stake in 1536.

In 1770, a fragment of about 70 Hutterites—virtually all who remained—accepted an invitation from Catherine the Great of Russia to settle in newly conquered parts of southern Ukraine. The Hutterite community thrived and grew there, but in the late 1860s it became increasingly pressured to assimilate as Russians under a policy enacted by the Tsarist government. In 1871 Hutterites and Mennonites in the Ukraine were declared no longer exempt from military service despite their pacifist beliefs.

Realizing a new wave of persecution was about to begin, the Hutterites and Mennonites looked to North America for possible refuge. In the mid- to late 1870s three groups comprising about 400 Hutterites immigrated to the United States, settling in South Dakota. Their pacifist life was again threatened in 1898 by the Spanish-American War and the possibility that Hutterites would be called up to serve in the military. This danger prompted some members to look northward to Canada, where their pacifist beliefs might be respected.

The Canadian government was eager to populate the Canadian west and encouraged the Hutterites to emigrate by granting them assurances in an 1899 agreement. That agreement promised the Hutterites respect of their pacifism, full religious freedom, the right to set up independent schools, the right not to make oaths of allegiance to the government or hold public office, and a guarantee they would be able to continue their communal way of life forever.

During World War I, the U.S. government aggressively persecuted the Hutterites living in South Dakota. As a result, when the war ended about 2,000 Hutterites accepted the Canadian offer and moved colonies north into Canada.

Hutterite settlement in the Prairies was controversial. Some non-Hutterites, in open contravention of the 1899 agreement, sought legislation to break up the communes, force Hutterite children to attend public schools, or prohibit the establishment of colonies. These attempts at repression served only to entrench among the Hutterites the view that the world outside their communes was Godless, hostile, and bent on destroying their way of life. In 1942, Alberta became the only province or state to introduce legislation prohibiting Hutterites, Doukhobors, and other "aliens" from purchasing additional lands. The Land Sales Prohibition Act, as modified in 1947, limited colonies to owning no more than 2,590 hectares and from establishing new colonies within 64 kilometres of one already in existence.

Alberta Hutterite women and children in the early 1900s, shortly after their immigration to the province from the United States. (Glenbow Archives photo, NA-4079-75)

Because of their high birth rate—the average Hutterite family had nine children—the need for colonies to expand or split off into new colonies was acute. The Act, with very few amendments to loosen its restrictions, remained in effect, however, until its repeal in 1972.

One unanticipated result of the legislation was the distribution of Hutterite populations throughout the province, as new colonies sought land lying outside the prescribed buffer zones. Originally concentrated in southern Alberta, Hutterites today are settled in all agriculturally viable parts of the province.

Hutterites believe their society can best be preserved in rural settings. Each colony is organized communally in a quasi-village settlement. Most colonies consist of about 13 families and have an average population of 80.

Houses are usually of a row nature, with each family occupying a private apartment. Traditional clothing is still worn at most Hutterite colonies. Men wear black denim pants and jacket, a coloured shirt, and broad-brimmed black hat. Women usually wear a long plaid or flowered skirt, an apron, and a polka-dot kerchief. Children dress similarly. German remains the common language.

Each colony has the same basic administrative structure. An executive council is elected and reports to the assembly, composed of all baptized males aged 20 years or older. Women have no official say in the colony's running but generally exert a high degree of informal influence on affairs. The colonies operate as independent units, but do cooperate with other colonies when it is advantageous to do so.

Hutterite colonies today are highly mechanized and practise efficient mixed-farming techniques. Most Hutterite colonies work 50 percent less land than would be owned by an equivalent number of non-collectivized farm families. Despite this, production yields are significantly higher than the provincial average. Working about 2 percent of the province's arable land, they generate approximately 3 percent of total receipts.

Hutterites constitute only about 0.3 percent of the province's **population**. Yet, unlike the Doukhobor community in British Columbia or the Mennonite community in the United States, Hutterite colonies are not in decline. The majority of young Hutterites who choose to leave the colonies and explore life in the outside world opt to return within a few years.

Some colonies are closed to visitors; others are not. Among those welcoming visitors is the Pincher Creek Hutterite Colony, located between Pincher Creek and Cowley. Visitors are asked to phone before coming, but little notice is required.

Icefields

From Kicking Horse Pass west of **Lake Louise** to the northwest corner of **Jasper National Park,** a string of icefields composed of large glaciers drapes across the shoulders of the **Rocky Mountains,** forming part of the **Continental Divide.** The Rocky Mountain icefields are concentrated at high elevations, sprawling across relatively level upland areas.

These icefields are remnants of a great ice shield known as the Laurentide sheet which—covering more than 13 million square kilometres—blanketed most of Canada until about 12,000 years ago. Although they have an ancient origin, the icefields are an ever-evolving force of nature that continually regenerate themselves.

The survival of these icefields is primarily due to the fact that the layered rock upon which they rest is mostly flat-lying. Erosion of flat-lying rocks occurs slowly, so these areas remain as high-altitude, very cold uplands where more snow falls each winter than can melt during summer months. Snow accumulation leads to ice buildup, which then feeds the major valley glaciers below in a manner similar to spring runoff feeding river headwaters. Clinging to the sides of many surrounding mountain peaks, and sometimes forming caps on top of the peaks, are hundreds of smaller glaciers.

A process known as spontaneous recrystallization combined with the compacting force of snow accumulation transforms snow into ice. This ice is slowly pressed deeper into the icefield lying beneath its snow covering. As the depth increases, the degree of compaction mounts. At a depth of about 10 to 20 metres it would take a jackhammer to penetrate the hardened ice. The bottom of a glacier is subject to such intense pressure that ice is literally squeezed outward along the edges. This oozing ice moves downhill from the heights of the icefield into the valley below.

The squeezing process accounts for the advance of icefields during the cold winter months when pressure exerted on them from behind and above is most intense. In summer the forward edge of the icefield is incapable of advancing at the same rate that it warms and melts so the icefield retreats—usually back roughly to its winter start position. This process has been repeating itself for millions of years, with most glaciers in the Alberta Rockies advancing an average of 15 metres per year. If a winter is particularly cold or a summer especially cool, the icefield may advance further than it retreats. Alternatively, if warmer winter temperatures and lower rates of annual snowfall combine with warmer summers the icefield will retreat.

Over the past 120 years the Athabasca Glacier has retreated 1.6 kilometres due to a gradual warming trend. Between 1945 and 1964 this withdrawal averaged 20 to 37 metres per year, but since the 1970s it has slowed to 1 to 3 metres annually.

Because an icefield constantly moves downward, the ice at the lowest level is usually the oldest. It will eventually melt, replaced by younger ice. On the Columbia Icefield the process of snow becoming ice and eventually reaching the glacier's foot takes about 150 years.

Snow and ice are insulating substances, so the bottom of a glacier is warmer than its centre or top surface. The rock upon which the glacier rests is not frozen, but is actually heated to above the freezing level. Despite the ice's density, the heat is sufficient to cause some melting, creating a thin film of water between the base of the glacier and the rock upon which it rests. This water moves downhill in a steady, thin sheet. A cirque lake at the foot of a glacier and the meltwater flowing out from under its leading edge largely result from this phenomenon. This water is greyish coloured because it contains tiny flecks of rock, known as rock flour, scraped away by glacial flow. Water running off the surface of the ice, by contrast, is virtually crystalline in colour.

The largest of the 17 icefields in the Canadian Rockies is Columbia Icefield, which covers 325 square kilometres and ranges in depth from 100 to 365 metres. It covers a high plateau between **Mount Columbia,** Alberta's highest mountain, and Mount Athabasca. This remarkable icefield lies astride the Continental Divide and is known as the "mother of rivers" because its meltwaters feed the North Saskatchewan, Columbia, Athabasca, and Fraser river systems. Meltwater from this icefield eventually reaches three oceans—the Pacific, Arctic, and Atlantic. This phenomenon is called a hydrological apex, one of only two on earth—the other is in Siberia. About 30 distinct glaciers are contained in the Columbia Icefield. The largest are called Saskatchewan and Athabasca.

The Athabasca Glacier is about 6.5 kilometres long, averages 1 kilometre in width, and has a maximum depth of 300 metres. Researchers estimate its total ice volume is 640 million cubic metres. The glacier's highest point is about 2,800 metres, with its foot 900 metres lower.

Icefields Parkway

The 230-kilometre-long Icefields Parkway (Highway 93) is renowned as one of the world's most beautiful roads because of the spectacular mountain scenery through which it passes. Extending from **Lake Louise** north to **Jasper,** the road parallels the **Continental Divide** for much of its length, running along the base of Alberta's most rugged and highest **Rocky Mountain** peaks. The southern 122 kilometres of the road lie in **Banff National Park,** the remainder in **Jasper National Park.**

This highway earns its name by passing near the foot of several of the Rocky Mountains' largest **icefields,** including the biggest of all—Columbia Icefield. Most of the glaciers of the various icefields visible along this stretch of highway are too far away to reach without extended hiking, but the Columbia Icefield's base is directly accessible.

It is possible even to travel onto this icefield aboard custom-built Snocoaches. Designed and built in **Calgary** by Canadian Foremost Ltd., these vehicles were created specifically for moving safely on snow and ice. Looking like a regular bus with massive tires, the buses carry 56 passengers. They depart from Parks Canada's Icefield Centre, a chalet-style stone building that provides interpretive information to about half a million visitors annually and has limited accommodation and meal service facilities.

Crowfoot Glacier Viewpoint is one of 13 scattered along the parkway. It provides the closest access by motor vehicle to an ice cliff.

Other highlights are: Bow Lake, set in an alpine bowl, overlooked by Wapta Icefield; 2,088-metre-high Bow Summit, the highway's highest point, with lush alpine meadows and a view over Peyto Lake; the Weeping Wall, where a thin slick of waterfalls runs down the face of a large limestone cliff; and Sunwapta and Athabasca Falls, south of Jasper.

The Icefields Parkway was originally constructed as a make-work project during the Great Depression. Called the Banff-Jasper Road, most of its construction was by hand, as the crew had only one medium-sized tractor and two smaller tractors. Completed in 1939, the single-lane gravel track opened in 1940. It was upgraded in 1961 to its present condition, with the new roadbed faithfully following most of the old route.

International Boundary Commission

In 1872, in response to concerns by both the United States and Canada that national borders were being violated, the International Boundary Commission was dispatched to chart and mark the border from one end of the western prairies to the other.

The decision that the 49th parallel would constitute the border between British North America and the U.S. had been reached during the U.S.-British Convention of 1818. Canada inherited this agreement when the North-West Territories became part of the new nation following Canadian confederation in 1867.

Demarcating the border was an immense task. In 1861 a border monument had been erected by surveyors on a mountain summit in the **Rocky Mountains** west of Waterton Lakes. This was virtually the only marker denoting the U.S.-Canada border in North America's west.

A group of surveyors, scouts, geologists, and army engineers from each nation set off together from the Red River area of Manitoba in May 1873. Using the stars and sun to guide them, they travelled 1,500 kilometres westward to the Waterton Lakes' monument. **Métis** scouts proved essential to keeping the commission on track and helping them survive the rigorous 15-month journey through wild, unsettled country.

A boundary marker was set up every five kilometres along the newly surveyed border. Since sod was the only plentiful building material across much of the **prairie,** many markers were earth mounds. Armed with pick and shovel, men wrestled with the deep-rooted **rough fescue** and other prairie grasses to dig up the sod. They then constructed the mound from sod bricks and circled it with a deep trench. A wooden marker inserted in the top provided directional information. Where rocks were available, stone cairns were built instead of sod mounds. By the time the party reached the Waterton Lakes site it had left behind 388 markers and 40 astronomical stations.

Almost immediately upon its creation the boundary became known by **First Nations peoples** as the medicine line. Plains First Nations peoples recognized it as a potential safe haven from the predation of the U.S. army south of the border. Sitting Bull led his people across the border to seek refuge after the Battle of the Little Bighorn, in which he annihilated most of the Seventh U.S. Cavalry under the command of General George Armstrong Custer.

The border also worked the other way. In 1870, before it had even been surveyed, Louis Riel, Métis leader of the Red River Rebellion, fled south to escape the closing Canadian military forces determined to quash the rebellion.

Without the formal border demarcation carried out by the boundary commission, however, it would have been almost impossible for the North-West Mounted Police to enforce Canadian law in the southern portions of the Canadian west. The border's clear identification meant U.S. liquor smugglers, traders, and profiteers were denied easy access to exploit Canada's First Nations peoples. Others were denied the opportunity to expand more legitimate mining and **ranching** activities into Canada without first becoming Canadian citizens or passing through immigration procedures.

The existence of a formalized border consequently assured that the Canadian west would be developed by Canadians or immigrants invited into the region by the federal government. Without doubt this resulted in more peaceful development and settlement of the Canadian west than occurred anywhere south of the 49th parallel.

Invertebrates

Between 90 and 95 percent of all animals living on earth are invertebrates, creatures lacking a backbone. Apart from this absence, invertebrates have little in common. They are generally soft-bodied animals without a rigid internal skeleton, but often have a hard outer skeleton (true of most molluscs, crustaceans, and insects) that serves, as well, for body protection. Every year new invertebrates are discovered and classified by wildlife specialists.

The most numerous subgroup of invertebrates is the arthropods, comprising insects, crustaceans, and spiders and their relatives. Roughly 85 percent of all invertebrates are arthropods. North America is known to have about 100,000 arthropod species.

The number of arthropod species in Alberta is unknown. Scientists have identified 20,000 arthropod species in the Canadian Rockies alone and there are at least 12,000 species of insects present across Alberta. Alberta bird species, by contrast, number only about 340.

The two most common groups of arthropods identified in Alberta are arachnids (spiders and their relatives) and insects. Arachnids typically have eight legs, insects six. It is believed that only about a quarter of all arachnids in Alberta have been identified and listed. Alberta has six arachnid orders: Acarina, composed of ticks and mites; araneida, or spiders; pseudoscorpionida, or book scorpions; scorpionida, or true scorpions; and solpugida, known as wind scorpions or sunfighters.

True scorpions and solpugida species are found under stones and logs in sheltered coulees of the southern short-grass regions, especially in the **Milk River** country. Only one species of scorpion lives in Alberta. Its sting is generally quite harmless, equivalent to that of a bee or wasp. The only poisonous Albertan spider is the black widow, which dwells in some of the gopher holes of this region. A black widow bite can be dangerous, even potentially fatal to children.

Of the insect species identified in Alberta, about 300 are caddis flies. Other common insects include dragonflies, damselflies, grasshoppers, cockroaches, Say's stink-bugs, and bed bugs. Alberta has a host of bloodsucking flies and related species, including mosquitoes, black flies, horse flies, and deer flies. At elevations of 1,300 to 1,800 metres, wingless crane flies and wingless scorpion flies walk on the snow on warm days. Another unusual mountain insect is the ice bug, often found under large rocks on avalanche fields. This bug is so sensitive to temperature change (preferring −2° Celsius to 5° Celsius) that the heat of a human hand touching it causes almost instant death. Water striders are commonly seen skating across the surface of ponds and lakes.

Familiar butterflies in Alberta are tiger swallowtail, cabbage white, and mourning cloak. Moths are also abundant.

Irrigation. *See* **Brooks Aqueduct; Lethbridge; Water.**

Jasper

The town of Jasper is located at the junction of the Miette and Athabasca rivers. Its name derives from Jasper House, a North West Company trading post built nearby in 1801 and managed by Jasper Hawes, which did not close permanently until 1884. The community's modern development began in September 1907 when Jasper Forest Park reserve was declared.

Like **Banff,** the initial impetus behind the park's development was commercial rather than intended to protect the natural environment. But the town and the park's relative isolation, compared to **Banff National Park,** meant both developed more slowly and modestly, so many adverse environmental impacts that plagued the more southerly area were averted. Jasper has had the distinct advantage of being able to learn from the mistakes made in Banff's development and expansion.

Tourism, however, was promoted here by 1915 and the first major hotels, the Athabasca and Jasper Park Lodge, opened in 1921 and 1922 respectively. The Athabasca is today one of the least expensive hotels, while Jasper Park Lodge remains Jasper's most famous and luxurious resort.

The Jasper-Yellowhead Museum catalogues the human history of **Jasper National Park.**

Jasper National Park

This 10,880-square-kilometre park was established in 1907 as Jasper Forest Park, originally encompassing 12,950 square kilometres. As was true of **Banff National Park,** Jasper's early history was closely linked to the railway industry. The park was created to provide a wilderness experience for tourists using Canada's second transcontinental line, built by the Grand Trunk Railway. Five years after the park's creation, the railroad finally reached the area, passing near Jasper House fur-trading post.

The Grand Trunk Railway did not have the route through the Yellowhead Pass to itself for long. Three years after Grand Trunk finished construction, Canadian Northern Railway also pushed tracks through. Sometimes the two lines were separated by only a few metres. By 1919, Grand Trunk, crippled by debt, including $28 million in federal subsidies and loans, was nationalized. The previous year, Canadian Northern had met a similar fate. Along with a number of other **railways,** the two were amalgamated by the government into one entity—Canadian National Railway (CNR)—and the two Yellowhead Pass lines were reduced to one.

While Grand Trunk Railway was still struggling for its existence, two entrepreneurs, Fred and Jack Brewster, established a tent camp on the shore of Lac Beauvert and called it Jasper Park Camp. In 1921, the CNR acquired the operation and built 12 log bungalows and a roomy dining hall. This main building was proclaimed by the railroad's promoters as the largest single-storey log building in the world. Even so, it could barely accommodate the many tourists flocking in to enjoy the area's scenery, hunting, and fishing. In 1927 and 1928, Jasper Park Lodge, as it was now called, underwent expansion. This structure burned on July 12, 1952, and was replaced by today's structure. Several of the original log bungalows remain.

Jasper National Park was officially designated in 1930, becoming the largest of the five **Rocky Mountain** national parks. The **Icefields Parkway** linked the heart of this park with its adjoining southern neighbour, Banff National Park, in the 1940s. The two parks share a similar natural environment—some of North America's most spectacular **icefields,** beautiful mountain lakes and streams, numerous waterfalls, rugged mountain terrain, lush forests, and broad expanses of alpine meadows. Jasper National Park is one of four linked parks that compose a world heritage site established by the United Nations Educational, Scientific and Cultural Organization (UNESCO) in 1985.

A 1,000-kilometre network of hiking trails makes this park's vast wilderness areas unusually accessible because the trails interconnect throughout the backcountry regions. This is one of the most extensive backcountry trail systems in the world. Day hikes, however, are more limited in the park. The most scenic day-hike trails are found at Maligne Lake, in the Tonquin Valley, and near the base of **Mount Edith Cavell,** as well as along the Icefields Parkway.

The park is home to seven species of ungulates—mule deer, white-tailed deer, a small herd of **woodland caribou,** elk, moose, mountain goats, and bighorn sheep—lynx, cougar, wolves, coyotes, black and grizzly **bears,** hoary marmots, and about 248 bird species (including at least a dozen pairs of ospreys).

Kananaskis Country

In 1977, the Alberta government used funds collected from oil and gas royalties to create Kananaskis Country, a sprawling 4,250-square-kilometre multiple-use recreation area west of **Calgary,** which encompassed **foothills** and front range portions of the **Rocky Mountains.** It remains one of the most lasting legacies created by the multibillion-dollar Alberta Heritage and Savings Trust Fund.

Kananaskis Country is not a unified park. In some areas, for example, logging is still permitted. It is, however, Alberta's largest provincial recreation area and encompasses three **provincial parks**—Bragg Creek, Bow Valley, and Peter Lougheed (formerly Kananaskis Provincial Park). Large blocks of land outside the park boundaries are set aside for motorcyclists and snowmobilers—an attempt to control and concentrate two sports that had previously caused extensive land abuse throughout the foothills. Several hundred kilometres of hiking and cross-country ski trails have been developed within the region. Kananaskis also contains a world-class 36-hole golf course and the Nakiska ski area on Mount Allan constructed for the 1988 **XVth Winter Olympics.**

The golf course and motorized vehicle areas were all attacked by environmentalists for damage caused to the environment. The $25.3 million ski area was even more controversial, as it transformed the slopes of a formerly pristine mountain into a high-tech ski area. The Nakiska also remains plagued by snow melting caused by **chinooks** throughout the winter. To ensure the presence of snow on its slopes, a $5 million snow-making system has been installed. It is capable of transforming 24 million litres of water daily into snow distributed on the slopes via a 40-kilometre network of piping and 343 hydrants.

Kananaskis Country contains four ecosystem zones. On its eastern edge, rolling sandstone foothills, with dry grassy areas and patches of lodgepole pine and aspen, dominate. **Mammals** include deer, hare, coyotes, moose, and black **bears.**

To the west of the foothills lies a montane zone covering the valley bottoms and lower mountain slopes from about 1,200 to 1,500 metres. The **climate** here is cooler and wetter, so the forest is mainly spruce and fir. This is the zone where the most bird life is found, especially warblers, thrushes, and wrens.

Higher up the slopes (1,500 metres to 1,800 metres) is an alpine meadow zone with carpets of wildflowers and small groves of larch and whitebark pine. Between elevations of 1,830 and 2,440 metres lies an alpine zone where rock is mostly barren except for lichen and saxifrage. Glaciers cling to the sides of the peaks that form the **Continental Divide** at the region's western boundary.

Kananaskis was named by the leader of the **Palliser Expedition,** Captain John Palliser. In 1858, Palliser recorded in his diary naming the Kananaskis Pass in honour of a legendary First Nations warrior who was said to have recovered miraculously from an axe wound to his head.

Klondike Gold Rush

In May 1897, word of the fabulous gold discoveries in the Yukon's Klondike River country reached **Edmonton.** A few weeks later eastern Canadians and Americans began flooding into the community by train. They all had their sights set on one destination—the Klondike. Edmonton lay at the end of the railroad lines reaching toward northwestern Canada, so it seemed a logical jumping-off point for gold seekers intent on travelling to Dawson City.

Many of those coming to Edmonton discovered it was safer and simpler to make money selling goods to other neophyte prospectors than risk the dangerous trip themselves. Prior to the rush, Edmonton's population was only about 1,000. The rush more than doubled Edmonton's permanent population and brought national attention to the area, serving to attract still more settlers. As a consequence, by 1905 Edmonton and neighbouring Strathcona had a combined population of 11,400.

While the Klondike Gold Rush brought nothing but good fortune to Edmonton, those passing through it en route to the goldfields fared poorly. Several routes were promoted by guides, outfitters, and scoundrels.

The most sensible involved travelling by water up the Athabasca or Peace rivers to the Mackenzie River. Once on the Mackenzie, various departure points led overland and via lesser rivers into the Yukon and finally to Dawson City. This trip entailed a journey of about 4,000 kilometres regardless of the route taken.

Going overland in a virtual beeline toward Dawson City was shorter, only 2,400 kilometres. Several routes were sketched out on maps; many showed fanciful topographical detail that included advantageous passes through the various mountain ranges, open grassland prairie plateaus where travel would be fast and easy, and supposedly clearly marked and cut trails. With pack horses, about 750 of the 1,600 men and women who set out from Edmonton for the Klondike headed off into the wilderness north of the community.

They soon faced a harsh reality. The trails were nonexistent, the country a tangle of mosquito-infested **boreal forest,** muskeg, and swamps. At best about 150 gold seekers made it through to the Klondike on a trip that took an average of two years to complete. At least 50 died, the majority of scurvy. Most of the rest straggled back to Edmonton, bitter and usually half-starved. A small number abandoned the idea of even returning to Edmonton and settled permanently around **Peace River,** establishing the first significant non–First Nations presence in the area.

Of those who opted for the water route, which also took about two years, about half succeeded in reaching the Klondike. They arrived, however, to discover the best gold claims long taken by the usually wealthier and perhaps less gullible prospectors who had opted for the less difficult Pacific coast routes.

Labour Force

About 1.5 million of Alberta's **population** of 2.77 million are employed, with another 7 to 8 percent seeking work. Alberta has Canada's highest workforce participation rate—718 of every 1,000 working-age Albertans, compared nationally to about 640 in every 1,000.

The province has one of the youngest populations in the industrialized world and one of the best educated in North America. About 40 percent of all Albertans hold a post-secondary certificate, diploma, or degree.

With only 10 percent of Canada's population, the province has about 23 percent of the nation's apprentices in training and annually graduates nearly 20 percent of the nation's certified apprentices.

The retail trade sector is the province's major employer. About 183,000 Albertans work in retail. The health and social services sector comes second, employing about 129,000.

Except for those working in **agriculture,** natural resource-based employment in Alberta is quite low. The **forest industry** has a direct participation rate averaging about 20,000. After the construction sector, forestry routinely tops the unemployment rate on a sector-by-sector basis. In recent years unemployment in the forest industry has sometimes reached as high as 17.5 percent. The **mining industry** employs about 78,000 Albertans and maintains a relatively stable unemployment rate averaging 7 to 9 percent per year.

Given that natural resource-based industries are often more heavily unionized than other economic sectors, it is not surprising that Alberta has a very low average of unionized workers. Only 26 percent of its workers are members of labour organizations, Canada's lowest percentage of unionized workers. The provincial government highlights this fact in its efforts to attract new business investment into the province.

The weakness of the province's labour unions results in few strikes in Alberta and very few work days lost to labour disputes. In most years, only about one person day per 10,000 is lost because of labour disputes.

Alberta's labour force is highly productive, apparent when gross domestic product (GDP) is measured against the population producing it. Using this measure, Alberta emerges with the highest per capita gross domestic product in Canada—between $30,000 and $31,000, or 20 percent higher than the national average.

Although the province has one of Canada's lowest minimum wage rates, of $5.00 an hour, average wages in all sectors are not among the nation's lowest. The average hourly wage paid in manufacturing jobs, for example, is about $14.85 an hour, which is higher than in all but four provinces—British Columbia, Ontario, New Brunswick, and Newfoundland. Nationally, the average hourly manufacturing wage is $16.40.

Despite the general strength of the province's **economy** and ability of its labour force, Alberta faces a serious problem plaguing all Canadian provinces. While its unemployment rate is lower than the national average, the province's youth unemployment rate fluctuates between 11 and 14 percent annually. As Alberta has led the country in reducing access for young people to government social assistance, the social and economic problems arising out of youth unemployment have increased.

Lake Athabasca

Located almost in the northeastern corner of the province and largely spilling over into Saskatchewan, Lake Athabasca is Alberta's largest lake. Altogether, it covers 7,936 square kilometres and is the fourth-largest lake found entirely in Canada. Fed by the Athabasca and Peace rivers, the lake drains north via Slave River into Great Slave Lake.

To the south of the lake, large areas of sand dunes created after the last ice age still slowly drift eastward on strong winds, burying jackpine forests in their wake. The Albertan part of Lake Athabasca is extremely wild, and virtually inaccessible.

Yet in the late 1700s it became a key entry port to the fur-trade operations that first opened the province to settlement by Europeans. One of the first trading posts in what is present-day Alberta opened on the northwestern edge of the lake in 1788. Fort Chipewyan remains the oldest continuously occupied settlement in Alberta. The community's small population of about 900 relies on seasonal fishing and trapping, plus some employment in the **oil and gas industry** and adjacent **Wood Buffalo National Park.**

Lake Claire

With a maximum length of 63 kilometres and encompassing 1,437 square kilometres, Lake Claire is the largest lake lying entirely in Alberta. This isolated western extension of **Lake Athabasca** is located in the southeastern corner of **Wood Buffalo National Park.**

The lake is a key component of the Athabasca Delta region, which is one of the world's largest freshwater deltas. It is fed by the Peace, Birch, and McIvor rivers and drains east through Mamawi Lake into Lake Athabasca.

When Europeans first ventured onto Lake Claire's shores they found it to be one of the deepest lakes in the delta region. Alexander Mackenzie, an explorer and trader with the North West Company, first named it Clear Water (*claire* is French for clear) because he could see so far into its depths. Over the years, however, the lake has become much shallower, a result of silt accumulation.

Lake Louise

In 1882, a horse-packer for the Canadian Pacific Railway construction crews building the railroad through the **Rocky Mountains** was guided to a cirque lake, known by the Stoney people as the "Lake of Little Fishes." Tom Wilson, the first non–First Nations person to see the lake, was awe-struck by this "gem of beauty beneath the glacier."

"I never in all my explorations of these five chains of mountains throughout Western Canada saw such a matchless scene," he later wrote. "I felt puny in body but glorified in spirit and soul." He named the "beautiful sheet of water" Emerald Lake because of its greenish, milky colour.

There are two versions of how the lake came subsequently to be called Lake Louise. The most accepted version is that in 1884 it was named after Princess Louise Caroline Alberta, fourth daughter of Queen Victoria and wife of the Marquis of Lorne, who was Governor General of Canada from 1878 to 1883 (and who named the territory of Alberta after his wife). Another version, however, maintains that Tom Wilson changed the name to honour the daughter of Sir Richard Temple of the British Association for the Advancement of Science. Temple led an excursion by society members to Canada in 1884. Unlike the Princess, Louise Temple did eventually visit the lake during her own Canadian excursion some years later.

Lake Louise stands 200 vertical metres above the Bow Valley floor at the foot of Victoria Glacier, which itself is overlooked by the peak of 3,459-metre-high Mount Victoria. Across the lake from the mountain stands one of the world's most photographed hotels, Chateau Lake Louise. This magnificent structure has undergone many changes and expansions since it was built in 1892 to replace a hotel erected two years previously that burned down. At that time it could accommodate about 12 guests. Today it has more than 500 rooms.

The lake's distinctive colour is a result of rock flour washing into it from beneath the glacier. (*See* **Icefields**.) Lake Louise is 2.4 kilometres long and 500 metres wide, has a maximum depth of 90 metres, reaches a summer-temperature high of only 4° Celsius, stands at an elevation of 1,731 metres, and has its outlet into the Bow River. In summer, about 10,000 people a day visit the lake.

To the east of the lake lies the village of Lake Louise. Across the Bow Valley is the Lake Louise Ski Area. With about 40 square kilometres of trails, mogul fields, steep chutes, and vast bowls filled with deep powder, this world-class attraction is Canada's largest ski resort. In summer, its quad chairlift is used by tourists to gain access to the views from the summit of

Mount Whitehorn. The view onto the Bow Valley, Lake Louise, and the rugged peaks of the **Continental Divide** from this mountain is considered one of the most spectacular in the Canadian Rockies.

Lake Newell

Developed as part of the Canadian Pacific Railway's ambitious turn-of-the-century southern Alberta irrigation scheme (*see* **Brooks Aqueduct**), Lake Newell is today Alberta's largest artificial lake. In addition to its continued key role in the irrigation of agricultural land, the 65-square-kilometre reservoir is also a major recreation area and waterfowl-shorebird habitat.

More than 100 species of **birds,** including American white pelicans and double-crested cormorants, use the small islands scattered throughout the lake as nesting sites, many of which are barred to human visitation. Kinbrook Marsh and Swen Beyer Peninsula are two prime birding spots where access is permitted.

Kinbrook Island Provincial Park, about 13 kilometres south of Brooks off Highway 873, provides camping, a beach, and boating access to the lake.

Languages

The **ethnicity** of Alberta's **population** is such that a diversity of mother tongues could be expected here. In reality, however, most Albertans claim only one tongue—English. Some 2,068,650 Albertans consider English their mother tongue. Of the remaining population of about 700,000, the dominant language is German, which is the first language of about 72,800. This is followed by **Francophone Albertans,** of which 51,100 of the approximate community of 74,600 claim French as their first language.

There are 104,350 **Ukrainian Canadians** in Alberta, but only 38,690 retain their language of ethnic origin as their mother tongue. By comparison, of the approximately 71,650 Chinese in Alberta, some 52,650 consider one of the Chinese languages their language of choice.

First Nations peoples in Alberta are successfully reclaiming their mother tongues. About 22,000 from a total population of 68,450 claim an aboriginal language as a first language. The Algonquian languages are the strongest, spoken by about 17,225 people; the majority of these speak Cree, known by 13,520 people.

The last significant linguistic group in Alberta is Vietnamese—the mother tongue of 10,400 Albertans.

Leaf Cutter Bees

In the alfalfa fields surrounding the tiny community of Rosemary, off

Secondary Highway 550 north of Brooks, large packing crate–sized boxes are evenly distributed throughout the fields. Most are painted blue, some with large black circles adorning their sides. The sides of the boxes facing east are open, the closed backs sheltering the insides from the prevailing westerly winds.

These curious-looking boxes are huts designed to attract and shelter colonies of leaf cutter bees. Farmers here have domesticated the leaf cutter bees to help pollinate alfalfa, which is harvested for seed rather than as a feed crop. The pollinating efforts of the bees make it possible to grow alfalfa for seed collection.

To ensure that sufficient numbers of leaf cutter bees are present when the alfalfa flowers bloom in the field, the farmers—most of whom are members of the Irrigated Alfalfa Seed Producers Association—manage an ingenious, but simple, bee-breeding program. Each box is filled with material female bees find attractive as a nesting site for laying eggs. The materials most commonly used are wood or Styrofoam blocks into which holes have been drilled. Each hole can accommodate up to ten bee larvae.

A female leaf cutter attracted to the boxes will select a suitable hole for her nest, then start cutting leaves from the surrounding alfalfa field to construct a network of cells. The leaves are used to build her nest inside the hole. From the alfalfa fields she will also gather pollen and nectar to store as a food source. She then lays an egg in each cell.

When an egg hatches it develops into a larva and spins a cocoon. It remains dormant in its cocoon stage until it is heated to 30° Celsius for 21 days, after which it emerges as an adult bee. Because of their design, the boxes work as perfect incubation containers for the 21-day period.

The warm summer temperatures enjoyed by Rosemary create ideal habitat for leaf cutter bees, which require temperatures of 22° Celsius or higher to fly and pollinate flowers. The hatching of young bees is carefully managed by the farmers, who time the distribution of the boxes so the emergence of the bees from nests coincides with the alfalfa bloom.

Forty percent of new bees hatched are female and these perform most of the field pollination. In a good season the bee population will multiply two or three times.

Leaf cutter bees do not sting. They will, however, sometimes inflict a slight, harmless bite if trapped against human skin.

Without the presence and careful management of the leaf cutter bee population, growing seed alfalfa in the Rosemary area would be impossible due to a lack of natural pollinating agents.

Leduc Oil

In February 1947, about 27 kilometres southwest of **Edmonton** near the small community of Leduc, Imperial Oil Limited was drilling at a depth of 1,500 metres. Engineer Vernon Hunter could tell by all the signs that Leduc No. 1 was going to yield a major strike. He also thought it was about time one of Imperial's wells proved out. In past months more than 133 dry holes had been drilled by the company at a cost of $20 million. Hunter was so certain of success this time he decided to stage a major media event.

Consequently, at noon on February 13, 1947, 500 reporters, businessmen, and government officials gathered together in the cold of a grain field. The drill at Leduc No. 1 had been operating since early morning, seeking the motherlode. By 4:00 p.m. the drill was still short of breaking through to the oil Hunter knew was there. The onlookers, shivering against the frigid winter chill, started skulking away toward Edmonton as darkness began to fall. Only a few had actually departed, however, when the drill broke through.

A ring of black smoke immediately erupted from the well's flare line at the top of the drilling stack, as the oil came in with a massive rushing sound. Gushing surges of oil, water, and drilling mud spewed into the flare pit surrounding the drill. At Hunter's direction, Alberta's Social Credit minister of mines, N. Eldon Tanner, turned a valve to divert the flow to a storage tank. The Leduc strike heralded the beginning of Canada's modern **oil and gas industry.**

Further drilling proved the existence of a large oil field at Leduc, the largest discovery to that point in Canadian history. In March 1948, Atlantic No. 3 well tapped into a gusher that blew wild for six months. More than a million barrels spilled out into the surrounding fields during a spectacle that captured world media attention. Soon it was confirmed that the Leduc field held 200 million barrels and 1,278 wells tapped into the valuable commodity.

An oil bonanza swept the province in the wake of the Leduc find. Hundreds of companies, mostly American owned, spent the late 1940s through to the mid-1960s drilling thousands of wells. There were many successes. Oil fields were found at Redwater, Golden Spike, Fenn-Big Valley, Wizard Lake, Acheson, Bonnie Glen, Westerose, Pembina, Swan Hills, Rainbow Lake, and other places.

This boom was largely responsible for the rapid growth in Alberta's **population** during this 20-year period, as people rushed in from outside the province to work in the oil industry or the larger service industries growing up around it.

Legal System

The Canadian Constitution gives the provinces jurisdiction over the administration of justice, consisting primarily of the operation of police forces (*see* **public safety**) and the lower court system. The highest courts in Canada fall under federal jurisdiction, where ultimate authority is vested.

The federal judicial system includes the Tax Court of Canada, the federal Court of Appeal, the Federal Court of Canada, and the Supreme Court of Canada. The Federal Court of Canada hears cases in limited areas of law falling exclusively under federal jurisdiction. It has both a division for hearing specific types of first-time trials and a division for hearing appeals of decisions made in lower courts. The federal court, for example, reviews decisions made by federal tribunals such as the Canada Labour Relations Board. The Supreme Court of Canada is the court of final resort and hears selected appeals from the federal Court of Appeal and provincial courts of appeal.

Federal jurisdiction applies to legal matters arising in trade and commerce, banking, bankruptcy, and criminal law—the latter covered by the Canadian Criminal Code.

The provincial court system in Alberta has a total of six divisions of first instance and one appellate court. First instance courts are Magistrate Court, Family Court, Surrogate Court, Juvenile Court, Division Court, and the Court of Queen's Bench. Magistrate Court involves no jury and hears few, if any, private lawsuits. Instead, it hears less serious criminal cases. The Division Court is a small claims court hearing cases not exceeding $2,000 in claims. The Court of Queen's Bench has unlimited jurisdiction in civil and criminal matters. Decisions in all these courts may be appealed to Alberta's highest court—the Intermediate Court of Appeal, which is strictly an appellate court for the province. Beyond that appeals must go to the Supreme Court of Canada for a final ruling.

Legislative Building

On September 1, 1905, Alberta was inaugurated with provincial status. The first provincial election was held November 9, 1905, with the Liberal Party winning 23 of the 25 legislative seats. At the time, **Edmonton** was staunchly Liberal, **Calgary** strongly supportive of the Conservative Party. The new government quickly decided to reward Edmontonians by declaring their city the capital.

Alberta's first session of government began on March 15, 1906. The session was, for want of a more suitable venue, convened in Edmonton's

Thistle Rink—a community-owned skating rink. Before that session was out a two-thirds majority vote confirmed Edmonton as the province's capital.

A site beside the still-operating Fort Edmonton was selected for the new legislature and construction began in November 1907. Although the province was small and relatively poor, the decision was made to build a grand structure that would provide a sense of stateliness, serenity, and tradition. Such an expensive building would also help ensure the provincial capital remained in Edmonton even if the government were lost to the pro-Calgary Conservatives.

Its architecture was based on the late Victorian Beaux-Arts style. The focal point of the granite and sandstone structure was a 16-storey vaulted dome that capped an open rotunda rising 53 metres from the first floor to the dome.

The granite came from quarries near Vancouver and the sandstone was drawn from quarries at Calgary, while marble imported from Quebec, Pennsylvania, and Italy graced the interior. Most of the interior wood was mahogany, and stained glass was used extensively throughout the building.

Although construction was not completed, the legislature first met inside the new building for a session beginning November 30, 1911. The legislative building was officially opened on September 3, 1912 after almost five years of construction.

Lesser Slave Lake

The third-largest lake in Alberta, Lesser Slave Lake covers 1,168 square kilometres. It lies about 200 kilometres northwest of **Edmonton.** The lake is fed by several small rivers that discharge eastward via the Lesser Slave River to the Athabasca River, which in turn feeds into Great Slave Lake in the Northwest Territories. This lake and river system served as a major transportation route for the Slavey First Nation. Both Great Slave and Lesser Slave lakes derive their names from this historical link to the Slavey people.

The oldest non–First Nations settlement near the lake is Grouard, which grew up around the St. Bernard Mission opened by Father Emile Grouard in 1884. The town enjoyed a brief boom as a stopover point on the **Klondike Gold Rush** Trail running from Edmonton to Dawson City, Yukon.

Today, Slave Lake on the southeastern shore is the primary community, with a population of about 5,600. The major economic force in the Lesser Slave Lake region is oil and gas development, but there is also a vibrant **tourism** industry based on Lesser Slave Lake's reputation as one of the province's best fishing lakes.

Lethbridge

With a population of about 64,000, Lethbridge is Alberta's third most populous city and the major commercial centre for the southernmost part of the province. It is situated on the heights of steep **coulees** cut by the Oldman River.

This site was used by some 500 generations of Blackfoot as an important camping area prior to the coming of Europeans. The first European settlement appeared in 1869 when American whiskey traders built **Fort Whoop-Up** on the river's edge. The **North-West Mounted Police** closed the fort in 1874 and for a few years the settlement was abandoned.

The year after Fort Whoop-Up's construction, a major battle between First Nations peoples took place here. On October 25, 1870, about 800 Cree warriors attacked a band of Bloods camping on the Oldman River's west bank. Unknown to the Cree, a band of Peigan, who, like the Bloods, were part of the Blackfoot nation, was also camped nearby. The Peigan came to the Bloods' rescue and the Cree attackers suffered a bloody defeat. About 300 Cree and 50 Blackfoot were killed in the battle.

Discovery of coal in the area led within a few years of Fort Whoop-Up's closure to the founding of a small coal-mining community known as Coal Banks. The community boomed when a large colliery opened nearby in 1885. Owned by the North Western Coal and Navigation Company, the mine's president was William Lethbridge. On October 14, 1885, Coal Banks was officially renamed Lethbridge in his honour.

By 1890, its population had reached 1,478 and it was linked to Montana by a railroad. In 1897, the Canadian Pacific Railway secured Lethbridge's future as a central transportation hub by extending an existing line west of the city through the **Crowsnest Pass.**

Although the surrounding country was **water** poor, its soil was fertile. To capitalize on the agricultural potential of the soil the Canadian North-West Irrigation Company was formed in 1900. The company developed the first large-scale irrigation system in Alberta. Several other major irrigation projects have since been completed that have diverted water from the St. Mary and Oldman rivers to transform the previously barren drylands surrounding Lethbridge into one of the province's richest agricultural regions.

In 1971 the University of Lethbridge opened. This impressive structure, set on a 185-hectare campus, was designed by world-renowned Vancouver architect, Arthur Erickson. The main building blends inseparably into the coulee country upon which it is built.

A replica of Fort Whoop-Up is a popular tourist attraction, as is the

$2.85 million Sir Alexander Galt Museum and the Nikka Yuko Japanese Gardens. The gardens serve as a monument to the contribution of Japanese Canadians to the region's development. Most Japanese Canadians coming to the Lethbridge area arrived as part of a small immigration wave to Canada between 1877 and 1928. They were called *Issei* and came from the islands of Kyushu and Honshu. While most *Issei* settled in British Columbia's coastal cities of Vancouver and Victoria or in the Fraser Valley, a few came to Lethbridge and **Edmonton.** When the Japanese Canadians were interned during World War II, some internment camps were built in the Crowsnest Pass and Alberta's national parks. After the war, some internees remained in southern Alberta and became part of the Lethbridge Japanese-Canadian community.

Lloydminster

With a population of about 17,300, Lloydminster traces its origin back to an ambitious scheme to bring thousands of British settlers to the Canadian **prairie** to keep Canada "as much as possible in the hands of people of British birth." In 1902, two Anglican clergymen—Isaac Barr and George Exton Lloyd—hatched the plan to create a British colony in the midst of the vast prairies.

Promoting the cause in Britain yielded 1,964 prospective settlers. They followed Barr and Lloyd to Canada in 1903. Few of the British immigrants had any experience in farming or breaking new land for settlement. They did, however, have high hopes and many possessions. A baggage train of 30 railroad cars was necessary to ship the belongings of the Barr Colony as far west as Saskatoon, where they arrived on April 17.

Barr had arranged for the colony to be established at a point where the Canadian Northern Railway survey would cross the 4th initial meridian (110° west longitude). This area lay 270 kilometres west of Saskatoon.

By the time the colonists reached Saskatoon, Barr was already being criticized for mishandling preparations and alleged incompetence. His strongest critic was the Reverend Lloyd. After two weeks of bickering in Saskatoon, which resulted in some desertions and various threats on Barr's life, the party straggled by wagon to its land parcel. The journey took two torturous weeks as the party fought and squabbled its way through mud holes and the slush of newly fallen snow. Barr, increasingly under fire and ever more disillusioned with his rebellious charges, quit the colony soon after the group's arrival. He went first to Toronto, then to the United States, and finally emigrated to Australia.

The colonists elected Lloyd their new leader and unanimously followed his advice in renaming the colony Britannia Colony. Lloyd soon proved himself a relatively capable leader and it was mostly due to his prudent guidance that the colony managed to organize itself sufficiently to endure the rigours of its first winter in a land of cold and snow unlike anything seen in Britain.

Their first townsite was located astride the meridian and incorporated Barr's abandoned homestead property. It was named Lloydminster. Lloyd wrote to Britain, "The name of the first town was decided to be Lloydminster but as this sounds somewhat personal I am not saying much about it." By March 1904, the village contained 100 homes. Lloyd went on to become bishop of Saskatchewan, dying in 1940.

Despite its early problems the colony survived, even prospered. The town's location, however, proved problematic. In 1905 it was split in two when the meridian upon which Lloydminster stood became the provincial boundary for the new provinces of Alberta and Saskatchewan. This led to some difficult administrative problems as each half had to abide by differing legislations.

The railway arrived at Lloydminster in 1905 and located its station on the Alberta side of the border. The settlers, however, had constructed most of the town's dwellings and businesses on the Saskatchewan side. The more populous side became a town, the Alberta side a village.

By 1930, everyone was tired of the confusion and an order-in-council approved by both provinces amalgamated the two communities. In 1958, the town of Lloydminster became the tenth city of both provinces.

Natural resource exploitation in the region, especially of oil and natural gas, led to a modest population boom in the 1970s. At that time the population of the Alberta side grew to match the Saskatchewan side.

There are some interesting aspects to living in a twin city. Although during Lloyd's tenure of leadership the sale of alcohol in the community was prohibited, it now has several liquor stores—but those on the Alberta side sell at lower prices. The legal drinking age is also 18 in Alberta, as opposed to 19 in Saskatchewan. The minimum wage is higher in Saskatchewan, but so is income tax and provincial sales tax is charged on retail purchases. Housing prices tend to run 30 percent higher on the Alberta side of the border.

The origin of the community is still honoured in Lloydminster, and the Barr Colony Heritage Cultural Centre traces the colony's development.

Lynxes. *See* **Wild Cats.**

Mammals

There are 90 species of mammals in Alberta. Mammals are generally regarded as the most evolved or advanced of the vertebrate species (animals having a backbone). They share a number of characteristics, including being warm-blooded and possessing mammary glands that produce milk for nourishing their young. Mammals in Alberta range in size from North America's smallest mammal, the pygmy shrew, and the province's eight bat species, all having virtually no discernible weight, to the largest land-based mammal in North America, the **bison.** Alberta has an unusual diversity of mammal life because of its complex mixture of topography, vegetation, altitude levels, and **climate.**

In the province's southeastern **grasslands** herbivorous mammals feed on grasses, shrubs, and wildflowers. These species include ground squirrels, cottontail rabbits, the rare kangaroo rat, and **pronghorns,** as well as white-tailed and mule deer. Coyotes and red foxes prey on the smaller herbivores, including the tiny grasshopper mouse. Beaver are occasionally found along the banks of the South Saskatchewan and Red Deer rivers. Unlike their darker-furred woodland cousins, beavers in this area have pale fur, enabling them to blend with the plains foliage and soil.

Alberta's **badlands** and **coulees** are home to white-tailed deer, coyotes, Richardson's ground squirrels, skunks, and badgers. Where the **prairie** starts rolling toward the **foothills,** pocket gophers, voles, shrews, long-tailed weasels, and mule and white-tailed deer are common, as well as a few cougars.

In the **parklands** snowshoe hares are numerous, along with coyotes, lynxes, and red foxes. The more northerly parklands regions are home to muskrat, beaver, mink, and long-tailed weasel. When the parklands start to blend with **boreal forest,** as near **Peace River,** black **bears** appear.

The boreal forest is home to many mammals, including wolves, foxes, black and grizzly bears, moose, and lynxes. In the Athabasca-Peace delta area wolves, foxes, and black bears encounter bison herds in **Wood Buffalo National Park.**

The foothills and lower reaches of the **Rocky Mountains** support a diverse and abundant mammal population. Moose, white-tailed and mule deer, elk, mountain sheep, mountain goats, mountain and **woodland cari-**

bou, black and grizzly bears, cougars, coyotes, and ground squirrels are all found here.

In the alpine country mountain caribou, wolverine, wolves, grizzlies, mountain goats, mountain sheep, moose, and mule deer live in the valleys. Along the mountain ranges themselves, hoary marmots, martens, pikas, golden-mantled and Columbia ground squirrels, least chipmunks, deer mice, and other small mammals are common.

Four Alberta mammal species are protected as **endangered species** under Alberta's Wildlife Act: the swift fox, woodland caribou, barren ground caribou, and wood bison. The swift fox was eradicated from the prairies in 1928 and considered extinct in Canada by 1970. Since 1980 swift foxes captured in the United States have been reintroduced into the short-grass prairie of southeastern Alberta near **Medicine Hat** and Manyberries. Some successful breeding in the wild has resulted and the population is making a slow comeback.

(*See also* **Wild Cats; Wild Dogs; Wild Horses.**)

Medicine Hat

There are at least five versions of how Medicine Hat was named. A First Nations legend tells of a Cree medicine man who lost his war bonnet here while fleeing across the South Saskatchewan River after a bloody battle with the Blackfoot. The name may also have originally applied to a hill east of the present-day city which bears a fanciful resemblance to a First Nations medicine hat. Whatever its origin, the townsite was first referred to as Medicine Hat in an 1882 **North-West Mounted Police** report.

In 1883 the Canadian Pacific Railway (CPR) crews constructing the transcontinental line arrived and the site became an instant tent town. That same year CPR drillers seeking water tapped into a natural gas deposit which ignited and destroyed the drilling rig. In 1890, drillers again struck gas near Medicine Hat, and by 1900 the town began using natural gas to light its streets—there being such an abundance that the lights were never turned off. In 1907, Rudyard Kipling visited the community and wrote that it had "all hell for a basement," because of the vast natural gas reserves lying under the town.

The gas provided a cheap fuel source for development of a manufacturing sector in the small community. Clay deposits also prompted establishment of pottery, brick, and tile manufacturing operations. Soon Medicine Hat was thriving as a manufacturing town based on clay-works, milling, canning, brewing, and some smelting. By 1911 its population was

5,600. Ten years later Medalta Stoneware became the first western Canadian plant to export a manufactured product east of Winnipeg. The high-quality china produced by Medalta was used exclusively by CPR-owned hotels throughout the early 1900s and Medalta became a household name in Canadian homes.

Medicine Hat's emphasis on manufacturing and industrial plants has continued to diversify the community's economic base. In 1955, Northwest Nitro Chemicals opened a large fertilizer plant in the city and five years later Goodyear Tire established a plant in the Brier Industrial Estates. Today, these manufacturing plants, petrochemical processing facilities, and other industrial operations generate about $1.5 billion annually. The city is also a major **agriculture** service centre, with a current population of about 46,000.

Within the city limits is the Saamis Archaeological Site, one of the most extensive and richest prehistoric First Nations' archaeological sites in the province. Overlooking this site from the heights of a coulee is Saamis Tipi. Originally erected at the **XVth Winter Olympics** in **Calgary,** this 65-metre-high structure was moved to Medicine Hat after the games ended. It has a base diameter of 50 metres and is constructed entirely of steel.

One of the city's prime tourist and educational attractions is the Clay Products Interpretive Centre, located on the abandoned Medalta Stoneware site. The factory—closed in 1954—is a national historic site.

The city has developed an extensive urban park system encompassing more than 400 hectares of natural landscape, linked by 50 kilometres of multi-use trails.

Medicine Wheels

On a high southern Alberta hill near Bassano lies one of the province's greatest archaeological mysteries. For 5,000 years prehistoric **First Nations peoples** periodically added rocks to a domelike cairn from which 26 to 28 rock-constructed spokes radiated outward to an encircling ring of rocks. Nobody knows the purpose of this or any of the other medicine wheels discovered in various parts of the plains east of the **Rocky Mountains.**

More than two-thirds of all discovered medicine wheels are in Alberta. The wheels have some common features, but no two are alike. Usually they are located on top of the area's highest hill. They are constructed of stones that often appear to have been carried to the site specifically for its building.

Variations in the design of wheels makes interpreting their function and importance to prehistoric peoples difficult. Some have central cairns consisting of only a few stones, others have large stone piles in the centre. One medicine wheel may have only four spokes radiating out from the hub, and another only concentric circles progressing outward.

Medicine wheels at Sundial Hill and at Majorville are among the most elaborate. Sundial Hill consists of a central cairn made of large boulders and two surrounding circles of smaller stones. A pathway breaks through the circles and leads to the cairn. The site appears to have been used in some ceremonial manner, and was held in reverence by the Blackfoot, who called it *Onoka-katzi.*

Construction of the Majorville medicine wheel began 5,000 years ago and evidence suggests that it was used continuously to historic times. When the site was archaeologically excavated, various objects were recovered that point to its having a ceremonial function. Among these objects were many *iniskims* (sometimes called buffalo stones)—fossil ammonites shaped to resemble **bison** and regarded by First Nations hunters as containing great power.

Given the diversity in the shape and size of various medicine wheels, archaeologists are wary of offering general theories on their purpose. One has suggested that to do so would be akin to "discussing aspirin and penicillin together simply because they are both drugs."

Some First Nations' sources describe certain medicine wheels as being commemorative monuments. Many Spotted Horses medicine wheel, near **Lethbridge,** is said to honour the Blood war chief after whom the wheel is named. The four spokes radiating from a circle enclosing two fireplace rings are believed to signify the battles this chief fought against his enemies. Cairns built at the ends of each spoke demonstrate his combat victories.

Another theory suggests that medicine wheels are part of a prehistoric calendar, with the stones, as at Stonehenge, England, designed to align celestial bodies at summer solstice. Summer solstice was the season of the Sun Dance and perhaps the wheels were used in conjunction with the dances. But a solar alignment cannot be made at all medicine wheel sites, so this theory can no more be substantiated than any of the others that have been offered.

Métis

The term Métis has been used generally throughout the Canadian Prairies to identify people of mixed First Nations and European ancestry. In French, *métis* means "mixed."

While today Métis is generally used throughout Canada for all First Nations people with mixed ancestry, its historical usage was more narrowly defined. This definition, however, differed during various time periods and at various places.

Métis are usually, however, considered to be Canadians who have a First Nations–French blood mix. In the 18th and 19th centuries most mixed-blood relationships were between First Nations women and French fur traders of the North West Company (NWC) and later the Hudson's Bay Company (HBC). The term Métis was commonly used to describe their off-spring. Other mixed relationships usually involved First Nations women and uplands Scottish traders; their offspring were known as half-breeds. Both mixed-blood communities concentrated in the Red River region of what is today Manitoba, where the HBC had supported development of a settlement in 1811 based on hunting **bison** and some farming. Generally, the less numerous half-breeds farmed, while the Métis organized their society and economy primarily around the bison hunt with the addition of limited farming activity. As many as 1,000 Métis were involved in the bison hunt at any time.

By 1869 the fur trade was dying and large-scale bison hunting was no longer viable. The Hudson's Bay Company negotiated the transfer of Rupert's Land and the North-West Territories to the Dominion of Canada, effective the winter of 1869. Conflict between Canadian government surveyors and Métis farmers prior to the transfer of the land to Canadian control led to the formation in mid-October of the Comité National des Métis (National Committee of the Métis), led by Louis Riel.

The Métis were concerned that the Canadian government would open their land to European settlement because neither Métis nor half-breed settlers in the Red River had deeds to prove land ownership. On December 10, 1869, a provisional Métis government was declared with Riel becoming president.

The Canadian government refused to recognize Riel's government and in the summer of 1870 an armed force was sent from Ontario to establish Canada's control over the Red River region. With the failure of the resistance movement in the Red River many Métis migrated west and northwest to areas where they could continue a traditional life based on hunting and trapping. Bison populations were in rapid decline throughout the Canadian west, however, and the market for furs was shrinking. Attempts to take up farming along the Saskatchewan River and in other parts of the prairies met with little success due to drought and lack of markets.

Many Métis eked out a narrow existence where food was short and there was little money to supplement the minimal farm production with purchased goods. First Nations who had signed various treaties with the Canadian government were also finding the disappearance of the great bison herds left them on the verge of starvation. Government indifference led many Métis and First Nations to join forces in the **North-West Rebellion** of 1885. When the rebellion was crushed many Saskatchewan Métis (where the majority of the rebellion was fought) fled west into Alberta, most settling in the Lac La Biche area.

Métis had lived in Alberta since the first fur traders to the region entered into relationships with First Nations women. It was, however, in the 1890s that large numbers of Métis settled here—primarily in communities formed by the Roman Catholic Church as part of a plan to sustain a large and strong Francophone-Albertan population. In 1896, for example, the Métis farming colony of St. Paul des Métis was formed near present-day St. Paul in eastern Alberta. The colony, however, was closed by the church in 1906 due to a series of agricultural failures and growing dissension between the church and the Métis settlers.

Throughout the early 1900s conditions worsened for the largely landless Métis of Alberta. Most "squatted" on Crown land in central and northern Alberta. With the transfer of control of natural resources from the federal government to the provincial government in 1929, much of this land was opened to homesteading, meaning the Métis could be forced off land where they had lived without legal title for 30 years or more.

In 1929, a small group of Métis living on a forest reserve at Fishing Lake near **Cold Lake** petitioned the government for land titles. The issue led to a government investigation of the condition of Métis throughout the province. In 1932 the Métis formed L'Association des Métis d'Alberta et les Territoires du Nord-Ouest (known today as the Métis Association of Alberta) to further advance their cause. The association identified 11 potential sites in an area between **Edmonton** and **Fort McMurray**. After years of negotiations the Métis Population Betterment Act was passed in 1938. It established eight settlements in central and northern Alberta jointly totalling 505,875 hectares. This act made Alberta unique as the only province or territory in Canada to set aside land for the use of Métis people in a way similar to the creation of First Nations land reserves. Since the late 1930s Métis communities have developed outside the eight settlements, but they remain a major base for Alberta's Métis **population.**

In recent years the term Métis has undergone redefinition to include all Canadians with a significant percentage (usually considered at least 25 percent) of First Nations ancestry, including non-status Indians. But the federal government continues to calculate Métis population according to French–First Nations ancestry. By this definition there are 27,100 Métis in Alberta today. If non-status Indians are incorporated into the figure the population numbers 35,700.

Metric System

Alberta, as in all of Canada, uses the metric system of measurement.

The decision to replace the historic British imperial system of units (based on yards, pounds, and gallons) with a metric system was made by the Canadian government in 1971. The metric system chosen is known as the Systeme international d'unites (SI). Conversion to metric was prompted by rapidly advancing technology and expanding worldwide trade, both of which made it clear that a country as dependent upon import and export trade as Canada needed an international measure system.

Converting to the metric system in Canada was a gradual process allowing for the re-education of a public used to the British imperial system. The first extension of metric unit measure into the realm of everyday Canadian life had the unfortunate timing of being introduced on April Fool's Day (April 1), 1975, when all temperature announcements were given only in degrees Celsius during weather forecasts. In September 1977, road signs showed distances in kilometres and speed limits in kilometres per hour. The national process of converting to metric was not completed until December 1983.

The adoption of the metric system has been controversial from the outset, both because of the mandatory nature of the government regulations and the fact that it was seen by many Canadians as an attack on the British-Canadian heritage. In the mid- to late 1980s some regulations were relaxed so that the two measures could be posted side by side and small businesses could continue to operate to a limited degree in the imperial system. But the metric system is clearly here to stay.

The following charts show common conversions.

To Change	To	Multiply by
centimetres	inches	.39
metres	feet	3.28
kilometres	miles	.62
square metres	square yards	1.20
square kilometres	square miles	.39
hectares	acres	2.47
kilograms	pounds	2.21
kilometres	nautical miles	.54

To Change	To	Multiply by
inches	centimetres	2.54
feet	metres	.30
miles	kilometres	1.61
square yards	square metres	.84
square miles	square kilometres	2.59
acres	hectares	.41
pounds	kilograms	.45
nautical miles	kilometres	1.85

Milk River

With its headwaters in northern Montana just across the U.S. border from Whiskey Gap, about 350 kilometres of the 1,000-kilometre-long Milk River gently curve through the extreme southern portion of Alberta before re-entering Montana south of the **Cypress Hills**. The Milk River is the only Canadian river to flow into the Gulf of Mexico's drainage basin.

It reaches the Gulf of Mexico via an enormously long trip. At Fort Peck in Montana, the Milk River joins the Missouri River, of which it is a major tributary. Its water then runs down the Missouri for about 3,050 kilometres to flow into the Mississippi River at St. Louis, Missouri, whereupon it continues almost due south to the Gulf of Mexico at New Orleans—an approximate distance of 3,725 kilometres. The entire run from the headwaters of the Milk River to the Gulf of Mexico tallies an incredible distance of about 7,775 kilometres.

The fact that the Milk River drains into the Missouri and Mississippi has led to this portion of southern Alberta falling under the jurisdiction of six different flags. In the 1700s France claimed all the Mississippi drainage basin as part of its empire, so the first European flag to fly over southern Alberta was that of France. Eventually France ceded control of the Mississippi region to Spain and the Milk River technically became part of its empire. After that the Hudson's Bay Company, the British, and the Americans all claimed jurisdiction, before the area was finally confirmed as part of Canada in 1873 by the **International Boundary Commission** survey.

The Milk River derives its name from the milky, murky colour of its water, which is darkened by silt from the light-coloured soil through which it passes. It was so named by the Lewis and Clark expedition. In the expedition's journal is the following entry dated May 8, 1805: "The waters of the river possess a peculiar whiteness being about the color of a cup of tea with the admixture of a tablespoon of milk. From the color of its waters we called it Milk River."

Milk River Formation

Sedimentary rock exposed in the Milk River Valley is known as the Milk River Formation and consists of four features, each formed under a different set of conditions.

The hardest of these features is the Lower Virgelle, which tends to erode into steep cliffs above the river. While the other layers were too soft for **First Nations peoples** to use for **petroglyphs and pictographs,** the Lower Virgelle formed a natural canvas for First Nations artists. It is these cliffs upon which the major rock art of **Writing-On-Stone Provincial Park** was created.

The four features of the Milk River Formation typically all occur together, one stacked upon the other. Usually grasslands tie into the back of the formation and effectively brace the entire formation up against the edge of the Milk River.

From top to bottom the features are: Deadhorse Coulee, composed of clays and where the clay mounds called **badlands** are found; Upper Virgelle, sandstone composition and home to the Milk River's distinctive **hoodoos;** Lower Virgelle, made up of hard sandstone; and Telegraph Creek, a mixture of shale and sandstone extending down to and including the river valley's basin.

It is this unique formation that gives the Milk River valley its distinct physical characteristics and desertlike beauty.

Mining Industry

The heart of Alberta's mining industry is coal. The province holds 60 percent of Canada's known coal supplies. Coal sales account for about $575 million annually.

Alberta also produces limited quantities of salt, sodium sulphate, peat moss, and minerals used in construction, such as limestone, sand, and clay. Small amounts of gold are mined and low-grade iron-ore and uranium deposits have been found in the **Lake Athabasca** region. The province is also the world's largest producer of elemental sulphur drawn from hydrocarbon sources.

The last major mining development in Alberta was the opening of the McIntyre Porcupine Coal Mine near **Grand Cache** in 1966, developed to provide coking coal for export to Japan.

(*See also* **Bellevue Mine; Crowsnest Pass; Grande Cache; Hillcrest Mine Disaster; Nordegg.**)

Mormons. *See* **Alberta Temple; Religion.**

Mountaineering

On April 30, 1827, Scottish botanist David Douglas may or may not have been the first European to successfully ascend a peak in the Canadian Rockies. The mountain in question was Mount Brown on the northern flank of Athabasca Pass. Douglas wrote that he set off on snowshoes at 1:00 p.m., apparently reaching the peak and descending again the same afternoon. That he described Mount Brown and the opposing McGillivray Ridge as both towering about 4,800 to 5,100 metres (the highest Canadian Rocky peak is 3,954-metre-high Mount Robson) makes this feat of prowess all the more incredible. From the summit, he wrote, was a view "too awful...to afford pleasure. Nothing can be seen in every direction, as far as the eye can reach, except mountains towering above each other, rugged beyond description."

As the years passed, Douglas further embellished his account until he claimed the mountain scaled was undoubtedly "the highest yet known in the Northern Continent of America." By this time the mountain had risen to a height of 5,485 metres. The possible existence of such a leviathan mountain in the Canadian Rockies tantalized European mountaineers, but it was not until the late 1800s that the search for fabled Mount Brown began in earnest.

Meanwhile other peaks of the **Rocky Mountains** were being climbed, but for science and surveying of railroad routes rather than sport. In 1888, James Joseph McArthur scaled a number of peaks in Rocky Mountains National Park (later renamed **Banff National Park**) in order to check triangulation points for his mapping work. Over a three-week period, the surveyor climbed 30 mountains.

By 1890, British and Swiss mountaineers were descending on the Rogers Pass area and ascending peaks of the Selkirk Mountain Range. Few stopped to climb in the Rockies. Possibly this was because Glacier House at Illecillewaet Glacier was the mecca for mountaineers coming into the western Canadian mountains.

In 1893, however, mountaineering in the Rocky Mountains started in earnest. Samuel Allen and Walter Dwight Wilcox unsuccessfully tackled Mount Victoria (then known as Mount Green) at **Lake Louise.** Although the ascent failed, they managed to identify a col connecting Mount Victoria and Mount Lefroy as offering the key to reaching the peaks of both mountains. Because the col served as a treacherous chute for avalanches off both mountains, Allen named it the Death Trap.

The same year, Dr. Arthur Philemon Coleman and his brother L. C.

Coleman continued a search started the previous year for the mythical Mount Brown. They found Athabasca Pass and climbed a lesser mountain of about 2,700 metres on its northern flank. Convinced that Mount Brown was still out there somewhere, Coleman concluded that Douglas must have been in a pass other than Athabasca when he scaled the mountain's slopes. The hunt continued without result, for the lesser mountain he had climbed was in reality Mount Brown.

By the mid-1890s, the serious mountaineering in Alberta's Rockies was being led by graduates of Harvard and Yale universities. Yale men focused on Lake Louise, Harvard climbers on the Rockies facing the Bow Valley. The mountain that increasingly obsessed the minds of mountaineers coming to the Rockies was Lefroy at Lake Louise. J. J. McArthur had calculated that Lefroy stood 3,553 metres, making it the highest known mountain in the Canadian Rockies.

Charles Fay, Charles Thompson, and Philip Stanley Abbot, all of the

Two climbers brave the slopes of Pinnacle Mountain to reach the peak in 1918. (Glenbow Archives photo, NA-4376-9)

Harvard-dominated Appalachian Mountain Club, determined to climb the peak. An attempt in 1895 was driven back. In 1896 Fay, Thompson, Abbot, and Professor George Little set out for the summit at dawn on August 3.

They rowed across Lake Louise, pulled on packs, and toiled up a long moraine, reaching the ice at 7:30 a.m.

By 8:40 they had roped up opposite a large snow couloir, visible from the Lake Louise chalet, and then started up the Death Trap, hugging the sheer, glacier-free cliffs of Lefroy. The sound of avalanches pouring down the sides of the two mountains was nearly constant.

At 11:50 the men reached a short yoke linking Mount Victoria and Mount Lefroy. The path to the summit appeared open—nothing more than a hard slog. For four and a half hours the climbers worked across ice and rock fields with Abbot leading.

They reached a vertical cleft up which Abbot decided it was possible to climb and attain the summit. He started up, taking the climbing ropes with him. The rock on the face was treacherous, with chunks breaking away continually. Professor Little called to Abbot, suggesting they try an alternate route. Abbot replied, "I think not. I have a good lead here." A moment later he fell, striking an ice slope 4.5 metres below, then rolling down its steep incline. The rope coiled around him snagged and prevented his limp form tumbling off a cliff edge. It took three hours for the other climbers to make the treacherous journey down to where Abbot lay. They expected to find the climber had died. To their surprise, none of Abbot's bones were broken and he seemed to be still breathing, despite a terrible injury to the back of the head. Minutes later, however, Abbot quietly died. He was the first sporting mountaineer to die in a climbing accident in North America.

Mount Lefroy was at last successfully climbed by a team led by English mountaineering veteran Norman Collie on July 30, 1897. Two days later Collie, Fay, Arthur Michael, and Peter Sarbach went back up the Death Trap and veered off to reach the summit of Mount Victoria. Collie went on to become a mountaineering legend in the Rockies, leading the team that successfully climbed Mount Athabasca (on August 18, 1898) and discovered the Columbia Icefields.

Since Abbot's death, mountaineering in the Canadian Rockies has continued to grow in popularity each year. Accidents happen, but rarely do experienced climbers perish. Four of the most popular mountains to climb in the Rockies are Mount Victoria, Mount Athabasca, **Mount Edith Cavell,** and Mount Robson. All are demanding ascents and none should be attempted by the inexperienced.

Mount Columbia

At 3,747 metres, Mount Columbia is the highest point in Alberta, and the second-highest peak in the Canadian Rockies. British Columbia's Mount Robson, at 3,954 metres, is the highest Canadian Rocky mountain.

All the big, majestic peaks in the **Rocky Mountains** have one common feature—they rest upon sedimentary bedrock that is flat-lying or only gently sloping. The angle of the bedding controls the height of the peak.

The present form of the Canadian Rockies landscape is the result of glacial carving. The big peaks, such as Mount Robson, Mount Columbia, Mount Assiniboine, Mount Temple, Mount Forbes, and Mount Alberta, were far more resistant to this form of erosion than their neighbouring peaks.

Many other peaks in the Rocky Mountains rest on bedrock that is layered on an angle, which renders the rock more vulnerable to glacial carving. The ice can work its way under or between rock layers and cause massive slabs to break away, some extending up the entire flank of a peak. As each slab breaks away, the peak is slowly, inevitably whittled away: gravity and carving by the glaciers combine to exhert overwhelming power.

The same glacier, however, can only erode a flat-lying peak by cutting directly into the edges of the bedding upon which the mountain stands. Because no big slabs can be undermined, small rock falls are all that occur as the glacier scrapes along the peak's virtually impermeable walls. The rate of erosion is consequently far slower and so the big peaks are left to dominate the Rocky Mountain skyline.

Mount Edith Cavell

One of the most visually striking mountain peaks in **Jasper National Park** is 3,363-metre Mount Edith Cavell. A saddle on its northeast slope is filled by Angel Glacier. Situated 29 kilometres south of Jasper at the end of a road running off Highway 93A (the original **Icefields Parkway**), the mountain is easily accessible and a favourite spot for day hikers.

Mount Edith Cavell was named in 1916 after a 50-year-old British nurse who was executed by a German firing squad on October 12, 1915. A matron at a Belgian Red Cross hospital in Brussels, she aided the successful escape of some 200 Allied soldiers trapped behind enemy lines before being arrested by the Germans.

German martial law declared her activities to be treason. Cavell admitted her actions and defended them with the argument that the men—mostly wounded—would probably have died if captured, so in helping them escape she was simply performing her nurse's sworn duty to save lives.

It was British Columbia premier Richard McBride who first suggested that a Canadian mountain be named after the nurse who, following her execution, became a popular World War I heroine throughout the Commonwealth. He proposed that the highest peak in the Canadian Rockies—3,954-metre Mount Robson—be renamed in her honour. Various other peaks in the Rockies and in Quebec were hastily suggested by other patriots.

To resolve the matter, Prime Minister Robert Borden asked the

Geographical Board of Canada to make the selection. In March 1916, they chose what was then known as Mount Fitzhugh for the honour.

French fur traders had known the mountain as La Montagne de la Grande Traverse (Mountain of the Great Crossing), so named because it served as the landmark for their route via the Whirlpool River and Athabasca Pass to the Columbia River and onward to the Pacific Ocean. Its First Nations' name translated into English as "White Ghost."

Nordegg

The only community on Highway 11 between **Rocky Mountain House** and the northeastern entrance to **Banff National Park** is Nordegg, home to only about 100 people and a minimum security prison. From 1911 to 1955, however, Nordegg grew to have a maximum population of about 2,500 and was a thriving coal-mining town.

Nordegg's story is inextricably linked to that of its founder, Martin Nordegg. The German-born Nordegg immigrated to Canada in 1906 and was soon prospecting in the area 92 kilometres west of Rocky Mountain House on behalf of the German Development Company. Several coal fields were discovered, surveyed, and staked. They were named the South Brazeau fields after a former clerk and postmaster of Rocky Mountain House, Joseph Brazeau. In 1909 the mining company Brazeau Collieries Ltd. was formed by a partnership of the German Development Company and the Canadian Northern Railway.

The coal was still inaccessible because there was no rail link into the area and it was unclear if the seams were sufficiently large to warrant development. In 1910, however, Nordegg paused by a lake to shoot some geese and noticed what looked like coal seams on a mountain face to the south. In the summer of 1911, the mountain face was inspected and rich coal deposits were discovered and staked. This time there was no doubting that the prime steam coal ran deep.

As Canadian Northern started pushing a railroad branch line into the area, Nordegg brought in a mine crew and began to dig. He promised 91,000 tonnes would be ready for shipment when the railroad arrived. Nordegg delivered on his promise when the railroad was completed in 1914.

With a railroad link established, Nordegg was able to embark upon realizing a personal dream, the creation of a modern town built to his own grand design—modelled on the Town of Mount Royal in Montreal.

At the town's hub was the railroad station and a service centre containing a bank, company store, drugstore, and hotel. From this hub extended a semicircular pattern of streets bordered by 100 modern three- and four-bedroom cottages. The houses were all painted in soft pastel shades to blend with the surrounding landscape. Some were serviced with sewer and water. Nordegg even supplied the residents with flower seeds for their gardens. Two churches, a school, and a hospital were soon added.

No sooner had Nordegg concluded initial construction of his town and fully developed the mine than World War I broke out. Soon Nordegg fell victim to the anti-German hysteria sweeping the nation. The government seized his property and he only avoided being interned by fleeing to New York. When the war ended, he returned to Canada and advised the federal government on its coal policy.

Living conditions in the community of Nordegg continued to be the best available to coal miners working the Alberta mines. This fostered great loyalty among the workers and the mine operation prospered accordingly. In 1923, production peaked at 447,593 tonnes, compared to a yearly average production of 226,800 tonnes. During the late 1930s, most Nordegg coal was converted to briquettes, which were more easily handled and burned. By the late 1940s, Nordegg's briquette operation, with four presses, was Canada's largest operation of this type.

But there were increasing signs that the future of Nordegg held little promise. In 1941, the formerly excellent safety record was marred by an explosion that killed 29 miners. To its credit, the Brazeau Collieries management immediately suspended blasting in coal shafts and became the first mining company in Alberta to use pneumatic picks. Disappearing markets for coal, as trains were converted to diesel fuel, increasingly plagued the mine. In 1950, a major fire destroyed several key mine buildings. They were rebuilt, but the mine finally closed on January 14, 1955. Within weeks the townsite was virtually abandoned. Few of the buildings remain.

In 1984, the Nordegg Historic Heritage Interest Group was formed, drawing much of its membership from former Nordegg miners and their offspring. This group has since worked to preserve and protect the minesite and remaining town buildings. It has leased the minesite and undertaken stabilization work on several of the larger colliery structures. The group operates interpretive tours of the site during summer months.

Northern Leopard Frog

The northern leopard frog is one of the most endangered of Alberta's ten known **amphibians.** Once this was the most widespread frog species in North America, but since the mid-1960s its population has declined drastically across the continent and it is now gone from some regions and scarce in others. In Alberta, the frogs began disappearing mysteriously from many central and south central habitats in 1979. By 1990 northern leopard frogs were known to occur in only 32 sites in the province. At half of these sites there was no evidence that the species was breeding. At most sites fewer than 10 adults were counted. Only one numbered more than 20 adults. These surviving sites are mostly located in southeastern Alberta in the mixed **grasslands** and the **Cypress Hills.**

Researchers are unsure of the exact cause for the rapid decline in northern leopard frog populations. Locally, droughts, frosts, diseases, acid rain, and the most important threat of habitat loss are causing amphibian populations in Alberta to decrease. Globally, amphibian and reptile species are all declining in the face of global warming, rising ultraviolet radiation levels, and contamination of air, soil, and water.

Northern leopard frogs are generally green in colour, with darker spots prompting the leopard comparison. Alberta's largest common frog, they average 50 to 130 millimetres from nosetip to tailbase. Tadpoles can range up to 80 millimetres in length.

Usual habitat for northern leopard frogs is along the edges of streams, springs, ponds, and lakes. They prefer clean water in open or lightly wooded areas. Capable of conserving relatively large water reserves, the northern leopard frog can stray up to half a kilometre from water in dry weather and even farther when it rains.

In Alberta, northern leopard frogs hibernate from November to early April. During hibernation, they rest on the bottom of lakes or hide under stones in springs, streams, or rivers. They draw oxygen to breathe from the water. In their active season, the frogs rest by day and hunt at night. They usually eat insects, but will also eat mice, small fish, and even young northern leopard frogs.

The females give birth in May by depositing up to 3,000 eggs underwater in a large flattened spherical mass of greyish jelly. The eggs hatch 10 to 20 days later. Despite the large numbers of tadpoles hatched, few will survive to reach adulthood. By late July or early August the handful of surviving tadpoles mature into juvenile adult frogs.

The Alberta population of northern leopard frogs is not only small but survives in seriously fragmented habitat. Each frog enclave is too distant from another to allow for breeding between colonies. This weakens species diversity. The small size of each colony means the slightest change to their habitat may kill its inhabitants. Draining of wetlands, increased use of a slough by cattle or other livestock, or a chemical spill can devastate an entire colony of frogs in days. When a population does thrive, some of the adults will attempt to disperse to a new area of wetland. There are, however, usually no suitable areas nearby. These frogs die during their attempted migration across the dry land surrounding their home.

Northern leopard frogs are a favoured food of many species of predators ranging from waterfowl to **fish** and snakes. They are also illegally hunted by humans for bait, food, or sale to biological supply houses. Collection by children is also a constant threat to the species' survival.

The Alberta Fish and Wildlife Division is working with the World Wildlife Fund (Canada) on a provincial management plan for the species. Increased legislative protection for northern leopard frogs, reintroduction programs, and captive breeding programs are all contemplated or being implemented.

North-West Mounted Police

In 1873, Canadian prime minister Sir John A. Macdonald was increasingly concerned by reports of both lawlessness in the Canadian west and of growing numbers of Americans entering Canada in what amounted to an undeclared invasion by U.S. citizens. As the U.S. government was still flirting with its Manifest Destiny doctrine, which held that God meant North America to be united under the Stars and Stripes, Macdonald decided it was imperative to establish Canada's authority over the western territories. He was particularly concerned by reports that an outpost named **Fort Whoop-Up,** constructed at the junction of the Oldman and St. Mary rivers, was serving as the primary base for an increasingly active, American-controlled whiskey trade into the Canadian prairies.

Macdonald ordered the creation of a paramilitary unit called the North-West Mounted Police. On July 8, 1874 at Fort Dufferin in present-day Manitoba, a tiny force mustered to begin a march west across the **prairie.** Their task was to establish the rule of Canadian law to 777,000 square kilometres of near wilderness.

The force, comprising 275 officers and men, with 339 horses, 142 draft oxen, 93 cattle for slaughter, 114 **Red River carts,** 20 **Métis** drivers, 73 wagons, two nine-pounder muzzle-loading field guns, two brass mortars, several mowing machines, forges, and field kitchens, formed a long line stretching more than three kilometres. Each soldier was outfitted in a scarlet jacket, white cork helmet, white gauntlets, grey breeches, and black riding boots. His personal weapon was a Snider-Enfield carbine. The colours of the horses were detailed by unit divisions. "A" division rode dark bays, "B" dark browns, "C" chestnuts, "D" greys, "E" blacks, and "F" light bays.

It would take the force 94 days to march 1,450 kilometres from Fort Dufferin to Fort Whoop-Up. Their orders were to close the fort down, stop the whiskey trade, and force any Americans refusing to accept their authority back across the 49th parallel.

The NWMP arrived expecting a fight, but the traders had fled into Montana and the fort was closed peacefully. To prevent smuggling parties from easily slipping across the border, a thin line of lightly manned forts and outposts was constructed close to the U.S.-Canada border, which had been demarcated by the **International Boundary Commission** in 1873.

For the most part, the NWMP's mission in the west proved one of drudgery and tedium. Living conditions were poor. Desertion rates were high, so it was hard to keep the outposts properly manned. Many, such as the post at Outpost Lake, near the Waterton Lakes, went through fitful periods of being open, then closed due to lack of manpower, and was finally abandoned entirely.

Despite these problems the Thin Red Line served its purpose. The lawlessness that often preceded the movement of settlers into a region of the

NWMP sergeants of D and H divisions pose at Fort Macleod on December 27, 1890. (Glenbow Archives photo, NA-1177-2)

American west never established itself on the Canadian side of the border. There was also little incidence of armed conflict between European settlers and **First Nations peoples** as the NWMP intervened successfully before disputes could erupt into open violence.

The North-West Mounted Police was redesignated the Royal North-West Mounted Police in 1906. In 1920, it merged with the Dominion Police to become the Royal Canadian Mounted Police, as it remains today.

North-West Rebellion

In 1885 discontent and near starvation among **Métis** and **First Nations peoples** throughout the North-West Territories culminated in an armed uprising under the leadership of Louis Riel. While the rebellion was primarily confined to present-day Saskatchewan, some violence and confrontation also occurred in areas now part of Alberta.

The Alberta phases of the North-West Rebellion occurred primarily in the **Lloydminster** area. The rebels here were mostly members of the Cree nation, led by Chief Big Bear.

Although he had refused to join most Cree leaders in signing Treaty Six in 1876, his people's subsequent near starvation (due to the almost total eradication of **bison** from the plains by this time) led to his agreement in 1882. Big Bear, however, refused to confine his people to the assigned reservation in the Frog Lake area and continued agitating for a better deal than was contained in the treaty. The government responded by cutting off rations in an attempt to force Big Bear's people to settle on the assigned reserve.

By spring of 1885, when the rebellion broke out, it was almost inevitable that Big Bear would join the rebels. Although Big Bear was the chief, his own authority was waning, especially among the younger warriors of the Plains Cree who were more warlike than the Woodland Cree. When word reached the Cree that Riel's forces under command of Gabriel Dumont had defeated government troops at Duck Lake, Big Bear's young warriors were elated. "We are doomed, and will be killed one after another by the whites. But before we die, or disappear altogether...we must plunder stores and kill as many white people as we can," one warrior said.

On April 2, a band of warriors, acting against Big Bear's wishes, attacked the small community of Frog Lake. The warriors were commanded by Wandering Spirit, the Crees' war chief. Upon entering the village they found most of the whites celebrating mass in the Roman Catholic church. Wandering Spirit ordered them to come out, intending to take them all hostage. The community's Indian agent, Thomas Quinn, emerged from the church but refused to go with the warriors. Wandering Spirit shot him through the heart. Father Fafard rushed to the fallen man's side and was also shot. Within minutes nine whites were dead, including Fafard and another priest. Several whites, including two widows of men killed, were spared—the two women and one man being taken prisoner. Most of the village was burned.

Following this massacre, Big Bear saw no alternative but to lead his people in the undoubtedly doomed rebellion. Under his and Wandering Spirit's leadership, the Cree pillaged stores from Lac La Biche, Saddle Lake, Beaverhill Lake, Lac Ste. Anne, Bear Hills, and Beaver Lake. They also besieged Fort Pitt on the Saskatchewan River in present-day Saskatchewan—forcing the **North-West Mounted Police** (NWMP) detachment to abandon the fort on April 15, after one of their men was killed in a skirmish.

Big Bear hoped the sizable Métis population in the area of Fort Edmonton and the Blackfoot and Bloods in the south would join the uprising. Although sympathy for the rebellion was strong among all these peoples, their leaders recognized the rebellion's futility. Big Bear's entreaties were refused.

White people in **Fort Macleod, Calgary, Edmonton,** and other communities near reserves feared for their lives in the wake of the Frog Lake massacre. The federal government responded by authorizing creation of a special military unit—the Alberta Field Force—based in Calgary. Military units rushed from eastern Canada to constitute the majority of the force. Commanded by Major-General Thomas Bland Strange, the Alberta Field Force consisted of two NWMP units, the 65th Mount Royal Regiment from Montreal, the Winnipeg Light Infantry, and the 9th Battalion from Quebec City. It numbered approximately 700 men.

While three companies of the Winnipeg Light Infantry remained to protect Calgary and surrounding communities, the rest of the force marched north in three columns for Edmonton. At Fort Macleod, meanwhile, an ad hoc militia dubbed the Rocky Mountain Rangers was formed to patrol between High River and **Medicine Hat.**

During the march from Calgary to Edmonton, the Alberta Field Force's 65th Mount Royals constructed and manned three blockhouses near present-day **Red Deer,** Ponoka, and Wetaskiwin. At Edmonton, the Alberta Field Force split up, with some detachments dispersed to protect Edmonton-area communities.

Strange, intent on smashing Big Bear's Crees, took the majority of his units east to Fort Pitt. He reached the fort on May 25, nearly two weeks after the seminal Battle of Batoche between Canadian and Métis forces in Saskatchewan had quashed any chance of the rebellion's success. Big Bear's Crees were dug in at nearby Frenchman's Butte. His force consisted of about 370, including women and children, plus about 40 white hostages taken in the earlier raids. His warriors occupied rifle pits completely dominating the surrounding countryside. Strange's troops took up positions beneath the butte, but were unable to advance further. After several days of desultory skirmishing, Big Bear abandoned the position on May 28 when Strange brought up a field gun and lobbed a few shells at his position. Strange set off in pursuit. Soon more than 1,000 troops were unsuccessfully scouring the nearby dense woods in search of Big Bear's force.

Fully six weeks after Louis Riel surrendered, Big Bear gave up on July 2 at Fort Carlton (which had been burned in March), near Duck Lake in present-day Saskatchewan. He was sentenced to three years in prison, but was released after serving two years. A broken and sick man, Big Bear died in 1888.

Oil and Gas Industry

Alberta's oil and gas deposits constitute the majority of Canada's reserves and give the province some of the largest stocks found anywhere in the world. Sixty percent of the nation's total known crude oil reserves lies within Alberta's boundaries. The province also contains 85 percent of Canada's natural gas, and all of its bitumen and oil sands reserves.

It is estimated the remaining reserve of marketable natural gas in Alberta is 53 trillion cubic feet, with ultimate potential reserves of 200 trillion cubic feet. In 1995, the Alberta Energy and Utilities Board reported that the province had 375 million barrels of conventional (crude) oil reserves left.

In terms of gross domestic product (GDP), Alberta produces about $10 billion annually in crude oil, $8 billion in natural gas, and $1.5 billion in natural gas by-products. This accounts for approximately one-fifth of the province's entire GDP.

Since 1947 when the petroleum industry boomed with the discovery of the **Leduc oil** field, oil and gas exploration, development, and sales have transformed Alberta from being a "have-not" province to one of the most prosperous in the nation. Despite world market trends which have since caused various booms and busts in the oil and gas industry, the province's **economy** has continued to prosper through the sale of its petroleum resources.

Those resources, however, are a finite commodity. Some experts say, given current rates of production, the marketable supplies of oil and gas will be exhausted by 2025. Even the Alberta Energy and Utilities Board reported in 1995 that at current production rates there were only enough conventional (not including natural gas and oil sands supplies) oil reserves in Alberta to last another 6.6 years.

The National Energy Board (NEB) has warned that if current production rates are sustained Canada's entire known natural gas reserves will be depleted by 2006. Despite these predictions the provincial government has encouraged increased oil and gas production and tries to keep natural gas prices low. In 1994, for example, natural gas production increased over the previous year by 7 percent to 118 billion cubic metres. The share of natural gas exported to the United States has been steadily increasing and accounts for about 57 percent of all petroleum and oil sales.

Alberta has hinged much of its effort to attract new industry to the province on having some of the lowest utility rates in the industrialized world. Its natural gas rates are Canada's lowest.

While known marketable reserves are rapidly dwindling, there are still believed to be large reserves of natural gas yet to be discovered, or which current technology is incapable of tapping. The NEB estimates Alberta has an additional 75.1 trillion cubic feet of undiscoverd natural gas. This does not include "tight" gas, which is unrecoverable through conventional drilling, or coal-bed methane reserves. Coal-bed methane supplies are believed to exceed by three times the estimated conventional reserves.

If these reserves can be developed as were the originally unrecoverable **Athabasca oil sands,** Alberta may gain another generation or more of economic strength on the basis of continued oil and gas sales.

(*See also* **Athabasca Oil Sands; Cold Lake; Leduc Oil; Turner Valley Oil and Gas Field.**)

Okotoks Erratic. *See* Erratics.

Palliser Expedition

For three years an expedition sent from Britain by the Royal Geographical Society and funded by the British government explored, mapped, and conducted scientific studies on the natural resources of the Canadian prairies. Ultimately the expedition's reports, published in 1859, 1860, and 1863, its comprehensive maps, and the various memoirs of its participants, would constitute the major source of information available to the British government about the vast lands lying from Lake Superior to British Columbia's Okanagan Valley. On the basis of this information the British government and later the Canadian government developed strategies for opening and settling the Canadian west.

The expedition's name derived from its leader, John Palliser, an Irish-born sportsman and explorer. With him were geologist and naturalist James Hector, botanical collector Eugène Bourgeau, secretary and astronomical secretary John W. Sullivan, and magnetical observer Lt. Thomas W. Blakiston. Supported by **Métis** scouts, the expedition set out according to its letter of instruction to record "the physical features of the country, noting its principal elevations, the nature of its soil, its capability of agriculture, the quantity and quality of its timber, and any indications of coal or other minerals."

In 1858 the party began exploration of what would become Alberta. They conducted a detailed and exacting exploration of the province south of an east-west line drawn directly through Fort Edmonton, which served as their main operational base.

Palliser, knowing next to nothing about **agriculture,** singled out the most arid region of the plains in the southern portion of Alberta as a viable agricultural zone. The area remains known today as the Palliser Triangle. The more sober and informed Hector declared the area useless, but noted that it was surrounded by much fertile land. Hector, however, was less than impressed by Alberta's **boreal forest.** Its spruce, he wrote, was "coarse and worthless" for anything but an "inferior quality of firewood." The expedition was excited to discover a great abundance of coal in various parts of the province. They also charted six Rocky Mountain passes, through several of which they felt a railroad could be built to link British Columbia with the rest of Britain's North American empire. The Canadian Pacific Railway would eventually be constructed through one of these passes—the Kicking Horse (so named because one of Hector's horses kicked him in the chest while fording a stream).

Parklands

Parklands in Alberta refers to a physiographic region rather than to lands contained within parks. This is made more confusing by the fact that until recently naturalists in Alberta tended to denote the province as having only four natural regions, one of which was called aspen parkland. Alberta's **Special Places** strategy now identifies six natural regions in the province, with the parkland region encompassing and generally limited to the same terrain originally categorized as aspen parkland.

The parklands are a transitional ground lying between the **grasslands** to the south and the forests to the north. They exist nowhere else in the world except in Canada's **prairie** provinces. Their landscape is a combination of rolling hills and flat plains formed during the last glacial retreat.

There are three subregions in the parklands, classified on the basis of geographic and vegetation differences.

- The central parkland subregion extends in a broad arc up to 200 kilometres wide between the grasslands and the **boreal forest.** Surface features include hummocky and ground moraines, glacial lake beds, kame moraines (sand or gravel hills and ridges), and dune fields. Elevations range from about 500 metres above sea level where the Battle River enters Saskatchewan to around 1,100 metres in the west. Lakes and permanent wetlands are common.

  Within this subregion there is gradual transition from grassland with groves of aspen in the south to closed aspen forest in the north. Native vegetation is scarce because most land has been cultivated to grow agricultural crops. The majority of remaining natural land is situated on rougher terrain or poorer soils.

  Aspen and balsam poplar forests are the primary forest types occurring here. Both are characterized by a lush, species-rich understorey. Within the grassland areas, plant species are essentially the same as those found in the northern fescue subregion of the grasslands. Shrub communities of snowberry, rose, chokecherry, and Saskatoon become increasingly common in northern parts of the subregion.

  Wildlife is a mixture of grasslands species and those of the northern forests. On the southern edge of this subregion upland sandpiper, Sprague's pipit, and Baird's sparrow are common but are less often seen in the northern section. Along the northern fringe, boreal forest species such as woodchuck, broad-winged hawk, and rose-breasted grosbeak are prevalent. Nearly all of Alberta's population of Franklin's ground squirrel and piping plover exists in the central parkland sub-region.

- A narrow band following the eastern edge of the **foothills** from **Calgary** south to the Porcupine Hills, and from Pincher Creek to the U.S. border, is known as the foothills parkland subregion. Its topography is rougher than the central parkland. Elevations are higher, ranging to more than 1,300 metres above sea level. Surface composition includes hummocky and ground moraine as well as gravel and sand left by rivers of the glacial melt, and glacial lake deposits.

  Grasslands here blend with aspen groves and turn to closed aspen forest over short distances of one to five kilometres because of rapid changes in topography and **climate.** This compression results in small geographic areas containing much **biodiversity.**

  Grassland communities of the foothills parkland are similar to those of the foothills fescue subregion of the grasslands. Fescue and oat grasses are dominant, with aspen forest in the upland areas mixed with balsam poplar in the wetter sites. Willow groveland is a distinct community occurring only in the northern part of this subregion.

  Many animals found in the central parklands are absent here, but common Rocky Mountain species are present, such as dusky flycatcher, MacGillivray's warbler, and white-crowned sparrow. In the far south, black-headed grosbeaks and blue grouse are found in the aspen forests.

- The last subregion is the **Peace River** parkland subregion, characterized by broad, gently rolling plains with scattered uplands and deeply incised, steep-sided river valleys. The main portion of this subregion is found in the **Grande Prairie** and Peace River areas with smaller pockets extending north to Fort Vermilion. Most of the extensive original grasslands of this subregion have been cultivated and only small, scattered remnants have retained native cover.

  The Peace River parkland experiences short, cool summers and long, cold winters. More precipitation falls than in the other parkland subregions, and it is less windy. Upland forests of aspen and white spruce meld indistinguishably with the surrounding mixed-wood boreal forest. Grasslands are dominated by sedges, intermediate oat grass, western porcupine grass, bearded wheat grass, and low goldenrod. On steep, south-facing slopes porcupine grass, sedges, and pasture sage-wort dominate.

Wildlife is virtually the same as that of the boreal forest's dry mixed-wood subregion, with which it is intermixed. The lakes and ponds of the Peace River parkland serve as important nesting areas for many **birds,** including rare **trumpeter swans.**

Peace River

Near **Lake Athabasca,** on the edge of the Peace River, is a spot named Peace Point in their respective languages by the Cree and Beaver people because here the two tribes negotiated a war settlement. According to explorer Alexander Mackenzie, the Cree called the river *unijigah,* meaning peace, in honour of this settlement.

About 20 kilometres up the Smoky River from its junction with the Peace River, Mackenzie discovered two Europeans building the first trading fort for the area—Fork Fort. He wintered there, using the fort as a base from which to continue his western journey of 1793. This part of the Peace River country has been continuously occupied by non–First Nations people ever since.

Missionaries arrived at Peace River in 1879 and in 1893 Reverend J. Gough Brick dramatically proved the area's agricultural potential by winning the world wheat championship at the Chicago Exposition. By 1913 a permanent settlement had developed. It was known as Peace River Crossing, a name it retained until 1916. The year before the community was officially renamed Peace River, the Edmonton, Dunvegan and BC Railway crossed the Peace River through the townsite.

With the coming of the railroad, the Peace River country was opened to immigration. The mixed **ethnicity** of the immigrants flooding in ensured the ethnic diversity for which it is known today. Peace River's current population is about 6,700. It is a distribution and administration centre for the vast surrounding agricultural region.

The community is also well known for being the burial site of Henry Fuller "Twelve Foot" Davis. Sturdy, strong, but small of stature, Davis derived his nickname from the fact that he had staked a claim in B.C. during the Barkerville gold rush that measured 12 feet along the shore of Williams Creek. The claim yielded about $20,000 worth of gold. Davis never lived in Peace River itself; rather he operated a trading post near **Fort Dunvegan.** He died in 1900 and was buried at Grouard, but in 1910, to honour his deathbed wish, his body was moved to a hill overlooking Peace River. A tombstone of Vermont marble was placed on the grave. A larger monument has since been erected and the old tombstone now stands in the Peace River Centennial Museum, along with a 12-foot-high carving that is supposedly in Davis's image.

Performing Arts

Alberta has a rich and diversified performing arts community. With 13 professional companies performing from May to September, **Edmonton** is home to the second-biggest English-language theatre community in Canada. The Citadel Theatre is Canada's largest theatre facility, encompassing an entire downtown block. It contains five theatres: the Maclab theatre which showcases work by teens and children; the Rice theatre, home to primarily experimental and innovative productions; Zeidler Hall, a venue for films, lectures, and children's theatre; Tucker Amphitheatre, a concert and recital hall; and the complex's main stage, Shoctor Theatre. In Edmonton's Old Strathcona district the nation's oldest and largest fringe festival, the Edmonton Fringe Theatre Festival, performs about 100 plays from countries around the world on more than 20 stages over ten days. About 450,000 people attend annually.

The city also hosts the Jazz City International Festival, the world-famous Folk Music Festival, and the Summerfest Street Performing Festival. The Northern Alberta Jubilee Auditorium provides a home for the Alberta Ballet Company, Edmonton Symphony Orchestra, and the Edmonton Opera Association.

In **Calgary,** the Centre for the Performing Arts has three superb theatre venues and one of Canada's most acoustically perfect concert halls. There are some ten professional theatre companies, an opera company, the Calgary Philharmonic Orchestra, and a ballet troupe, the Alberta Ballet. The city also holds an international jazz festival each June, has its own folk festival, and in August hosts the International Native Arts Festival with performances by native dancers and musicians.

Since 1933, the **Banff** Centre for the Arts has become a major international focal point for the study and celebration of a diverse range of artistic disciplines. Throughout the year various concerts, displays, and live performances are held here. The Banff Festival of the Arts, the Banff Festival of Mountain Films, and the Banff Television Festival are among a few of the major annual events.

Petroglyphs and Pictographs

Alberta's prehistoric inhabitants left behind a legacy in the many sites throughout the province where they carved or painted images on rocks.

More than two dozen major pictograph and petroglyph sites have been found, and others may still be undiscovered.

A pictograph is a painting done on rock walls with a combination of red ochre, water, and animal grease. It is executed by using fingers or a rough brush. A petroglyph is a carving etched or pecked into the rock's surface with tools made of stone or bone.

Archaeologists refer to the two forms collectively as rock art. Both share common imagery and subject matter. Why some artists opted to create pictographs and others petroglyphs, or whether the same artist might have used both forms, is unknown.

Rock art scenes range from simple human or animal figures to full battle stories including dozens of warriors, animals, and details of camps.

Human figures vary greatly in style. Some are statically posed, simple stick figures. Other show sticklike feet and a head protruding from the edges of a shield. Many figures seem to be moving, often as if in the midst of a hunt or battle.

Animal figures are commonly depicted. **Bison, bears,** sheep, elk, deer, dogs, snakes, **birds,** and horses are easily identifiable. A great variety of geometric and abstract shapes was employed. The meaning of many of these shapes is impossible to interpret. Some archaeologists believe they represent the spirits thought to inhabit the rock upon which the art was rendered.

While differences in artistic style are thought to represent artistic development over the ages, it also probably derives to some extent from varying styles among the **First Nations peoples** of the time. Plains peoples, such as the ancestors of the Blackfoot, created some sites. Others were the product of the Ktunaxa (formerly Kutenai or Kootenay), who travelled into southern

This petroglyph is just one of the many found at Writing-On-Stone Provincial Park. (Glenbow Archives photo, ND-34-21)

Alberta's plains country from the Rocky Mountain **foothills** and parts of British Columbia on **bison hunting** forays.

Archaeologists believe rock art had definite purposes and did not represent mere doodling or graffiti. Rock art sites appear to have been considered sacred. Some rock art was at least partially ceremonial, as human burial sites have been found close by. A few sites were known to have been used in vision quest ceremonies, whereby individuals sought to communicate with the spirit world. In some places **medicine wheels** and rock art occur together. Others, such as the pictographs at **Head-Smashed-In Buffalo Jump,** appear to mark and possibly honour the sites at which bison were commonly killed.

Most rock art sites in Alberta occur in the southwestern portion. Many are in caves or shelters, while other etchings have been discovered on high exposed rock faces that are almost inaccessible today. Pictographs have been found on stone **erratics** scattered across the **prairie.** Some large boulders have had a rib pattern pecked into them. These distinct patterns have been named buffalo rib stones.

It is difficult to date rock art except from the content of the work itself. Those showing European trade goods, or guns and horses, can be no older than 1730, when horses first appeared in southern Alberta. But some of the art is believed to be more than 3,000 years old. Other older works have likely been eroded away by wind and water, leaving no trace.

The most extensive collection of rock art found anywhere in North America is at **Writing-On-Stone Provincial Park,** along the banks of the **Milk River** and within sight of the Sweetgrass Hills of Montana. Here, more than 50 rock art sites have so far been discovered.

Population

In 1891 a census of the North-West Territories determined that there were about 9,000 **First Nations peoples** and 17,500 **Métis** and white settlers in what would in 1905 become the province of Alberta.

Following the election of a federal Liberal government in 1896, population growth in Alberta accelerated as the new administration actively encouraged immigration to the Canadian Prairies. Clifford Sifton, the cabinet minister responsible for immigration in the Wilfred Laurier government, dedicated his political career to peopling the west. By altering the rules of the land-grant system, through which speculators and colonization companies had tied up much of the Prairies' best land, Sifton made it simpler for individuals to secure homesteads.

Sifton decided the way to populate the Prairies was to attract farmers. Although Anglo-Canadians in the Prairies and the rest of Canada hoped to settle the west with people from Ontario, Great Britain, and northwestern Europe, Sifton recognized that these regions had populations too small to generate the kind of immigration needed to fill a vast land. So Sifton looked to central and eastern Europe, promising prospective immigrants 65 hectares of land for a $10 fee. In most parts of the Ukraine at the time a peasant was lucky to work 3 hectares of land. For many impoverished European peasants Sifton's offer was irresistible. Sifton's "stalwart peasants in sheepskin coats" poured into Canada. (*See* **Ukrainian-Canadian Albertans.**)

At the same time as Sifton was establishing his immigration policies, the United States' frontier was reaching a point of settlement saturation. Canada's North-West Territories became widely known as the "last best west" and immigration turned from the U.S. to Canada.

In 1900 Canada numbered 5 million people. By 1910, 1.25 million immigrants had been added. Alberta's population increased by over five times—from 73,000 in 1901 to 374,000 in 1911. First Nations and Métis in Alberta represented only 3 percent of the population by 1911. Despite the influx of non-British immigrants, by 1914 more than half of Alberta's population still traced its roots to Britain. In roughly equal portions this majority came mostly from Ontario, the U.S., and Britain.

A post–World War I depression stretching into the early 1920s, combined with the fact that most of the best land in central and southern Alberta had been taken, slowed the flow of new settlers. In the five years between 1921 and 1926 the province's population grew by only 20,000 to 608,000. A new influx of immigrants arrived in the latter part of the decade, settling primarily in new agricultural areas that were further north, such as the **Peace River** country. Here, area population by 1931 had more than doubled from 21,000 to 44,000. Altogether 732,000 people lived in Alberta by 1931.

The Great Depression struck Alberta hard and population growth during the 1930s stagnated—increasing to only about 769,000 by 1941. This was a smaller rate of growth than experienced in any other 20th-century decade, with just 12,500 people immigrating to Alberta during this period.

World War II also slowed the province's growth. Between 1941 and 1946 the population increased to 803,000. A net emigration of 72,000 Albertans occurred during this time, including those who left to serve in the armed forces and war-industry jobs in other provinces.

The war years also saw the beginning of a continuing trend—movement of Albertans from farms to urban jobs. Although the role of **agriculture** in

Alberta's **economy** remained dominant, the number of people working in this sector was declining rapidly.

With war's end and the **Leduc oil** discovery on February 13, 1947, the province's economy started undergoing a profound change that encouraged rapid population growth. By 1951, 939,000 people lived in Alberta, rising to 1.332 million by 1961—a 40 percent increase, mostly the result of the "baby boom." Only 13 percent of the growth in this period stemmed from immigration to the province, with people coming primarily from the United States, Europe, and Saskatchewan.

The populations of **Edmonton** and **Calgary** boomed in the post-war years. By 1971 Edmonton's population had quadrupled from 100,000 in 1946 to 400,000. Calgary tripled its population during the same period to over 300,000.

In 1946, 41 percent of Albertans lived on farms. Twenty years later only 19 percent were still farming. Many small hamlets and villages disappeared during this period, as Albertans moved to large urban centres.

The massive oil boom of the 1970s increased Alberta's population by over a third, from 1.6 million in 1971 to 2.2 million in 1981. Both Edmonton and Calgary contained over 500,000 people by 1981, surpassing 650,000 by the late 1980s. The small northwestern city of **Grande Prairie** doubled its population between 1971 and 1981, reaching 24,000. This growth was driven by local developments in the **oil and gas industry** and **forest industry.**

Alberta's prosperity during this period attracted Canadians from other provinces. The portion of Alberta's population born in other provinces increased from 21 percent to 29 percent, with Ontario-born immigrants constituting the largest group—almost 8 percent of the total population.

Canada liberalized its immigration laws in 1967, enabling immigration from Asian countries and other developing nations for the first time. About half of Alberta's annual 10,000 immigrants during the 1970s and 1980s came from the developing world, especially Asia. Alberta's Chinese community increased to well over 50,000. Over 80 percent of these immigrants settled in Edmonton or Calgary, adding a new range of **ethnicity.**

First Nations people—now calculated as including Métis—continued to represent 3 percent of the population. In 1981 72,000 First Nations people lived in Alberta—35,800 status Indians, 8,600 non-status, 27,100 Métis, and 500 Inuit. Most First Nations people in Alberta were under 30 and 40 percent lived in urban centres.

The 1980s through to the present have seen Alberta's population continue to grow, but at a slower pace. During the oil bust in the 1980s population in many areas of Alberta declined or stagnated. Today, some 2.77 million people live in Alberta. Half are concentrated in Edmonton and Calgary. In all, approximately 80 percent of Alberta's population lives in urban centres.

A population corridor between Edmonton and Calgary follows Highway 2, passing through **Red Deer.** From Calgary two population strings extend south and east along the highways leading to **Lethbridge** and **Medicine Hat.** Other Alberta population centres are **Lloydminster, Fort McMurray, Grande Prairie,** and **Peace River.** Another population corridor extends from Canmore to Drumheller and north to Stettler.

Outside these narrow corridors the province is sparsely populated, especially in the north. Overall, there are only about 3.8 persons occupying every square kilometre.

More than two-thirds of Alberta's population is under the age of 40, giving the province one of the youngest populations in the industrial world. It is also one of the best educated populations in North America, with more than 40 percent of the workforce holding a post-secondary certificate, diploma, or university degree.

Given the percentage of people under 40, Alberta has Canada's highest labour force participation rate—about 718 out of every 1,000 working-age Albertans.

Post-Secondary Education

Just under 100,000 full-time students are enrolled annually in degree, diploma, or certificate studies at Alberta's 35 post-secondary schools. This degree of access to higher **education** facilities, combined with the fact that immigrants to the province from other provinces and nations generally hold some level of post-secondary education, results in the **population** of Alberta having the highest level of educational attainment of any province in Canada. Approximately 14 percent of Albertans over the age of 15 possess a bachelor degree or higher.

Alberta has four universities, three technical institutes, and a province-wide network of community colleges. Additionally, there are numerous private colleges, vocational schools, and training centres. Eighteen Alberta-based public and private institutions offer programs leading directly, or through transfers, to an academic undergraduate degree. These include the University of Alberta, University of Calgary, University of Lethbridge, Athabasca University, the Camrose Lutheran University College, Concordia College, and Kings College. Other colleges, such as Grant MacEwan in

Edmonton, Mount Royal in **Calgary,** and Red Deer College offer university-transfer programs.

About one out of every four full-time students in Alberta attends Edmonton's University of Alberta, which offers a total of 19 degrees at the bachelor, master, and doctoral level. The University of Calgary, with a full-time student population of about 20,000, is the second-largest post-secondary school in Alberta. About 10 percent of this university's student population are engaged in master's and doctoral degree studies. The rest are seeking one of 15 possible degrees offered in a wide variety of academic subjects.

The University of Lethbridge is a smaller facility with an average annual full-time enrollment of 3,000. It offers six degree programs at the baccalaureate level and a Master of Education program, as well as 12 professional transfer programs.

The University of Athabasca is a university without a campus. This unique facility offers home-study courses to more than 7,000 students across Canada. Its 120 courses are focused in four major fields: administrative studies, social sciences, natural sciences, and humanities—enabling students to pursue three undergraduate degrees in either administration, arts, or general studies.

Alberta operates three technical colleges—Northern Alberta Institute of Technology (NAIT) in Edmonton, Calgary's Southern Alberta Institute of Technology, and the Westerra Institute of Technology in Stony Plain, 30 kilometres west of Edmonton. NAIT is one of Canada's largest polytechnical institutes.

Across the province there are 11 colleges, including two specialized colleges. Olds College, located 90 kilometres north of Calgary, specializes in agricultural sciences. Calgary's Alberta College of Art, which specializes in visual arts education, is one of Canada's four diploma-granting art colleges.

Prairie

The Alberta prairie is part of a vast grassland called the Great Plains, which stretches from the Gulf of Mexico north and west to encompass much of western and central North America. Southern parts of Alberta, Saskatchewan, and Manitoba are all part of this prairie region. Approximately 12 million hectares of Alberta can be considered true prairie. It stretches from about the latitudinal line cutting through Olds, south of **Red Deer,** to the international boundary and from the **foothills** to the Saskatchewan border. North of the true Alberta prairie is a region of about

5 million hectares often termed "mixed prairie," which extends northward to **Edmonton.** This area was slightly more forested than the largely treeless prairie until European settlers cleared it for farming and **ranching**.

The common myth of the prairie is that it is singularly flat and feature-less. Reality is far different. With its **coulees, badlands, cottonwood forest**-bordered rivers, wetlands, lakes, rolling hills and plateaus, broad reaches of plains, and other features, the prairie is as diverse in physiography, veget-ation, and wildlife as any other part of North America.

The word *prairie,* meaning meadow, was employed by early French explorers to describe the interior of North America. In Canada, the term Prairie is employed collectively to describe the three provinces of Alberta, Saskatchewan, and Manitoba. It is common for Prairie-born people to first think of themselves as being from the Prairies and then from the province of their birth. This has led to the misconception that the three provinces share many things in common that extend far beyond their natural envi-ronment. Politically, federal governments have often clumped the three provinces together in terms of policies and attempts to win regional pol-itical support. This happens despite the fact that each province has its own distinct political tradition which differs greatly from those of the other Prairie provinces.

Culturally, intellectually, and artistically, there are similarities among the Prairie provinces. Prairie painters, writers, filmmakers, musicians, and other creators tend to draw closely upon the specific prairie communities of their birth and the surrounding landscape as a fertile source of inspiration. This tendency to employ local imagery and subject matter, however, has in no way limited the ability of Prairie artists to speak successfully to national and international audiences.

In recent years the prairie landscape and wildlife habitat has become increasingly popular with international travellers and artists, especially those from European countries, looking for a new, largely undiscovered and untrammelled North American frontier for **tourism** and creative exploration. There are indications that the prairie regions of North America, especially those such as the **Milk River** country of **Writing-On-Stone Provincial Park** that have expanses of natural grassland, may eventually eclipse the North American desert and the Pacific northwest coastal rainforests in popularity.

Pronghorns

During the Pliocene Period ending about 1.5 million years ago a host of ungulate species dwelt in **ancient Alberta** and across the rest of the North

American plains. Fossil evidence shows that some of these had long, bizarre-looking, forked horns, the horns of others spiralled, and still others had four horns. All but one of this diverse ungulate family are now extinct. The survivor is the American pronghorn, which lives today in Alberta in the southeastern corner of the province.

Pronghorns are small, with slender limbs, short necks and tails, long pointed ears, and a distinct white rump. Their heads are large in comparison to body size and their eyes are remarkably large (as big as a horse's). A male pronghorn weighs about 50 kilograms and a female about 41.5 kilograms.

Males and females both carry black horns that prong into curved tips. The horns of bucks can reach 50 centimetres, while those of does are either smaller or lacking. Hooves are small, daintily pointed, and sharp. The horns of the pronghorn are not the same as antlers in other North American ungulate species. Antlers are solid bone developing out of the frontal bones of such ungulates as deer and elk. Pronghorns have a proper horn, composed of keratin (the same complex protein contained in hair and fingernails), a core base of bone extruding from the top of the skull, and layers of skin and specialized hairs. Pronghorns rub the tips of their horns on bushes, making them shiny and black. The horns are shed annually, regrowing quite quickly.

Pronghorns are highly gregarious, congregating in small herds for most of the year. Does break off by themselves to give birth in the spring and bucks also disperse at this time. In a few weeks when the kids are relatively mobile the does reform the herd, but the bucks do not return until the fall.

Pronghorns have almost unlimited energy and are extremely curious, but are also highly skittish and easily frightened. Their eyesight is remarkably keen, enabling them to see small moving objects as far off as seven kilometres. However, if an object or animal is stationary pronghorns usually ignore it, no matter how close it is. Their hearing and sense of smell are also quite acute. They move and feed at all times of day and night, resting intermittently.

There is no other North American mammal as fleet as the pronghorn. They have been clocked at speeds ranging between 80 and 100 kilometres per hour during short bursts and can sustain a speed of 60 to 70 kilometres per hour for distances of seven kilometres without exhaustion. Their normal walk is stiff-legged. They can bound, but not over objects. For this reason, when wire fencing of the **prairie** and plains became common, pronghorns learned to squirm under the fences rather than jump over. They will even go under fences easily jumped by far less agile and powerful animals.

Forbs (herbaceous plants other than grass) constitute more than two-thirds of their diet, with woody browse largely making up the rest. Favoured forbs are clovers, sourdock, wild onion, lupin, larkspur, buttercup, and alfalfa. Browse food is sagebrush, saltbrush, and rabbit brush. Pronghorns also eat such grasses as cheatgrass, wheatgrass, timothy, and sedge.

Their primary predators are coyotes, especially in deep snow when the coyotes can match their speed. During summer months coyotes focus on taking down young kids, but the does are usually able to drive them off by trying to spear the **wild dogs** with their horns or kicking them with their sharp, quite deadly, hooves. Bobcats are also occasional predators, as are golden eagles and ravens.

Pronghorns once ranged the western North American prairie and steppes in numbers equivalent to those of the **bison.** As with the bison, the coming of European hunters resulted in a mass slaughter, so by 1908 only about 20,000 survived on the entire continent. By 1922 just 1,400 were left in Canada, but the establishment of sanctuaries resulted in this population growing to about 2,400 ten years later. By 1945 Canadian numbers had rallied to 31,000, considered a sufficiently strong population to ensure the survival of this species within its limited remaining Canadian range of southeastern Alberta and southwestern Saskatchewan.

Provincial Museum of Alberta

The Provincial Museum of Alberta in **Edmonton** traces the history of the province over a billion years of natural and human history. The habitat gallery covers the province's diverse natural regions; the natural history section examines the forces that shaped the province and takes visitors from the Cretaceous-age **dinosaurs** through to the emergence of **mammals.** Other sections detail the precontact culture of Alberta's **First Nations peoples** through the arrival of European explorers and settlers.

Occupying one-quarter of the museum's exhibit space is the new Syncrude Canada Aboriginal Peoples Gallery. This is the largest and most significant permanent gallery developed by the museum since the facility opened in 1969. The gallery has been funded jointly by the provincial government and Syncrude Canada Ltd., with Syncrude covering one-third of the estimated $2.4 million cost.

The gallery displays many of the museum's 3,500 artifacts—ranging from stone tools to contemporary art and music—for the first time. It provides a backdrop for the museum's Blackfoot, Cree, and Athapaskan collections, which are considered some of the best in Canada. Pre-European contact history and culture are key components of the gallery. But the displays also explore the erosion and loss of traditional lifestyles, identity, and beliefs following the incursion of Europeans into Alberta, as well as the recent cultural renewal and growing sense of identity and pride that mark First Nations' culture today.

The Provincial Museum of Alberta also houses the Provincial Archives, containing photographs, maps, government records, and other documents relating to Alberta history.

Provincial Parks

In the late 1920s, then Alberta premier John Edward Brownlee visited Great Britain and was impressed with how attached the British were to the beauty of their countryside. He decided to foster similar attitudes among Albertans. On May 28, 1929, Brownlee directed his deputy minister of public works, J.D. Robertson, to "form a committee to investigate the feasibility of park development in the province."

At the time Brownlee was negotiating with the Canadian federal government for the province to gain control over its natural resources—this power having been retained by the federal government when it created the province in 1905. Lacking jurisdiction over natural resources, nothing concrete in the way of park creation could be undertaken until the federal government ceded control. On December 14, 1929, that agreement was finally signed.

Three years later, on November 21, 1932, Aspen Beach Provincial Park on Gull Lake west of Lacombe became the province's first park. Seven others were soon declared.

Since then the provincial parks system has grown to more than 300 provincial parks, provincial recreation areas, ecological reserves, and wilderness areas.

Additionally, the Alberta Forest Service maintains more than 175 recreation areas, including 109 vehicle-access campgrounds and 22 group campgrounds.

(*See also* **Dinosaur Provincial Park; Kananaskis Country; Writing-On-Stone Provincial Park.**)

Public Safety

Alberta is policed by two separate forces—the Royal Canadian Mounted Police (RCMP), who are responsible for enforcement of federal law, and municipal police forces. Policing in municipalities with populations under 1,500 people is through the RCMP via a contract with the provincial government. Policing in urban areas with populations exceeding 1,500 is provided either by a community contract with the RCMP or by establishment of a distinct municipal police force. Most of Alberta's medium- to larger-sized urban areas, such as **Calgary, Edmonton, Red Deer,** and **Lethbridge,** have their own non-RCMP forces. In total there are 10 municipal forces, 60 contracted RCMP municipal forces, and a province-wide contracted RCMP force.

Fire protection is provided in Alberta through a network of 400 fire protection departments. Eight of these employ strictly full-time fire fighters, 23 use a composite of full-time and volunteer fire fighters, and 369 are run exclusively by volunteers. The eight full-time fire departments are found in Calgary, Edmonton, **Fort McMurray,** Lethbridge, Red Deer, **Medicine Hat,** St. Albert, and Hinton. Population centres of less than 25,000 are serviced by composite or volunteer forces. There are about 10,500 fire fighters across the province, 25 percent being full-time professionals.

Most cities in Alberta operate 9-1-1 telephone contact services for police, fire, and ambulance emergencies.

Pysanka

The world's largest pysanka stands in Vegreville, a small community of about 5,100 located 105 kilometres east of Edmonton on Highway 16. Pysankas are exquisitely and intricately decorated eggs traditionally created by Ukrainians to celebrate Easter. Pysanka comes from the Ukrainian verb *pysaty,* meaning "to write." Vegreville lies in the heart of a region extensively settled by Ukrainian immigrants in the early 1900s.

In 1973, the Alberta government encouraged communities to erect monuments to the Royal Canadian Mounted Police, as part of the force's centenary celebrations. (*See* **North-West Mounted Police.**)

The giant Easter egg at Vegreville is the world's largest pysanka and is also an engineering wonder. (Mark Zuehlke photo)

The Vegreville and District Chamber of Commerce decided that a giant pysanka would be a fitting memorial to the police force which brought peace and security to the region where **Ukrainian-Canadian Albertans** settled.

The unique nature and complicated geometry of the egg shape made designing a huge pysanka a highly complex project. Professor Ronald Resch, a University of Utah computer scientist, agreed to design the $25,000 egg. Resch was breaking new ground, the pysanka being the first egg-shaped structure ever built and the first computer modelling of an egg ever undertaken. It was also the first completely closed architectural shell structure. In all, nine mathematical, architectural, and engineering firsts were involved in its design and construction. Among these was the first practical application of the theory of a mathematical curve definition known as B-splines. It is the first geometrical structure whose geometry requirements are as complex as the aerodynamic surface definition of an aircraft or missile cone.

The pysanka created by Resch is really an immense jigsaw puzzle containing 524 star patterns, 1,108 equilateral triangles, 3,512 visible facets, and 6,978 nuts and bolts. It measures 7.83 metres long, 5.49 metres wide, and stands 9.45 metres high. The 907-kilogram aluminum skin is attached to a central mast at a 30-degree angle with 177 turnbuckle struts. Its internal structure weighs a further 1,360 kilograms. All this weight rests on a 12,247-kilogram base of concrete and steel designed to turn in the wind like a weathervane.

Paul Sembaliuk, an expert on traditional Easter egg design, used three colours—bronze, silver, and gold—to symbolize prosperity. The predominant colour of bronze represents the "good earth" on which the Ukrainians struggled for survival and existence. Five distinct symbols, all in silver and gold, make up the design. Three-pointed stars, in alternating gold and silver, represent the Trinity and reflect the strong Christian devotion of the Ukrainians who came to Alberta. A band of silver circumscribing the pysanka symbolizes eternity. Gold and silver windmills with six vanes and points painted on the central barrel section stand for a rich harvest. The design's most prominent motif, silver wolf teeth pointing toward the centre from the silver band, stand for the protection and security afforded the early pioneers by the presence of the then North-West Mounted Police.

The pysanka is situated in Vegreville's Elks' Park.

Railways

Although, as is true for the rest of Canada, the number of branch lines in Alberta is ever shrinking, the province retains an extensive and efficient railroad service. Two railways provide the province with east-west transcontinental service. Canadian National (CN) serves the northern part of the province, with **Edmonton** at the hub. Canadian Pacific (CP) serves the southern portion, centring on **Calgary.**

These two mainlines are linked through the Edmonton-Calgary corridor, which passes through **Red Deer.** Each railroad company operates numerous branch lines for rail car transport of bulk commodities such as grain, lumber, and petrochemicals. Container traffic passes through terminals in both major cities.

The provincial railway grid is linked to the United States' rail networks of Burlington Northern and Southern through the Shelby, Montana, container terminal, which is about 55 kilometres south of the border.

VIA Rail Canada provides limited passenger service using the CN rail line, which runs from Vancouver through **Jasper** to Edmonton and east into Saskatchewan.

Rocky Mountain Railtours offers luxurious rail trips, primarily intended for tourists, that run from Vancouver through **Banff** to Calgary, or alternatively to Jasper via the Monashee Mountains.

Ranching

The first ranches in the Canadian west were established in the 1850s in British Columbia's interior plateau country to supply meat to the Cariboo gold rush fields. But the true bonanza of the Canadian ranching industry was destined to occur in the **foothills** of the eastern slopes of the **Rocky Mountains.** Blessed by warming **chinooks,** this part of Alberta had the best grazing conditions in Canada for fattening cattle. Until 1877, however, the combined factors of an absence of local markets and the occupation of the land by Blackfoot First Nations tribes kept prospective ranchers away.

In 1873 prairie missionary John McDougall and his brother David McDougall arrived at Morley in the Bow Valley, west of present-day **Calgary.** They came from Fort Edmonton with 12 head of cattle and about 50 horses. The next year, when the **North-West Mounted Police** (NWMP) built **Fort Macleod,** the brothers brought a small herd of cattle up from Montana and sold some animals to the NWMP. During this time no attempt was made by the McDougalls or several other small operators who followed in their footsteps to let cattle herds roam and graze freely. The cattle were brought in from outside as mature stock and kept alive for only a short period before being slaughtered and sold.

In 1876, NWMP Sergeant Robert Whitney, intent on leaving the force the following May to try his hand at ranching, bought 25 head of cattle from a Montana rancher. Lacking the feed to carry the animals through the winter, Whitney turned them loose to fend for themselves in the fall. The following spring he succeeded in rounding up the entire herd. They were all healthy and strong after a winter of grazing on grass exposed by chinook melts.

With the signing of Treaty Seven (*see* **First Nations Land Claims** and **First Nations Peoples**) in 1877, the foothills and the great grassy plains fronting them were opened to white settlement. The construction of NWMP posts throughout southern Alberta created a demand for cattle. As well, some retiring police officers opted to establish ranches rather than return to eastern Canada.

No sooner was the treaty signed than Fred Kanouse brought 21 cows and a bull from Montana, allowing them to roam freely across the open range. In the spring of 1877, about 30 NWMP troopers left the force and accepted land grants in the Macleod and Pincher Creek districts.

The first true roundup took place in 1879, with 16 men participating. They discovered that some of the cattle were falling prey to the displaced Blackfoot, who were struggling to avoid mass starvation on their meagre reserve lands. The federal government consequently approved importation of a herd of about 1,000 head from Montana to the Porcupine Hills area west of Fort Macleod. Cattle from this NWMP-administered herd were intended to furnish the Blackfoot with beef. While the herd was poorly managed, resulting in many deaths, it became evident that large herds could thrive in the foothills country.

In 1881, a number of developments opened the way for a ranching boom in southern Alberta. First, the Canadian Pacific Railway was pushing its way rapidly west of Winnipeg and the federal government was obviously committed to its extension to the Rocky Mountains. The **bison** had been mostly slaughtered by this time, so there was no natural competition for the lush grassland. Most important of all, the Land Act of 1881 provided for 21-year leases for up to 40,000 hectares (100,000 acres) per lease for only a penny an acre. (*See* **Cochrane Ranche Historic Site.**) Cattle imported from the U.S. to populate the leased land were allowed in duty free.

Soon such large ranches as the Cochrane Ranche, the **Bar U Ranch,** Oxley Ranch, Winder Ranch, Walrond, and the Quorn were in full swing. In 1883 it was estimated the region had a population of about 75,000 cattle. But in the winter of 1886–87 heavy snows caused nearly half of the cattle in the range lands from the Red Deer River to Texas to perish from starvation. In Alberta, the death rate probably reached three-quarters in most areas. This disaster, which still ranks as the worst in Canadian ranching history, led to the adoption of cutting and storing hay to supplement winter feeding.

Another problem plaguing the ranchers was that open grazing denied them any control over breeding. Bulls wandered freely and mated with any cow they encountered regardless of its brand. Diseases, especially mange, also became a problem, causing Britain to place an embargo on Canadian cattle in the early 1890s.

In 1896 the industry was pushed into serious decline by the election of Wilfred Laurier's Liberal government. The Liberals were determined to open the Canadian west to homestead settlement. To give homesteaders land to settle on the government began dismantling the ranch lease system. Soon many of the vast grazing ranges were lost to an influx of hundreds of settlers bent on farming. Unlike in the United States, however, where cattle ranchers in some areas resisted the changes by terrorizing homesteaders and in isolated cases resorting to violence, the Canadian ranchers confined their resistance to unsuccessful political lobbying.

A High River round-up crew in the 1890s after bedding down a cattle herd for the night. (Glenbow Archives photo, NA-466-19)

In the winter of 1906–1907, the great cattle empires were dealt their final death blows by a bitter, chinook-free winter. Stock losses were in the thousands and the cattle companies never recovered. Thereafter the ranches of Alberta were smaller operations. Albertan cattle seldom graze free today, most fattened instead in confined feedlots. Only a few larger operations and some ranches owned by steadfast traditionalists still run significant herds over the foothills country rangeland.

Ranching, however, remains a significant sector of the **agriculture** industry. Cattle and calf sales account for about $2.2 billion of the $4.2 billion in annual agricultural exports.

Ratless Alberta

There are no rats in Alberta. This is the result of a remarkable, ongoing rat extermination and control program.

Rats first appeared in North America as refugees from the sailing vessels of European explorers. The Norway rat, for example, is believed to have jumped ship in 1775. Over the years, North American–born rats pushed inland from the coastal ports and were eventually established in almost all parts of the continent. While the **Rocky Mountains** serve as an effective, uncrossable hurdle for rats coming from British Columbia, the expanses of the prairies were eventually crossed.

The first rats appeared in southeastern Alberta about 1950. By the fall of 1951, rat infestations were reported in numerous southeastern communities. Three years later the Alberta Department of Agriculture initiated a comprehensive rat control program. The program concentrated on a 29-kilometre-wide rat-control zone along the Saskatchewan border. Utilizing poison and traps, the anti-rat patrols managed to contain and ultimately eliminate the rats that had crossed the border into Alberta.

The program continues today under the auspices of Alberta Agriculture and regional municipalities. About $250,000 a year is spent to keep Alberta ratless.

Rattlesnakes

The open **grasslands** and rocky outcroppings of much of southern Alberta provide ideal habitat for the prairie rattlesnake. This region is at the northern extent of the snake's range. The harsh northern **climate** of Alberta, however, forces prairie rattlesnakes to spend most of their lives in a dormant state, huddled in dens below the frost line.

In May, just after the rattlers emerge from their dens, the females give birth. A baby rattler is born fully equipped with fangs, venom, and a small button on the end of its tail. As the snake grows larger, it must shed its restricting skin. This may occur from two to five times per summer. With each shedding, a new rattle is added to the tail, so the number of rattles does not indicate the precise age of the snake. Adults reach between 1 and 1.5 metres in length.

During the summer months, rattlers range a few kilometres from their dens in search of the small rodents and **birds** that constitute their primary diet. By day, rattlesnakes lie in wait for prey to approach within striking distance—about half the length of their body. A rattler strikes with lightning speed, injecting venom from its extended fangs similarly to the action of a hypodermic needle. The venom soon immobilizes the prey, which the snake then swallows whole.

Rattlers have poor vision, but a keen sense of smell. At night, they also use special heat-sensing pits found between their eyes and nostrils to detect potential victims.

As fall approaches, rattlesnakes return to their dens in preparation for the long winter. By mid-October, they will be underground, waiting for the arrival of warm spring weather.

Prairie rattlesnakes range in colour from olive green to dark brown, making it sometimes difficult to distinguish them from harmless bull snakes. Rattlers, however, always have dark blotches along the back. They can most easily be distinguished from bull snakes by the fact that rattlers have a triangular-shaped head and a tail rattle that can be up to five centimetres long.

Although they are venomous, prairie rattlesnakes are very timid of large animals and will try to avoid humans if given a chance to escape. Their bites are seldom fatal to humans. They will rarely strike at large moving objects unless provoked. Usually, if cornered, they will try to warn away people by making a distinctive buzzing noise with their rattle.

The prairie rattlesnake is an **endangered species,** listed on the province's red—or most threatened—list.

Red Deer

Located halfway between **Calgary** and **Edmonton,** Red Deer takes its name from the river flowing through it. The river received its name as a result of the numerous elk frequenting its shores. The elk were mistakenly identified by Scottish factors of the fur-trading companies for the red deer of their native land.

The original settlement was built in 1882 where the Calgary-Edmonton

Trail crossed the Red Deer River. During the **North-West Rebellion** the Canadian militia constructed a blockhouse named Fort Normandeau at this site. The **North-West Mounted Police** used this site until 1893, but in 1891 the settlement proper was moved seven kilometres downstream to stand beside the newly completed Canadian-Edmonton Railway.

By 1900 the community was prospering due to an influx of homesteaders. It developed primarily as an agricultural service and distribution centre, a role it retains today. Following World War II, discovery of oil and natural gas deposits in the area caused the town to undergo a major boom. By the late 1950s, it was renowned as the fastest-growing city in Canada.

In the late 1970s world-scale petrochemical plants were constructed east of the city at Joffre and Prentiss. This development ensured the petroleum industry's importance to Red Deer's continued prosperity. Its population is about 60,000.

Red River Carts

In 1852, the North Pacific Railway reached the Mississippi River and offered a new route for moving furs to world markets. The Hudson's Bay Company (HBC) realized that furs could be shipped south into the United States to St. Paul, Minnesota. There, they could be loaded onto steamboats and transferred to rail cars further south. The new route would be faster and less expensive than the unwieldy all-water route extending from **Rocky Moun-**

Red River carts such as this one were used by the Hudson's Bay Company to move furs from trading posts throughout Alberta overland to the Mississippi River for export to Britain. (Mark Zuehlke photo)

tain House near the headwaters of the North Saskatchewan River to York Factory on the shores of Hudson Bay. Additionally, the cost and lack of an all-season, ice-free port for shipping furs by boat from Hudson Bay to overseas markets made the St. Paul route more desirable because the furs could be routed out of such ports as New York City or New Orleans.

Unfortunately for the fur-trading company, no network of rivers and lakes linked this route so **York boats** could not be used to haul the cargo. Instead a means of overland travel had to be found.

HBC soon found its answer to this transportation dilemma in the Red River cart. Developed in about 1801 by pioneers at Pembina Post on the Red River, the carts were initially used to carry settlers' goods. With their oversized wheels and rugged, functional construction, the carts were precisely what the HBC needed.

Cart construction was simple and relatively crude; function was more important than design or aesthetic considerations. Two deeply dished wooden wheels up to two metres high were connected by a rough axle. Extending from the axle were two shafts that could be hitched to a horse or ox. The axle and shafts provided a foundation capable of supporting a large box. The various parts of the cart were either connected by wooden dowels or lashed together with leather straps. Metal was seldom involved in any of the construction. Axles were often nothing more than a stout poplar log stripped of its bark.

The oversized wheels enabled the cart to roll easily over bumpy terrain or through thick mud. Relatively light, because of its all-wood construction, the cart was also buoyant and could be floated across rivers. Yet it was amazingly sturdy, capable of carrying loads of 450 kilograms. The turning of the wooden axles within the wheels produced a distinct grinding and squeaking sound. Convoys of HBC carts often extended in a line for two to three kilometres and the sound of their approach could be heard several kilometres away.

At first the HBC used the carts only to haul furs from Fort Garry on the southern shore of Lake Winnipeg over 885 kilometres to St. Paul. But soon an overland route was developed that ran from Fort Edmonton to Upper Fort Garry at the confluence of the Assiniboine and Red rivers, then on to St. Paul—a journey of some 2,400 kilometres.

Religion

Most of Alberta's 2.77 million **population** consider themselves Christians, but the variety of Christian denominations is great. Catholicism is dominant,

*St. Vladimir's
Ukrainian Greek
Orthodox Church at
the Ukrainian
Cultural Heritage
Village. (Mark
Zuehlke photo)*

with about 666,800 Catholic Albertans. Of these, 640,500 are Roman Catholic and most others Ukrainian Catholic.

The United Church follows in prominence with 419,600 members. The numbers drop significantly for the third and fourth most popular Christian churches: some 173,000 Anglicans live in Alberta and 137,000 Lutherans.

From these is another large step down to other Christian denominations: Baptists with 63,750, Pentecostals with 53,000, and Presbyterians with 48,400. The Church of Jesus Christ of Latter-day Saints (more commonly known as Mormons) numbers 45,800.

Non-Christian religions have a relatively small presence in Alberta. There are only about 31,000 Islamic, 20,000 Buddhist, 13,500 Sikh, and 10,750 Hindu followers. A further 2,000 **First Nations peoples** follow traditional aboriginal or Inuit spiritual practices.

A significant population of Albertans profess no religious belief—about 496,000.

Remington-Alberta Carriage Centre

"This hobby can drive you buggy," carriage collector Don Remington once confided. Remington, a Cardston-area rancher, referred to his fascination with horse-drawn carriage collecting.

Remington started collecting carriages in 1954 after the Cardston Rotary Club asked him to organize that year's Santa Claus Parade. Having decided Santa Claus should come into town aboard a sleigh, Remington could only find a small cutter needing restoration. He set to work and shortly before Christmas Santa glided into town aboard a faithfully restored horse-drawn snow sleigh.

Over the next 30 years, Remington assembled a collection of 49 horse-drawn vehicles ranging from elegant carriages to delivery vans. He then offered them all to the provincial government if they agreed to build an interpretive centre to house the collection.

The government agreed and greatly expanded it with vehicles held by the Historical Resources Division of the Department of Community Development and others offered on a long-term loan by **Glenbow Museum.** In 1993, the $13 million Remington-Alberta Carriage Centre opened on an eight-hectare plot of land just off Highway 2 immediately south of Cardston's downtown centre.

Containing more than 200 horse-drawn vehicles, the 5,200-square-metre centre has one of the largest collections of its kind in North America and is considered one of the world's finest displays of any technological history. The main gallery features interactive settings from the 19th-century era of horse-drawn transportation. These include a fire hall, street scene, carriage factory, and various audiovisual productions. The carriage restoration workshop is also open to the public.

Reptiles

Only 8 species of reptiles live in Alberta, although there are about 6,000 in the world. Six of the province's reptile species are snakes, and four are on Alberta's red or blue **endangered species** lists. The blue list includes the western hog-nosed snake and the short-horned lizard. On the red list are **prairie rattlesnakes** and **western painted turtles.**

The western painted turtle has a carapace ranging from 60 to 250 millimetres in size, with those of hatchlings being about 25 millimetres. It is usually found near ponds, lakes, streams, ditches, or marshes where waters are quiet, bottoms sandy or muddy, and aquatic plant life plentiful. This turtle likes to bask on logs, rocks, or banks near water. In winter, it hibernates by burrowing into underwater mud. It eats insects, earthworms, **fish,** frogs, and aquatic plants. Average lifespan is 40 years. Western painted turtles are native to the **Milk River.** They also live in isolated sites in the **Cypress Hills, Banff National Park, Edmonton,** and Hines Creek. These populations are believed to have been introduced.

Alberta has just one lizard species—the short-horned lizard. This is a small lizard, just 40 to 70 millimetres long. Females are considerably larger than males. It lives primarily on south-facing, sagebrush-covered slopes where **prairie** grass meets the rims of **coulees.** The lizard's major food is beetles and ants, a few grasshoppers, and small **invertebrates** that come within its reach. It is active from mid-May to early September. The lizard is found from the southern banks of the South Saskatchewan River to the Montana border, ranging west from the Saskatchewan border to Del Bonita.

The western hog-nosed snake ranges from 400 to 900 millimetres in length, with females larger than males. It prefers sandy locations and damp lowlands, especially areas near water in the **badlands.** It has an upward-lifting snout used for digging. This snake eats toads, frogs, salamanders, other snakes, lizards, turtles, and small rodents. If threatened it spreads a hood at the back of its head, hisses, and strikes. Although mildly venomous to small prey, its venom has no effect on humans. Its range is limited to the short-grass prairie of the southeastern corner of the province—north of the Montana border to the Red Deer River and from the Saskatchewan border to a line running up from Orion to **Medicine Hat.** There may be a small population of western hog-nosed snakes around Drumheller.

Bull snakes are large, ranging from 900 to 2,000 millimetres in length. They have stout bodies and males are sometimes larger than females. Bulls are found mostly in dry grassland or sagebrush areas, where the soil is sandy and there are rock piles and boulders. Killing prey by constriction, bull snakes eat rodents, rabbits, and other small **mammals,** as well as **birds,** birds' eggs, and lizards. They hibernate in dens during winter. Their Alberta range is limited to short-grass prairie from the U.S. border north to about **Calgary,** from Saskatchewan west to the **grasslands** of **Waterton Lakes National Park.**

Alberta's three garter snake species—wandering garter snake, plains garter snake, and red-sided garter snake—are all similar in size and habitat preference. Size ranges from 450 to 1,300 millimetres long. They prefer to live in the vicinity of ponds, marshes, ditches, dugouts, and streams, but the red-sided is also found in forests, farmlands, and urban environments. They eat just about anything small enough to digest, including insects, worms, fish, **amphibians,** other reptiles, small mammals, and birds. All three are mildly venomous but their venom is harmless to humans.

The wandering garter snake is distributed widely south of 52° north latitude to the 2,000-metre level, with scattered populations on the Athabasca and Peace rivers. Anywhere south of **Cold Lake** and east of Calgary can be home for the plains garter snake. It is most common in the province's southeastern corner, however. The red-sided garter snake occurs at scattered locations throughout Alberta. It is mostly confined to **boreal forest** and aspen **parklands.**

The prairie rattlesnake occurs primarily in the province's dry grassland

and sagebrush country. Rattlesnakes are the only venomous snake in Alberta that can be harmful to humans.

In addition to the eight reptile species known to exist in Alberta there are three species whose presence is unconfirmed but possible. These are the snapping turtle, which was introduced in the Battle River area and may exist naturally in the Milk River or creeks south of the Cypress Hills; the rubber boa, a small, 800-millimetre boa snake that may be found in the **Crowsnest Pass** and Waterton Lakes country; and the racer, a snake ranging from 680 to 1,800 millimetres in length, which may occasionally stray across the Montana border into the country south of Milk River.

Reynolds-Alberta Museum

The provincially operated Reynolds-Alberta Museum celebrates the "Spirit of the Machine." More than 100 displays and interactive demonstrations in the main exhibition hall chronicle the history and development of a vast array of machinery used in Alberta from the 1890s to the 1950s.

On display are over 200 antique tractors and steam engines, as well as snowplanes, stationary engines, motorcycles, bicycles, music boxes, telephones, clocks, lamps, military vehicles and equipment, airplanes, and automobiles.

The collection contains more than 90 military vehicles, including trucks, jeeps, tractors, weapons carriers, half-tracks, crash tenders, and amphibian vehicles. There are also firearms, war relics, toys, signs, appliances, and aviation and military memorabilia.

Aircraft range from a 1928 American Eagle to a 1951 Chipmunk. Automobiles include a 1929 Duesenberg Phaeton Royale, donated to the museum in 1993 by its original owner.

The museum regularly mounts special displays. In 1996, for example, it unveiled the largest exhibition of motorcycles ever held in Canada. Entitled Motorcycles Forever, the exhibition featured 120 motorcycles ranging from a 1903 Kerry (the oldest known operating motorcycle in Canada) to 1970s-era bikes, such as a 1973 Triumph Hurricane.

Attached to the museum is Canada's Aviation Hall of Fame. It recognizes the contribution many Canadian flyers and plane owners made to Canada's aviation history. The displays are gathered amidst a collection of vintage aircraft housed in the museum's hangar.

The museum is located one kilometre west of Wetaskiwin, a community of about 10,800 people, situated 68 kilometres south of **Edmonton** via Highway 2A.

Rocky Mountain House

In 1799, both the North West Company (NWC) and Hudson's Bay Company (HBC) constructed fur-trading posts near the junction of the North Saskatchewan and Clearwater rivers. Both companies were hoping to attract Ktunaxa (formerly Kutenai or Kootenay) **First Nations peoples** living on the western side of the **Rocky Mountains.** The NWC post was called Rocky Mountain House, the HBC post Acton House. Following the 1821 merger of the two companies, the NWC post was abandoned and Acton renamed Rocky Mountain House.

In 1835, this post was replaced by a newer one built nearby. The Ktunaxa trade the company sought never materialized because the Blackfoot tribe, determined to keep their traditional foes from getting firearms through trade, violently stopped the Ktunaxa from reaching the fort. As the fort was situated at the northern extremity of their sphere of control, the Blackfoot were, however, unable to prevent the Stoney, Assiniboine, and Cree (all Blackfoot enemies) from trading with Rocky Mountain House.

When the HBC temporarily abandoned the post in 1861, the Blackfoot tried to discourage the traders from returning by burning the post buildings and stockade wall. In 1864 a party of HBC traders returned and hastily erected a small, temporary post to provide protection while they worked on a permanent fort. Construction began in 1865, but a variety of problems, including the near-starvation of personnel during two harsh winters, delayed completion until 1868. This fort remained in operation until its abandonment in 1875.

Today, the only remains of the post are two restored chimneys that have been protected since 1926 as part of Rocky Mountain House National Historic Site. The 228-hectare site contains remains of the five historic forts, one burial ground, an unknown number of buried cultural remains, and a **bison** paddock. Visitor centre and trail interpretive displays detail the history of the forts, the fur trade, and western exploration.

To the northeast of the historic site, on the opposite shore of the North Saskatchewan River, sits the community of Rocky Mountain House, with a population of about 5,400. Its economy is based on **agriculture,** natural-gas processing, the **forest industry,** and **tourism.**

Rocky Mountain Region

The Rocky Mountain region along the **Continental Divide** is underlain primarily by upthrust and folded limestone, dolomite, and quartzite. The breadth of this region varies from about 10 kilometres wide in **Waterton Lakes National Park** to more than 100 kilometres wide west of **Grande Prairie.** It contains Alberta's most rugged topography. Elevations rise from east to west, from most river valleys at 1,000 metres above sea level to ridges of 3,700 metres along the Continental Divide.

The provincial government's **Special Places** natural area protection strategy identifies three subregions within the Rocky Mountain region. They reflect changes in environmental conditions associated with differences in altitude.

- The montane subregion in southern Alberta occurs on east-west trending ridges that extend out from the **foothills.** To the north, this subregion occurs mostly along the major river valleys of the Bow, North Saskatchewan, and Athabasca rivers.

    Chinooks are common and in winter the area is intermittently snow-free. The montane landscape is characterized by a pattern of open forests and **grasslands.** Its forests are among Alberta's driest. The diversity of habitats found in the forests makes them species-rich. Limber pine grows on the most exposed rock outcrops and blends with Douglas fir in more soil-rich areas. Lodgepole pine occurs on upland sites, white spruce grows along streams, and aspen forests are found on terraces. Grasslands are dominated by bluebunch wheat grass, fescue grasses, and oat grasses.

    Douglas fir and limber pine habitats support blue grouse, mule deer, elk, **bears,** and Columbian ground squirrel. Aspen forest is home to **birds,** such as lazuli bunting and MacGillivray's warbler, and **mammals** such as moose, coyotes, and chipmunks. Alberta's spotted frog and long-toed salamander population exists only in this subregion's wetlands.

- The subalpine subregion occupies a band running between the montane and alpine subregions in the south and between the upper foothills and alpine subregions in the north. Freezing temperatures occur in all months here and the frost-free period is likely to be less than 30 days. Winter precipitation is higher in this subregion than in any other part of Alberta, with often more than 200 centimetres of snowfall.

    The lower subalpine is characterized by closed forests of lodgepole pine, Engelmann spruce, and subalpine fir, while the upper subalpine has open forests near the treeline. Whitebark pine forests are scattered in pockets throughout the subregion and subalpine larch grows to the south of Bow Pass. High elevation grasslands are found on steep south- and west-facing slopes. Snow avalanches create a diverse mix of shrubby and herbaceous communities.

Wildlife species of the coniferous forests include spruce grouse, marten, snowshoe hare, black bear, deer mouse, and red squirrel. Subalpine forest birds restricted to Alberta's Rocky Mountain region are Stellar's jay, varied thrush, and willow ptarmigan.

- The alpine subregion includes vegetated areas, bare rock, snowfields, and glaciers above the treeline. It is the coldest subregion in Alberta. Bedrock dominates the landscape and soils are thin, scarce, and weakly developed.

Alpine vegetation is diverse. Deep, late-melting snowbeds are occupied by black alpine sedge communities. Moderate snowbed communities contain dwarf shrub heath and tundra dominated by heathers and grouseberry. Shallow snow areas on ridgetops and other exposed sites shelter snow willow and moss campion. Diverse, colourful herb and wildflower meadows occur in moist sites below melting snow banks or along streams. At the highest elevations lichen is present on many rock surfaces.

Many **mammals** range regularly in both the subalpine and alpine subregions, including Columbian ground squirrel, pika, hoary marmot, grizzly bear, mountain goat, and bighorn sheep. White-tailed ptarmigan, rosy finch, and American pipit are restricted to the alpine subregion, appearing here only during nesting season.

Rocky Mountains

The Canadian section of the Rocky Mountains extends for 1,450 kilometres from **Waterton Lakes National Park** in the south to the Liard River in northern British Columbia. For almost its entire length this mountain range is about 150 kilometres wide. It encompasses a total area of 180,000 square kilometres.

At the Kakwa River, north of **Grande Cache,** a continuing westward drift takes the Rockies outside the western border of Alberta. They also start to subside at this point, dropping to a maximum height of 2,542 metres, with their summits becoming more rounded and forested.

South of Kakwa River to the U.S. border are found the classic summits that typify the popular image of the Canadian Rockies. Here the mountains take on spectacular forms, commonly exceeding 3,000 metres. To its east the range is bordered by low rolling **foothills,** to the west by the longest valley in North America, the Rocky Mountain Trench.

The Rocky Mountains were built by geological forces between 65 and 57 million years ago. During this time enormous pressure caused by the consecutive piling of drifting land masses, known as plates, was exerted in a downward thrust along the western edge of the North American continent. As a piece of paper pushed toward the middle rises in the centre, so too did the land that would become the Rocky Mountains. When the land could rise no further it broke along fracture lines to form faults. Along these faults massive blocks of rock, known as fault blocks, moved upward and northeastward along the major faults. These blocks rose up and over younger rocks, pinning them beneath the larger blocks. All of Mount Rundle, for example, is a huge fault block thrust up over the younger rocks on the floor of the Bow Valley below.

Thrust faulting, as this process is called, proceeded from west to east, so the greatest movement of fault blocks occurred in the western portion. The rocks forming the mountains of **Lake Louise** moved horizontally from 50 to 80 kilometres and were displaced vertically by about 4,300 metres. The thrust-faulting period is believed to have ended about 40 million years ago, although some scientists believe that rock layers continue moving at an imperceptible rate.

To the west of the Rockies, British Columbia's other mountain ranges were subjected to far more violent geological processes that resulted in massive volcanic action. Intense heat and pressure caused by volcanic action formed igneous rock (mainly granite) and, where the heat was intense but incapable of actually melting the rock, metamorphic rock.

The mountain-building forces in the Rockies were much less violent, so the rock here was untouched by such intense heat and pressure. For this reason the rock of the Rockies is sedimentary, usually sandstone, shale, and limestone. There is some metamorphic rock, such as gneiss and slate in the Rockies, and very little igneous rock. **Banff National Park** contains only one small outcrop of igneous rock. It is found alongside the **Icefields Parkway** near the Crowfoot Glacier viewpoint.

Once the mountains had been formed, they began to undergo erosion by wind, water, and ice. It is erosion that has given the Rockies their rugged character and distinctive shape. Ice-age glaciers gouged U-shaped valleys between peaks. After the ice ages, young rivers flowed down from the peaks, cutting narrow canyons and deep V-shaped valleys.

Nine types of mountains are found in the Rockies. They are anticlinal, synclinal, thrust fault, sawtooth, dogtooth, castellate, complex, horn, and totally glaciated.

Anticlinal mountains have rock layers that are arched up into a huge upfold, or anticline. This upfolding usually produces fractures that expose the mountain to erosion. Consequently, anticlinal mountains are extremely rare, but several mountains in the Lake Minnewanka area of Banff National Park are anticlinal.

The rock layers of synclinal mountains downfold into a trough, or syncline. These are quite common, often resulting from erosion of the land surrounding the syncline because the rock at its centre is so intensively compressed it is very resistant to erosion. Cirrus Mountain and Mount Kerkeslin are examples.

Thrust fault mountains have been cut into a mass of layered sedimentary rock inclined at an angle of up to 45°. Often they have a smooth slope following the dip of a rock layer. On the other side a more broken, very steep slope is found. Mount Rundle is a classic thrust fault mountain.

When rocks in a long ridge are upthrust to nearly vertical angles of 60° to 90°, erosion often produces rows of angular mountains resembling the teeth in a saw. The Sawback range parallelling the Bow River between **Banff** and Castle Junction is an example.

Dogtooth mountains are sharp, jagged mountains resulting from erosion of masses of vertical or nearly vertical rock. The peaks are formed of particularly resistant rock left standing after less resistant layers have been eroded away from the flanks. Mount Louis and Mount Norquay are dogtooth mountains.

Castellate rocks are composed of flat-lying sedimentary rock and look somewhat like European feudal-age castles. **Castle Mountain** is the best example.

Complex mountains have been so deformed by intense folding and faulting that classification is impossible. These mountains are simply called complex mountains.

Bowl-shaped depressions called cirques commonly result from glacial erosion on a mountainside. When several glaciers carve a mountain from different sides an isolated tower of rock, known as a horn, is sometimes produced. Mount Assiniboine in the southwestern corner of Banff National Park is a prime example.

When a mountain is totally glaciated its upstream side (the southwest in the Rockies) is rounded and gently sloped, while the downstream side (northeast in the Rockies) is cut sheer by the plucking action of the passing ice. **Tunnel Mountain** is the most accessible example of this kind of mountain.

The Rockies are still young geologically. Their sharp peaks and soaring heights will, over the course of several hundred million years of erosion, eventually be lost, the mountains wearing down to a low plain.

Rodeo

Including the **Calgary Exhibition and Stampede,** there are more than 30 professional rodeos held in Alberta each year. Additionally, countless amateur and community rodeos are staged.

Rodeo traces its roots back to the Spanish verb *rodear,* meaning "to go around." In the 16th century, *vaqueros,* Mexican herdsmen, worked cattle herds from the backs of sturdy horses. They used *la reata* (rope), wore *chaperajos* (leggings), and their styles of riding and roping created a tradition of élan that has shaped the practice of rodeo ever since 1847, when the first rodeo probably took place in the streets of Sante Fe, New Mexico.

Prior to the end of the 19th century, amateur rodeo infected the local giant cattle ranches of what was to become present-day Alberta. Cowhands pushed themselves to the limit to prove they could rope, wrestle, and ride the toughest bulls, steers, and broncos.

By the 1880s, the Fort Macleod Agricultural Fair routinely featured rodeo events. In 1892, renowned Walrond cowboy John Ware was regularly wrestling steers. Raymond, Alberta hosted Canada's first rodeo in 1903. The first major rodeo occurred on September 12, 1912 when "The Last and Best Great West Frontier Days Celebration" mesmerized **Calgary.** The six-day event drew 14,000 people and offered a collective purse of $20,000 to the **cowboys** participating.

In 1944, the Canadian Rodeo Cowboys Association was formed. As time passed more events were added to the slate of typical rodeos and many community rodeos feature unique sports of their own devising, such as greased-pig wrestling, wild cow milking, and mutton busting (children riding sheep).

Rodeos generally contain the following events: bareback bronco riding, saddle bronc riding, bull riding, calf roping, steer wrestling, and barrel racing (the only event for women). Alberta has produced a long list of world rodeo champions. The tradition of rodeo is celebrated at the **Western Heritage Centre** near Cochrane, west of Calgary.

Rough Fescue

The so-called "queen of the grasses," rough fescue is the characteristic native grass of Alberta's **grasslands** region. It is a large, tufted bunchgrass that throws down extremely deep roots—usually close to a metre in depth.

Rough fescue shared its habitat with other native grasses, wildflowers, and shrubs. Together these plants constituted the grasslands plant community.

A highly nutritious grazing grass, rough fescue provided the backbone upon which the Alberta **ranching** industry rested when ranches commanded vast grazing lands—especially those located in the **foothills** country, such as the **Bar U Ranch,** which held over 63,000 hectares of rangeland.

The native grass, however, was slow to grow back when overgrazed. Eventually it was largely pushed aside by plants more tolerant of heavy grazing and—as farming eclipsed ranching in the grasslands tracts—by cultivated crops. Today, rough fescue grasslands exist only in remote, uncultivated areas of the province where there has been minimal livestock grazing.

The rest of the grasslands have been so modified by human use they bear no more than a surface resemblance to the grasslands that thrived here a century ago.

Royal Tyrrell Museum of Palaeontology

The Royal Tyrrell Museum of Palaeontology is one of the world's largest and most prestigious palaeontological museums. It is also an internationally renowned research and exhibition centre. No other museum is devoted entirely to palaeontology—the study of life existing in preceding geological periods through examination of **fossils.**

Situated in the Red Deer River **badlands,** six kilometres west of Drumheller, the museum was opened in 1985. While **dinosaurs** are the museum's main draw, the 11,200-square-metre facility has displays tracking the complete history of **ancient Alberta** over 4.5 billion years. The museum's ever-growing fossil collection contains more than 80,000 specimens, many of which are on display.

Just as they ruled the world during their 150-million-year existence, dinosaurs dominate the museum. In the main gallery, about 50 complete dinosaur skeletons stand within realistic dioramas of the natural habitat in which these monstrous creatures lived. Further insight into the nature of dinosaur habitat is provided by a two-storey subtropical arboretum containing more than 100 living plant species, many of which existed during the Mesozoic Era.

The museum is more than just a showpiece for palaeontology, it is also a research facility. A major part of the complex contains workrooms and laboratories for studying, identifying, quantifying, and storing fossil remains.

In the spring of 1884, 26-year-old Joseph Burr Tyrrell led a Geological Survey of Canada expedition into the largely unstudied southern heart of

Alberta. While paddling down the Red Deer River in a folding canvas canoe, Tyrrell was awestruck by the surrounding badlands. At Kneehills Creek, he discovered an assortment of dinosaur bones that greatly intrigued him. He returned to Kneehills Creek again in August and this time found a dinosaur skull, which was classified as *Albertosaurus sarcophagus,* a three-quarter-size relative of *Tyrannosaurus Rex.*

What Tyrrell had discovered on the shore of Kneehills Creek was a dinosaur graveyard, virtually unmatched in its size or importance anywhere in the world. This massive dinosaur quarry lies close to the present-day museum. Tours and museum-organized day digs enable visitors to go into the digging sites themselves.

Until the late 1970s, most fossils unearthed in Alberta left the province to go to other museums and university facilities possessing palaeontological research staff and equipment. Dismayed by this practice, Albertan Dr. Philip Currie started promoting the creation of an Alberta palaeontological museum and research facility. His work was principally responsible for the establishment of the museum.

More than 400,000 people visit the Tyrrell Museum annually. The museum also operates a satellite facility, the Field Station, at **Dinosaur Provincial Park.** Opened in 1987, the Field Station houses permanent and changing displays based on ongoing research in the park. It offers educational programs and tours. Both the Royal Tyrrell Museum and Field Station are operated by the Alberta government.

Special Places

In Alberta the phrase special places has unique meaning. It refers to an initiative called Special Places: Alberta's Natural Heritage, sometimes also called Special Places 2000. This provincial government program is a strategic plan for coordinating the designation and preservation of Alberta's many diverse natural landscapes. The strategy is part of a larger program aimed at conserving the world's natural heritage and so supports similar initiatives at provincial, national, and international levels.

In the early 1990s the Canadian federal and provincial governments committed to the World Wildlife Fund Endangered Spaces Program, whereby a commitment was made to adequately preserve self-sustaining and representative samples of all forms of natural landscapes found within a government's jurisdiction. Special Places is a made-in-Alberta strategy intended to meet the province's commitment to the World Wildlife Fund program.

The vision of Special Places is to create a network of landscapes that together preserve the environmental diversity of Alberta's 6 natural regions and the 20 subregions found within them. Rather than aggressively protecting this network inside a system of parks where no development or exploitation of natural resources would be permitted, the province opted to try balancing preservation with three other goals, which it termed cornerstones. These are heritage appreciation, outdoor recreation, and **tourism**/economic development. The government describes this approach as ensuring "there is a balance between our environmental priorities and our economic realities and will help meet the objectives of sustainable development."

Some areas are closed to such economic pursuits as oil exploration and drilling, livestock grazing, mining, logging, and development of ski resorts. In other areas, including some **provincial parks** and wilderness areas, these kinds of activity are permitted with varying degrees of restrictions. Environmental critics have argued that opening up any special places to such uses derails the central objective of the strategy—to preserve the purity and ecological integrity of the landscapes.

While the debate over the value of the program continues, the effort to identify, classify, and designate special places throughout the province proceeds. In some cases, such as **prairie** grassland, many remaining natural areas are privately owned. One of the biggest challenges facing the special places initiative is to create the means whereby private landowners can be enticed to allow these lands to be protected.

The designation of special places is based upon trying to protect representative samples of each of the six natural regions: **grasslands, parklands, foothills, Rocky Mountain region, boreal forest,** and **Canadian Shield.** Within each of these broader regions is a series of subregions totalling 20. The land classification for each protected area is based on natural or biogeographic features, such as geology, landform, soils, and hydrology. Other factors affecting classification include an area's **climate,** vegetation, and wildlife.

Each region and subregion, whether large or small, contains a pattern of features clearly distinguishable from other regions and subregions. Even the subregions may be broken down to smaller categories referred to as either level I, level II, or level III themes. Level I themes contain a complex of physical and biological features that are readily apparent. Twenty level I themes have been identified in Alberta. An example is sandy upland–dune fields, which is one of 13 level I themes in the dry mixed-grass subregion of the grasslands natural region, which encompasses most of southern Alberta west of the foothills. The dunes of Middle Sand Hills National Wildlife Area are an example of level I area.

A level II theme contains a distinct mix of vegetation, habitat type, or highly visible geology. Active sand that is not held in place by vegetation within the sandy upland–dune fields is an example of a level II theme.

Level III themes are even finer breakdowns of level II themes. They include specific plant community types and wildlife habitats, rare plants and animals, and specific bedrock and landform types. The Ord's kangaroo rat is a level III theme because it is found nowhere else in Alberta but in association with areas of active sand (a level II theme). The western spider-wort flower is a level III theme because it occurs in only one Alberta location, the active sand dunes around Pakowki Lake, northeast of **Writing-On-Stone Provincial Park.**

Stephansson House Historic Site

On June 27, 1888, 50 Icelandic settlers from North Dakota homesteaded at Markerville, southwest of present-day **Red Deer.** For many this was their third attempt to develop a successful farming-based community in North America. Drought, debt, and crop failures had doomed their earlier attempts in Wisconsin and North Dakota. The following year another Icelandic group from North Dakota joined the first in response to reports of Markerville's plentiful feed for livestock, wood for homes and fuel, and readily available **water** and **fish.** Among the new arrivals was Stephán Gudmundsson Stephansson, who had fled western Iceland because of its tenant-farmer system, crop failures, and incessant volcanic activity.

Like his neighbours, Stephansson made his living primarily by working a small homestead farm. At night, however, working by the light of a coal-oil lamp, he wrote poetry. Writing in Icelandic, Stephansson turned out a massive collection of work. His poetry and articles were initially little acclaimed in Canada but by 1894 he emerged as a leading literary force in his native Iceland and in Icelandic immigrant communities around the world.

His poetry focused on his concern with contemporary political issues, his Icelandic heritage, and his ever-deepening love for Alberta—especially the natural landscape of the **Rocky Mountains** and its **foothills.** Romantic realist, socialist, pacifist, advocate of women's rights, and a satirist, Stephansson by the early 20th century gained a reputation as an advocate of radical leftist politics that did not sit well with many contemporary non-Icelandic Albertans. Despite this, his poetry about Alberta won him the sobriquet "Poet of the Rocky Mountains" and soon he was recognized internationally as one of the greatest poets in the western world.

Throughout his life Stephansson remained highly active in Markerville's community organizations, including the cooperative creamery, which became a community economic mainstay.

He died in 1927. Today, Stephansson's homestead house has been restored to its appearance at the time of his death. Costumed guides provide interpretive programs and house tours. Interpreters engage in wool spinning, baking, household chores, and farm work. Poetry readings are also staged in the same way they would have been during the 1920s.

Nearby, the Historic Markerville Creamery, which closed in 1972, also profiles the lives and traditions of the community's Icelandic settlers. Descendents of the Icelandic settlers still constitute a significant percentage of the community's population.

Symbols

Alberta has a number of official symbols and emblems that serve to represent the province both at home and abroad and reflect its natural and historical heritage.

The coat of arms was granted by King Edward VII on May 30, 1907. The arms consist of the following: at the base a wheatfield surmounted by **prairie,** overlooked by **foothills,** the snow-capped peaks of the **Rocky Mountains,** an azure sky, and then St. George's Cross. Above this is the crest composed of a helm with wreath argent and gules, a beaver couchant upholding on its back the royal crown. Supporting the shield on one side is the lion, on the other a **pronghorn** antelope. Beneath the shield is a grassy mount with the floral emblem of the province. The province's official motto is printed at the bottom of the coat of arms: *Fortis et Liber* (Strong and Free). The crest and supporters were granted to Alberta on July 13, 1980 by Queen Elizabeth II.

The provincial flag consists of the province's shield taken from the coat of arms centred against a blue background. It was adopted on May 1, 1968, with approval granted by Queen Elizabeth II. The flag's proportions are two by length and one by width, with the arms covering seven-elevenths of the flag's width.

The following are other official symbols: flower—wild rose, bird—great horned owl, mammal—bighorn sheep, tree—lodgepole pine, stone—petrified wood. Blue and gold are the official provincial colours. The province's tartan has the following colours: green, representing Alberta's forests; gold, for its wheat fields; blue, symbolizing the skies and lakes; pink, reflecting the official flower; and black, standing for the coal and petroleum industries.

Threatened Wildlife. *See* **Endangered Species.**

Tipis

The conical skin-and-frame dwelling called a tipi provided an efficient form of shelter for the nomadic **First Nations peoples** of the Great Plains, including the plains peoples of Alberta. Combining both aesthetic and utilitarian features, the tipi was a perfect solution to the problem of constructing a dwelling in an often harsh, largely treeless environment.

It was a highly sophisticated construction. The high roofline and the smoke flaps allowed a fire to burn within, while an inner liner prevented drafts.

An average tipi was four to seven metres in diameter at the base and about seven to eight metres high. Up to 24 overlapping poles constituted the frame and gave the structure its distinctive conical shape. A sewn cover of about 8 to 12 **bison** skins was cut and designed to fit snugly over the poles

Traditional Blackfoot tipi overlooking the plains of southwestern Alberta. (Mark Zuehlke photo)

and conform to their shape. The entire structure could easily be broken down into parts and transported to the next camp.

A tipi entrance usually faced east in deference to the Creator and the sunrise. In southern Alberta this also served the practical purpose of sheltering the opening from the prevailing western winds.

In ancient times, the tipi's bottom edge was held down by rocks, which were usually left in place when the tipi was moved. These circles of stone, called tipi rings, are still found in various parts of southern Alberta.

Tipi construction and size evolved over the ages. Prior to the appearance of the horse, tipis were smaller because of the need to transport them by dog-pulled travois. By the 19th century, however, horses could be used to transport tipis and they could consequently be much larger. Often, these tipis could house several nuclear families. Some were embroidered with quillwork and painted, such improvements greatly enhancing the status of the owners.

The space within a tipi was carved up and assigned various uses, just as a modern house's different rooms serve specialized purposes. Some areas were for sleeping, others for ceremonial use or cooking.

Tornadoes

Visible as funnel clouds hanging down from dark thunderheads, tornadoes (sometimes called twisters) are wildly rotating columns of air. In area terms, tornadoes are one of the smallest of storms, limited to the tens or hundreds of metres in diameter. The visible funnel cone moves erratically across the ground. Most tornadoes in Canada are considered weak; their speeds average only 40 to 65 kilometres per hour, compared to a potential speed of 509 kilometres per hour. Some Canadian tornadoes, however, have been extremely powerful and caused much damage, loss of life, and human injury. Alberta has often been struck by such devastating storms.

Damage from a tornado is caused at ground level where the narrowest part of the funnel touches the earth during its journey. A tornado storm can be composed of a single funnel, several funnels occurring simultaneously, one or more funnels reforming one after the other, or combinations of these states.

A tornado's life cycle consists of three stages. The first occurs when a funnel-shaped protuberance called a tuba develops beneath the southwest flank of a thunderstorm. The base of the storm cloud at this point will have begun rotating due to rapidly changing air pressure and opposing winds. The tuba elongates downwards from the cloud and is enveloped by a rotating sleeve known as the annulus. The annulus grows upward from the ground toward the descending tuba, both created by the tremendous changes in local air pressure. Once the two bodies of air have merged, a mature tornado vortex has been created. This is the stage that causes damage. The final stage occurs when the tornado degenerates and the tuba rises back into the cloud base and disappears.

Tornadoes almost always rotate in a clockwise direction in the northern hemisphere (anticlockwise in the southern hemisphere) when viewed from below the cloud. When a violent tornado exceeds 400 kilometres per hour, the air pressure inside the cone can drop to less than 90 percent of the normal atmospheric pressure outside the cone. The atmospheric disruption caused by the tornado will usually produce accompanying outbursts of lightning, torrential rain, and barrages of hailstones. The destruction caused by a tornado storm can be tremendous.

Because tornadoes strike suddenly, there is seldom much or any warning, so escaping from their path is virtually impossible. Escape is made even more difficult by the erratic tracks tornadoes follow and the possibility of multiple funnels striking a narrowly confined area. Powerful tornadoes can demolish buildings, derail trains, lift large vehicles off the ground, uproot trees, twist steel girders, and dismember people and animals.

Late June to early July is prime tornado season, and from 3:00 to 7:00 p.m. is the most common time for the storms. June is the peak month for tornadoes exceeding 180 kilometres per hour. Tornadoes do occur outside this peak period, at almost any time between April and October, or approximately 160 days of the year.

While Ontario and Manitoba are the worst areas in Canada for tornadoes, Alberta also has a significant danger zone. It extends through central Alberta from just north of **Edmonton** south to **Calgary** and east to the Saskatchewan border in an ever-narrowing front that extends from about Provost in the north to Sibbald in the south. Tornadoes can occur throughout most of the rest of Alberta, but are somewhat less frequent. They are extremely rare north of **Lesser Slave Lake** or along the **foothills.**

The worst tornado in Alberta's recorded history struck on July 31, 1987. It dropped a series of funnels that swept through parts of southeast and northeast Edmonton. As the storm passed it flattened residences, destroyed an industrial park, devastated a trailer park, blew apart a huge oil tank, wrecked hundreds of motor vehicles, and knocked over transmission towers. In its wake the storm left 27 people dead, most of whom were caught in the trailer park, and more than 300 injured. Thousands of others lost their homes. Insurance companies estimated the total claims at more than $250 million. Hailstones added to the damage and injury toll, with some stones weighing 2.64 kilograms.

There has been speculation that the number of tornadoes occurring annually is increasing, but climatologists say the number remains static. The perceived increase is really the result of improved reporting techniques and increasing human **population,** ensuring that tornadoes are sighted and reported.

This argument is backed up by the historical record. Although the total deaths are fewer and the damage recorded also less, incidences of tornadoes were recorded by early Europeans coming into Alberta. With settlement came increasing numbers of deaths from tornadoes. On July 30, 1918, a tornado killed three children in Vermilion. Either the same tornado or one nearby also destroyed the grandstand at Wainwright's exhibition grounds.

Forty tornadoes were reported in central Alberta over a two-day period on July 7 to 8, 1927. More than 60 farms had grain bins, barns, and homes destroyed. Three people were killed.

The worst tornado in Canadian history occurred in Saskatchewan at Regina on June 30, 1912. It left 28 dead, hundreds injured, and caused $6 million in damage.

Tourism

Alberta's third-largest economic sector is tourism, following energy and **agriculture.** Approximately 100,000 people work in this sector, which generates more than $3 billion annually in provincial revenues. Almost half of this income, about $1.4 billion, is realized from out-of-province visitors.

Most of this tourist activity has historically focused on Alberta's two major national parks—**Banff National Park** and **Jasper National Park**—with major events, such as the **Calgary Exhibition and Stampede,** drawing large numbers for a short period. Increasingly, however, tourist traffic is being drawn into other regions of the province. Encouraging this diversity of tourist destination is the development of some prime attractions and parks throughout the province, which often have the same effect as anchor stores in a shopping mall. The **Royal Tyrrell Museum of Palaeontology** at Drumheller, for example, packs in more than 375,000 visitors a year—visitors who are then likely to go on to visit **Dinosaur Provincial Park** and other nearby destinations. **Head-Smashed-In Buffalo Jump,** near **Fort Macleod,** is also emerging as one of the province's major tourist attractions.

The provincial government projects that the role of tourism in Alberta's **economy** will continue to grow, ensuring its position as the third most important economic sector.

Trumpeter Swans

The trumpeter swan is a North American species numbering about 20,000— the world's rarest swan. Of this population about 1,200 nest in Alberta, making the province a vital habitat for the world's largest waterfowl species. The trumpeter swan has been listed as rare by the Committee on the Status of Endangered Wildlife in Canada and the Alberta government has listed them as vulnerable to extinction.

Trumpeter swans used to breed in **boreal forest, parklands,** and **prairie** habitats throughout Canada and the United States from James Bay to the **Rocky Mountains,** south to Missouri and Wyoming. In Canada, they nested throughout central regions of Alberta, Saskatchewan, and Manitoba as well as along the James Bay coast of Ontario and Quebec. Indiscriminate hunting by European settlers for meat and down, as well as habitat disturbance, reduced the once vast flocks to virtual extinction by the early 1900s. In 1930, the only known breeding population was in Yellowstone National Park in Wyoming.

During the 1930s an international program to save the species was initiated. The program has proven relatively successful. Populations in the United States have increased to such numbers that they have been removed from endangered lists in that country. In Canada, the population remains vulnerable. Locations of breeding flocks in Canada are found in the Yukon, northern British Columbia, the southwestern Northwest Territories, and in the **Grande Prairie** and **Peace River** region of Alberta.

The majority of the Alberta flock is concentrated on lakes and sloughs near Grande Prairie. Bear Lake and Sinclair Lake are the two most common staging points here for the trumpeter flocks. Saskatoon Island Provincial Park, encompassing Little Lake, is one of the few areas in Canada where nesting swans can be easily observed by humans. Other nesting populations are found near Cardston, Edson, various lakes north of Peace River, and lakes north of St. Paul. Nesting pairs have been reintroduced to **Elk Island National Park.**

Trumpeter swans are identifiable by their loud, low-pitched buglelike call, which clearly distinguishes them from the more common tundra swan (formerly known as whistling swan), which has a more tuneful, whistling call. Their neck significantly exceeds body length. Except for a black bill and feet, and a red border on the lower mandible of the bill, they are completely white. Trumpeters average 150 centimetres in length, weigh up to 12 kilograms, and have a wingspan of 2.1 to 2.4 metres.

A migratory bird, they are found in Alberta in spring, summer, and fall. Unlike some migratory **birds,** trumpeters do not fly long distances—they will fly only far enough to reach suitable habitats for nesting or wintering. They arrive in Alberta in April, moving north as lakes and sloughs become free of ice. Trumpeters require shallow lakes with an abundant supply of aquatic plants, insects, and snails. With freeze-up, migration southward begins. Most birds from Grande Prairie will migrate only as far south as Yellowstone National Park or the Snake River in eastern Idaho.

Trumpeter swans retain strong ties to their nesting areas, returning to the same lake and even nesting site year after year. The birds live up to 35 years in captivity, but seldom longer than 12 years in the wild. Trumpeter swans usually mate for life or until one dies, pairing off at about three years of age. Average clutch size varies from three to nine eggs.

Swans will not nest on lakes intensively developed for recreation. Motorboat activity on Wembley and Crystal lakes near Grande Prairie, for example, drove away the trumpeter swan breeding population.

All swans are completely protected in Canada from hunting, and killing a swan is illegal.

Tunnel Mountain

This mountain east of **Banff** is named after an unrealized dream. In 1882 a surveyor working for the Canadian Pacific Railway suggested that the then under construction trans-Canada line should proceed westward via a 275-metre tunnel bored through the mountain's core. Although the same engineer subsequently found a route for the railway that avoided the costly enterprise of the tunnel, the mountain has since borne the name he gave it.

Turner Valley Oil and Gas Field

Along the Sheep River natural gas had bubbled out of the banks for centuries before the first Europeans discovered it. For decades they could see little use for the discovery, although legend holds that during cattle drives **cowboys** sometimes fried bacon and eggs over the gas seepages. In the early 1900s Okotoks rancher William S. Herron bought up the land bordering the Sheep River west of Black Diamond. After capturing some of the gas in a bottle and having it analysed, he formed Calgary Petroleum Products (CPP) and started drilling for oil.

Previously only traces of petroleum had been discovered in western

Canada, but the CPP wells in Turner Valley yielded more promising results. On May 14, 1914, the third well, drilled by A. W. Dingman and consequently named "Dingman No. 1," struck a rich deposit at a depth of 823 metres. The Turner Valley oil boom had begun.

Soon Herron, now with Dingman and many other Calgarians as partners in his CPP operation, brought in a compressor and installed a separator to recover the gasoline. Near the end of 1914 an absorption plant was constructed to improve the gasoline recovery process. This was the second such plant in the world. The rapid expansion repeatedly outran the company's revenues and CPP teetered perilously on the verge of bankruptcy.

On October 20, 1920, a fire demolished the expensive absorption plant. Herron was forced to sell out to the Imperial Oil Company. Imperial created a subsidiary, Royalite Oil Company Ltd., to develop a new processing plant and manage the Turner Valley fields. The company built a new absorption plant and started running natural gas through a 15-centimetre line to Okotoks. By 1922, Turner Valley was supplying **Calgary** with natural gas.

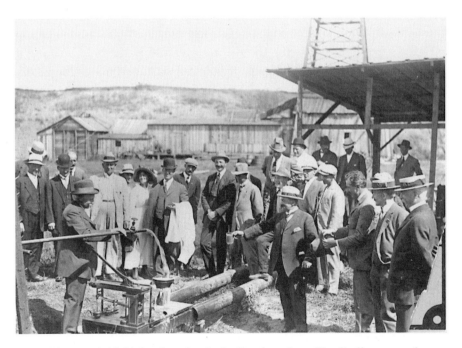

A. W. Dingman (with his hand on the pipe leading from the wellhead) offers mugs of crude oil to dignitaries during a visit by the Duke of Connaught to Dingman well No. 1 on July 28, 1914. (Glenbow Archives photo, NA-2119-4)

That same year Royalite began drilling deeper wells. On October 14, 1924, Royalite #4 reached 1,140 metres and pierced a reserve of sulphur-laden gas. The well burst into flames. Specialists from Oklahoma had to be called to put the blaze out with dynamite. By channelling the gas through two frost-encased pipes, the waste natural gas was flared off in a coulee northeast of the town. The seared coulee country was soon called Hell's Half Acre because of the ferocity of the blaze and its foul odour. This was the only solution the company could devise, until it could develop some way to eliminate the hydrogen sulphide content.

A solution was soon found. Using steam-driven blowers, Royalite mixed the hydrogen sulphide with air and propelled it up two tall stacks to be carried away by the prevailing westerly winds. This gave Turner Valley a dubious reputation for spreading foul, noxious odours all the way to Calgary when the winds were right, but some proudly declared it smelled "like money."

They were partially right because the gas processing plant was the main source of employment in Turner Valley, but oil yielded the greater profit. Well into the 1930s, the oil companies operating in Turner Valley continued to flare off much of the natural gas to keep oil production costs down and profits up. In 1938, however, the Alberta government recognized that flaring off excess gas was destroying the natural pressure in the field, making it harder to move oil to the wellheads. To stop the waste and maximize the oil-fields' economic potential the government founded the Petroleum and Gas Conservation Board, which established some measure of control over the industry's operations. By the end of World War II the Turner Valley oilfields were beginning to be depleted, but the natural gas operations would continue for many more years.

From the 1930s to the 1950s the Turner Valley Gas Plant was a technological leader. In 1935 and 1941 the first sour gas scrubbing plants of their type in Canada were installed, Canada's first propane plant was opened in 1949, and one of Canada's first two sulphur plants began operation in 1952. The plant remained operational until 1985. In 1988 the facility was donated to the provincial government and in 1996 it was declared a national historic site. Parks Canada and Alberta's Historic Sites Service now work together to protect, develop, and provide interpretive services at the large complex of gas works located just south of the community of Turner Valley.

Ukrainian-Canadian Albertans

Ukrainian Canadians constitute the third-largest ethnic group in Alberta. Although today largely distributed throughout Alberta's **population,** the historical roots of this community centre on land extending east of **Edmonton** to the Saskatchewan border.

Most Ukrainians came to Canada in one of three distinct immigrations. The largest and most influential immigration pulse was the first, occurring between 1891 and 1914. At the time of this immigration phase the Russian Empire controlled about four-fifths of the Ukraine, the remainder being part of the Austro-Hungarian Empire.

The majority of Canada's Ukrainian immigrants came from the provinces of Galicia and Bukovyna—both inside Austro-Hungarian borders. Over 75 percent were from eastern Galicia and a smaller, but significant, percentage from Bukovyna.

Galicia was dominated politically and economically by Poles; Bukovyna's local power rested in the hands of Romanians (both Romania and Poland formed part of the Austro-Hungarian Empire). Because of Polish domination, Ukrainians from Galicia were primarily members of the Greek Catholic Church—a hybrid that combined Russian Orthodox faith with elements of Roman Catholic doctrine. Bukovynian Ukrainians remained Orthodox in their faith.

Regardless of location or faith, most Ukrainians were desperately poor and politically oppressed. Landholdings were shrinking, rural areas were becoming overpopulated, malnutrition was widespread, farming methods were primitive, illiteracy was common, and most peasants were in debt. Many Ukrainians despaired of being able to survive in their native land and interest in emigration to other countries was high.

The desire of Ukrainians to emigrate coincided with a new initiative by the Canadian government to encourage immigration to the Prairies. This initiative, led by Clifford Sifton, actively established organizations to seek out settlers in east-central Europe. Sifton figured that these "stalwart peasants in sheep-skin coats" would make ideal settlers for turning more difficult regions of the west into productive farms.

In 1891, two Galician peasants, Ivan Pylypiw and Vasyl Eleniak, arrived in Canada to investigate the possibility of immigration. The following year the first Ukrainian immigrants arrived and established a colony at Edna-Star (now known as Vegreville), east of Edmonton. Pylypiw and Eleniak both homesteaded in this settlement, established here because a group of Galician Germans known to Pylypiw lived nearby.

Ukrainian immigration to Canada boomed. Most desired to settle between Edmonton and the Saskatchewan border where a strong community was becoming established. English Canadians in Alberta quickly became hostile to this concentration of people from another culture in an enclave of their own and the government moved to distribute new settlers into other areas. Despite this effort, however, Ukrainian immigrants continued to concentrate in the Vegreville region.

Prior to World War I, approximately 170,000 Ukrainians immigrated to Canada. Most settled in Manitoba, but many also came to Alberta and Saskatchewan. All immigration from Ukraine ceased for the duration of World War I.

Although 10,000 Ukrainian Canadians enlisted and fought in Europe for Canada, the Ukrainian community found itself increasingly under attack because the Austro-Hungarian Empire had aligned with Germany against the British Commonwealth and other Allied nations. The pretext that Ukrainian Canadians were enemy sympathizers or "enemy aliens" was used to justify extensive discrimination and repression.

About 6,000 Ukrainians were interned in labour camps, mostly built inside the boundaries of Banff and Jasper national parks. All Ukrainians were required to register with the government and to report regularly to the nearest government office. Anyone failing to do so was interned, as were all unemployed Ukrainian men—including those who were fired from their jobs because they were considered enemy aliens. Ukrainian immigrants who had not been naturalized Canadian citizens for more than 15 years were disenfranchised by the Wartime Elections Act. This Act was introduced by Prime Minister Robert Borden, leader of the coalition pro-conscription Conservative and Liberal Union government. Historians have since generally agreed that Borden's motivation was to ensure that the generally pro–Liberal Party and anti-conscription–minded Ukrainians and other ethnic groups would not be able to cast ballots that might endanger his government's chance of re-election.

The anti-Ukrainian actions taken in World War I were reflective of widespread discrimination against eastern European immigrants by the Anglo-Canadian majority. As most Anglo-Canadians believed that the British Commonwealth and British society were the penultimate expression of humankind's potential, they disdained people of visibly different cultures and races.

The highly visible peasant dress of Ukrainians and their agricultural and cultural practices distinguished them dramatically from Anglo-Canadian society. Ukrainians were stereotyped by Anglo-Canadians as dirty, immoral, unintelligent, unenterprising, drunkardly, and fond of fighting among themselves. Yet, they were also recognized as necessary for the hard work of settling hostile tracts of agricultural land.

The solution was to undertake an extensive program of anglicization, primarily carried out in the public schools. In addition to teaching English, and generally prohibiting the speaking of Ukrainian inside the schools, public school teachers working in Ukrainian communities sought diligently to instill Ukrainian children with a sense of British patriotism and British social values. Attempts by the Ukrainian community in Alberta to introduce bilingual, certified Ukrainian teachers into some schools resulted in the Department of Education refusing to accept their certification (obtained in Saskatchewan and Manitoba), cancelling their permits, and refusing to pay salaries owed. With the ability to preserve their language and culture blocked in public schools, many Ukrainians turned to private educational institutions. Not until 1959 would Ukrainian be taught in Alberta public schools, and then only in high school.

Assimilation policies and efforts by the government, and Presbyterian, Methodist, and later United churches largely failed. By 1931 only 1.6 percent of Ukrainian Canadians in Alberta were members of the United Church. Most remained faithful to the Greek Catholic or Orthodox faiths.

In the period between the two world wars another surge of about 68,000 Ukrainians immigrated to Canada. In 1941, the Ukrainian population in Alberta stood at 71,868.

A further wave of Ukrainian immigration to Canada occurred with the resettlement of Europeans displaced by World War II. About 34,000 Ukrainians came to Canada as displaced persons, but most settled in Ontario.

The immigrants from these last two pulses differed from the first in many ways. The majority were well educated and from nonagricultural backgrounds. Although some settled in the traditional Ukrainian-Canadian enclaves, most sought out homes in the country's urban areas.

By 1981, the number of Ukrainians in Alberta had risen to 136,710, eclipsing both Manitoba and Saskatchewan. But by the 1980s, Ukrainian Canadians were—like most other Canadians—primarily urban, Canadian born, and indistinguishable from their neighbours. By 1981 only 17.9 percent of Ukrainian Canadians used Ukrainian as the dominant language in their home, although studies show that Ukrainian is used more often on a daily basis in Edmonton than in any other major Canadian city.

In recent years, perhaps in response to the federal government's encouragement of multiculturalism, there has been a strong resurgence of interest by Ukrainian Canadians in rediscovering their heritage. Ukrainian dancing, **pysanka** (Easter egg) making, embroidery, and cooking are attracting many Ukrainians who wish to preserve the culture of their ancestors. Other Albertans have also embraced aspects of Ukrainian culture, so its impact upon all Alberta is increasingly visible.

Ukrainian Cultural Heritage Village

The Ukrainian Cultural Heritage Village is an open-air museum of some 30 historic buildings and other attractions located 50 kilometres east of **Edmonton** on Highway 16, just east of **Elk Island National Park.** Displays and period-costume actors present the early history of east-central Alberta (from 1892 to 1930) through the eyes of the predominantly Ukrainian **population.**

This village never actually existed. Its buildings, their furnishings, and inhabitants are drawn from a cross-section of communities and periods of real life in east-central Alberta. The buildings have been moved from other sites and faithfully restored. The dress and actors' presentations of the experiences of early Ukrainian settlers are also accurate in detail.

The "living history" method of interpretation is highly developed at the centre. Visitors find themselves chatting in front of a *burdei* (sod hut) with a Ukrainian woman whose husband is off working in the mines to earn money to support

A period-costume actor at the Ukrainian Cultural Heritage Village portrays a Ukrainian pioneer woman living in a burdei. (Mark Zuehlke photo)

their land clearing efforts. Or visitors might be chastened in a public school for not showing proper respect for the King of England, or be suddenly cast as first-time farmers, learning the ropes of how to deliver grain to the elevator operator.

A keystone fixture at the village is the Historic Children's Program, a week-long summer day camp that has operated since 1989. Youngsters from grades two to six can experience Ukrainian immigrant life directly by becoming members of a family portrayed at the village. (Each household recreates the reality of a particular Ukrainian-Canadian family's experience.)

As part of the process, participants have to decide through debate whether to emigrate from Ukraine to Canada. Once they make the fateful decision passports are acquired and trunks packed. At the village the children learn a variety of once-common skills, such as how to grind wheat, cook on a wood stove, and feed farm animals. They also spend time roleplaying and interacting with other village visitors.

The village is open during the summer months. It is also the site of Ukrainian Day in July, an annual event that includes performances by dancers, singers, choirs, and bands from all over Alberta.

Unique Claims to Fame

Many communities across Alberta have unique attributes, works of public art, or museums that are used to promote **tourism** or to celebrate the town's identity.

St. Paul, northeast of **Edmonton,** has the world's only Unidentified Flying Object (UFO) landing pad. Construction of the pad was completed on June 3, 1967. It was built to celebrate Canada's Centennial. The platform stands alongside the town's main road. All the provincial and territorial flags are on display to add an element of formal ceremony should alien ambassadors arrive. There is also a time-safe built into the platform, scheduled for opening on June 3, 2067.

Chauvin, southeast of Wainwright, has the world's largest softball on display. Donalda, near Stettler, is home to the world's largest lamp museum. Torrington, south of **Red Deer,** offers a gopher museum where more than 50 stuffed gophers are dressed up and displayed in scenes ranging from a wedding to a fashion show. The idea is to illustrate what life would be like in Torrington if the community were occupied by gophers given to human behaviour and dress. Glendon, west of **Cold Lake,** has the world's largest pyrogy. Hardisty, southwest of Wainwright, claims to be the "Flag Capital of the World." Sexsmith, Vulcan, and Three Hills all lay claim to the title of

Glendon celebrates its status as the pyrogy capital of Canada with a statue depicting the world's largest pyrogy, fittingly speared by a fork. (Regan Paynter photo)

wheat capital of Canada. To the west of Edmonton, Wildwood, with some 140 regularly scheduled bingos, asserts itself as the bingo capital of Canada.

Morinville, north of Edmonton, has the largest toque in the world. It took 136 volunteers six weeks to knit and measures 13 metres wide by 5 metres high.

Edmonton boasts all sorts of world's largest things besides the **West Edmonton Mall.** On display at various commercial locations around the city are the world's largest hammer (weighing 315 kilograms), the world's biggest shopping bag (10.5 metres high by 5.5 metres wide), the world's largest milk bottle (built in 1928 and weighing 8 tonnes), the world's largest Santa Claus (a nine-metre balloon with a deflated weight of 149 kilograms), and the world's largest cowboy boot (12 metres tall and weighing 35 tonnes).

Vegreville. *See* **Pysanka.**

Water

More than 90 percent of the entire water supply of the Canadian prairies originates in Alberta, primarily in the watersheds of the **Rocky Mountains** and their **foothills.** The resulting distribution system flowing out of these watersheds runs mainly to Hudson Bay via the North and South

Saskatchewan rivers and to the Arctic Ocean via the Slave River system. The **Milk River** drains the extreme southern portion of Alberta to the Gulf of Mexico.

The Slave River, receiving all of the vast Peace River and Athabasca River drainage, has the largest flow and relatively small annual and seasonal variations. Other rivers drain much smaller basins, with most of their flow obtained from the mountains and foothills of the Rockies. The rivers and streams of the southern plains are even smaller and experience highly variable seasonal and annual fluctuations.

Many of Alberta's rivers draw water from glaciers and snowfields in the Rocky Mountain main ranges (*see* **Icefields**). The flow from the glaciers is light in spring, heavy in early and mid-summer, and lighter in late summer and autumn. By contrast, outflow from snowfields is heaviest in the spring and dwindles to little or nothing by mid-summer.

Streams originating out of the Alberta foothills and front ranges of the Rockies derive most of their outflow from melting snow, although summer precipitation also influences water levels. By mid-summer these streams have passed their peak and in semi-drought years their channels will be relatively dry.

Despite the fact that Alberta's water base is critical to all of the Canadian **prairie,** Alberta's total water supply constitutes only about 2.2 percent of Canada's total water resource base. The prairies are profoundly water poor compared to the rest of the nation.

Yet Alberta is the country's largest water consumer—accounting for more than 50 percent of consumptive use. Irrigation and the water needs of the **oil and gas industry** are primarily responsible for Alberta's extremely high levels of water consumption. Well over half of Canada's irrigated land is in Alberta. The province has almost all the secondary oil and gas recovery operations, which entail pumping water into geological formations to replace the oil and gas being drawn out. Although water conservation techniques have been introduced in many urbanized parts of Alberta, the oil and gas industry and irrigation demands continue to increase the province's share of Canada's water consumption.

Because of the manner in which the province's drainage system is distributed, most of the water is not near the province's **population** base. About 87 percent of the total water supply is in the north, flowing out of the Slave River system to the Arctic Ocean, via Great Slave Lake and the Mackenzie River. The water running in a more southerly direction through the North and South Saskatchewan rivers is governed by agreements with

Saskatchewan, Manitoba, and the federal government so that one-half of these rivers' flow is allocated for downstream use outside Alberta.

All this means that during drier than average years, acute water shortages (especially in the extreme southern part of the province) have become an increasing risk.

Waterton Lakes National Park

The 525 square kilometres of terrain encompassed by Waterton Lakes National Park is spectacularly diverse. In less than one kilometre, dry rolling foothill **prairie** gives way to dense woodlands, glacial ice sheets, and soaring peaks rising to heights of almost 3,000 metres. About 1,200 plant species are found within the park's boundaries—representing prairie, wetland, parkland, montane forest, subalpine forest, and alpine flora zones. The park also contains some of the oldest exposed bedrock in the Canadian **Rocky Mountains.**

Because the park includes so many landscapes, the wildlife here is extremely varied. **Pronghorns** and coyotes are found in the park's northeastern corner of prairie; a small herd of moose frequents the wetland area; mountain goat, bighorn sheep, grizzly and black **bears,** and marmots are present in the subalpine and alpine areas. The park is also home to a small cougar population. Waterton Lakes sits astride two major flyways. From September to November thousands of waterfowl stop at Maskinonge and Lower Waterton lakes.

There are 255 kilometres of trails in the park, ranging from a short stroll to steep treks of several days' duration. The park has designated hiking, cycling, and horse trails. Trails provide links to other trails in Montana's Glacier National Park and British Columbia's Akamina-Kishenina Provincial Park. Waterton Lakes is also a popular park for **mountaineering** and rock climbing.

The abundant wildlife in this region attracted many **First Nations peoples.** Archaeological evidence reveals a First Nations presence in the area as early as 11,000 years ago. More than 200 archaeological sites have been identified in the park's boundaries.

Lt. Thomas Blakiston of the **Palliser Expedition** was an early European explorer of the region. He named the lakes after the 18th-century British naturalist Charles Waterton. The park's first settler was John George "Kootenai" Brown, who later became its first warden when it was set aside as a forest reserve in 1895.

Shortly thereafter, Brown noticed beads of oil floating on the surface of

Cameron Creek. He and a business partner siphoned the oil off, bottled it, and sold the substance in **Fort Macleod** and Cardston. Soon the bottled oil came to the attention of entrepreneurs seeking oil in Alberta and the Rocky Mountain Development Company began exploratory drilling—leading to western Canada's first oil well being drilled within the park's boundaries in September 1902. Although the forest reserve status protected the forest from development, prospecting and mining were allowed. The drillers struck oil at a depth of 311 metres. A townsite was quickly established alongside Cameron Creek and named Oil City. High transportation costs and the failure of successive wells to produce significant oil flows, however, led to the city's hasty abandonment.

In 1910, the U.S. government set aside Glacier National Park immediately across the border from Waterton Lakes. The Canadian government followed suit by redesignating the forest reserve to Waterton Lakes Dominion Park in 1911. Brown became its first superintendent and remained so until his retirement at 75 years of age.

Great Northern Railway in Montana soon took an interest in the Waterton Lakes area. The company already operated several grand hotels within the adjacent U.S. park. In 1926, it began construction of a seven-storey, gabled resort overlooking Upper Waterton Lake. One year later, the 81-room Prince of Wales Hotel opened for business. Tourists were bused to the hotel from a railroad station across the border.

As the boundaries of Glacier National Park and Waterton Lakes National Park met at the border, the Rotary Clubs of Alberta and Montana started lobbying for the parks to be linked in some official form. As a result, in 1932 Waterton Lakes and Glacier national parks were designated as the world's first International Peace Park. The park's designation commemorated the long friendship of the United States and Canada. Since then the park has come to symbolize the need for cooperation between nations in a world where sharing resources and ecosystems is essential. In 1995, UNESCO designated the Waterton/Glacier International Peace Park a World Heritage Site. Both parks have also been designated Biosphere Reserves by UNESCO's Man and the Biosphere program, which provides information about the relationships between people and their environment.

Weather. *See* **Climate.**

West Edmonton Mall

One of Alberta's biggest tourist attractions, drawing more than 20 million people annually, is a totally enclosed environment—the West Edmonton

Mall. This is the world's largest shopping centre and also the world's largest indoor amusement park. The mall sprawls across 483,000 square metres, the equivalent of 100 Canadian football fields or 48 square city blocks.

Inside its walls are 11 department stores and more than 800 smaller shops. Shoppers can choose between 210 stores for women, 35 men's stores, 55 shoe shops, 35 jewellery stores, and more than 100 eateries. There are also 7 amusement parks, a chapel, 10 bird aviaries, a bingo hall, a casino, 25 salt-water aquariums, 19 movie theatres, an indoor water park with the world's largest wave pool, a National Hockey League–sized ice rink, a life-sized replica of Christopher Columbus's flagship the *Santa Maria,* an underwater world complete with sharks and dolphins that can be visited by four submarines, 11 fountains including one fashioned after that at the Palace of Versailles, and an 18-hole miniature golf course built to replicate the course at Pebble Beach.

The mall consumes the same amount of power as a city of 50,000, requires five postal codes for mail delivery, and, with parking for 20,000 vehicles, has the world's largest car park. Adjacent to the mall is a 351-room Fantasyland Hotel and Resort. Each floor of the hotel features rooms with a theme, ranging from Arabian, to Victoria Coach, to Hollywood.

That the mall would become a consumers' mecca heightened to fever pitch by a vast carnival air was not apparent when the first phase opened in 1981. With only 225 stores it seemed merely an over-sized shopping mall. But in 1983 the ice rink and Fantasyland opened, and two years later the other theme parks and entertainment facilities were added. Final construction cost topped $1.1 billion.

The brain child of the Iranian-born Ghermezian brothers, who made their first fortune as **Edmonton** carpet retailers, the mall has been controversial. Financial critics claim the mall can never realize a profit. Supporters of Edmonton's downtown-core commercial area argue that the mall has seriously compromised efforts to revitalize the older shopping area. Social workers and others worry that some young people are spending virtually every non-school waking hour of their lives in an enclosed mall because it is more interesting and, for most of the year, warmer than the city's outside environment.

None of this seems to phase the 55,000 customers who every day flow through its 58 entrances, providing direct employment for more than 15,000 people.

Western Heritage Centre

The Western Heritage Centre is a 7,830-square-metre interpretive centre illustrating the past, present, and future of farming, **ranching,** and **rodeo.** Located just north of Cochrane, the $8 million facility opened in 1996 after ten years of development and controversy over the facility's cost and funding.

The concept for the centre was born in 1985 when the Stockmen's Memorial Foundation and the Canadian Rodeo Historical Association decided there was a need to preserve western heritage through creation of an interpretive centre. The provincial government also supported the establishment of the centre.

Visitors are able to learn about western life through its interactive displays. Many of these displays involve using computers equipped with touch screens and laser equipment, so one can virtually experience operating different agricultural equipment and participating in various ranching activities, such as confronting a 1,000-kilogram angry bull, roping a calf, or running the business side of a ranch.

Displays showcase western life from the earliest cattle drives to today's technologically advanced industry, where computer links enable instant commodity market transactions.

Another major facet of the centre's operation is its chronicling of rodeo history. The centre is home to the Canadian Rodeo Hall of Fame. Many artifacts from rodeo history are displayed in this section of the centre.

Wild Cats

All three species of wild cats in Canada are found in Alberta—the cougar, lynx, and bobcat. The historical range of cougars in Alberta extended throughout southern and central Alberta, as well as in the most westerly part of the **Peace River** country and up the Athabasca River to about **Fort McMurray.** Lynxes dwelt throughout northern Alberta's **boreal forest** and **Canadian Shield** fragment, down the length of the **Rocky Mountains** and **foothills,** and across the southern **grasslands, badlands,** and **coulees.** Bobcats have the smallest range in Alberta, confined to the southern Rockies east to the Saskatchewan border, but seldom straying north of the South Saskatchewan River.

Much of Alberta has become too settled and too developed by **agriculture** and other habitat changes for the cats to survive there. In most areas densely populated by humans the cats have either retreated or been hunted down and killed. They survive today primarily in the enclaves of provincial and national parks large enough to support them and in areas of unprotected wilderness isolated enough that conflicts between cats and humans are unlikely and prey is sufficiently numerous.

The largest Canadian wildcat and one of the most powerful predatory animals in the nation is the cougar, sometimes called mountain lion. In Canada, only **bears** are larger carnivorous animals. Cougars were extirpated from most of their traditional range in Alberta by the mid-1900s. They occur seldom outside of the Rocky Mountains and higher foothills country. In these areas, populations are small but generally stable. There are, for example, only about 20 cougars believed to be in **Banff National Park.**

Cougars are so extremely wary of humans that observation of their habits in the wild is difficult. They are also solitary except during mating season, primarily nocturnal, and capable of moving with great stealth through heavy undergrowth. All their senses are keen. They are excellent climbers. Their lairs are usually built in caves or rocky crevices, but cougars may also use overhanging banks or trees, hollow stumps, or even dense thickets. Each cougar's range covers about 93 square kilometres. Males mark their territory by clawing trees upon which they have urinated to create a scent post. This warns other cougars away.

Male cougars are far larger than females, weighing between 67 and 103 kilograms, compared to females' weight of 30 to 63 kilograms. Both males and females are long and lithe of body, with small heads. Hind legs are much longer than forelegs, pushing the hindquarters up higher than the front of the body. Cougars are usually tawny coloured.

A cougar feeds primarily on larger **mammals,** stalking prey much as a domestic cat will a bird. When close enough, the cougar breaks from its hiding place and springs onto the prey's back. If cover is scarce, it will make a short, very fast dash before leaping. Deer are its favoured food, usually accounting for about 77 percent of an individual cougar's diet. The cougar takes a deer by landing on its shoulder, biting deep into the back of its neck, and raking the head and flanks with its long, deadly claws. Usually the deer is knocked flat by the impact and death is almost instantaneous. Once an animal is killed, the cougar will usually drag the carcass to a safe eating place. Besides deer, cougar hunt elk, moose, bighorn sheep, mountain goats, porcupines, beaver, snowshoe hares, mice, and **birds.** In rare instances they will also kill coyotes, foxes, lynxes, bobcats, and skunks. Occasionally they will prey on domestic stock, such as calves, pigs, dogs, and colts. On average a single cougar will kill 14 to 20 deer a year to meet its food requirement, supplemented by kills drawn from other species.

The southern boundary of the lynxes' Alberta territory has gradually withdrawn northward so they are seldom found outside the boreal forest and the subalpine reaches of the Rockies. Lynxes are medium-sized with a short body, long legs, large padded feet, and a stubby tail. A prominent ruff surrounds the face, and ears are tipped with long pointed black hairs. The facial ruff and forehead are striped with black and other indistinct dark spots are present on the belly and insides of the forelegs. Adult males weigh about 11 kilograms and are about 90 centimetres long; females are about 30 percent smaller.

Researchers working in the Rocky Mountains and foothills estimate that in this region lying southwest of **Calgary** only about 24 to 36 lynxes live in an area encompassing 800 square kilometres. It is unlikely lynx populations in other similar-sized parts of the Rockies are much greater.

Lynxes are solitary, silent hunters who prefer to work in deep forest and pair up only for mating. Nocturnal hunters, lynxes seldom travel except during a period ranging from two hours before dark to an hour after sunrise. Their large furry pads enable them to stalk soundlessly. They rely primarily on sight and sound, apparently lacking a keen sense of smell.

Their favourite food is snowshoe hares, constituting about 73 percent of their diet. An average lynx will kill about 200 hares a year. Their other primary source of food is birds such as ducks, ptarmigan, sparrows, and flickers. They will also feed on mice, voles, and other small mammals. In rare instances they might pull down a deer, caribou fawn, or mountain sheep lamb.

Because of their colourful and attractive fur, lynxes are hunted by fur trappers. This is putting increasing pressure on their populations. An additional threat is loss of their dense woodland habitat to logging and other clearing.

Similar to the lynx in size and appearance, the bobcat dwells in more southerly locations and is the only wildcat to occur across Alberta's southern region—although it is limited here primarily to pockets protected by parks. Male bobcats seldom weigh more than 10 kilograms and reach lengths exceeding 83 centimetres, with females being 30 percent smaller. They are more tawny in colour than lynxes, have a longer tail, and have white bellies. Ears, like those of the lynx, are outlined in black but the tufts are shorter.

Bobcats behave quite similarly to lynxes and both hunt small mammals, although bobcats eat fewer snowshoe hares (only 48 percent of their diet) and more mice (28 percent). In some areas porcupines are important prey. Bobcats, in turn, fall prey to coyotes, wolves, and sometimes cougars. The kittens are hunted by great horned owls and foxes.

It is believed that bobcats were unknown in Canada until the early 1900s when they moved up into the southern boundaries from the United States, probably because of loss of habitat in the American grassland ranges. Outside of the southern reaches of the Rockies, bobcats are also found in the **Cypress Hills, Writing-On-Stone Provincial Park,** and other coulee-bad-lands areas along the **Milk River.** They have even been seen in Police Point Park in urban **Medicine Hat.**

Although bobcats are hunted for their pelts, they are generally considered not as attractive as those of the lynx, so the cats are less in demand with furriers and, consequently, trappers.

Wild Dogs

There are six species of wild dogs in Canada, four of which are found in Alberta—one, the swift fox, having been reintroduced after becoming extinct in the early 1900s. Alberta is home to the wolf, coyote, red fox, and swift fox.

Coyotes are Alberta's most common wild dog species. They are found throughout the province, even within the urban limits of **Edmonton** and **Calgary.** Coyotes are so highly adaptable they are among the few animals in the 1900s to have extended their ranges rather than having them eaten away by habitat changes. Between 1907 and 1931 coyotes pushed northward to occupy most of Alaska, Yukon Territory, and the Mackenzie delta.

Their scientific name, *Canis latrans,* means "barking dog," which is appropriate given their tendency to howl and bark nocturnally. **First Nations peoples** assigned this species the supernatural status of the "trick-ster" and ascribed to it many mysterious powers that rested on its supposed ability to fool and mislead people.

Coyotes are medium-sized dogs, with a slender muzzle, large pointed ears, long slender legs, relatively small feet, and a tail slightly less than half their body length. Their face is foxy, often giving them the appearance of laughing or looking wily. They are usually a grizzled grey colour, but can be tan as well. Males weigh between 13 and 20 kilograms with females being only a bit smaller. Although often mistaken in the **Rocky Mountains** for wolves, coyotes are half their size, and far less wary of humans.

Social animals, they form family packs. These consist of a mated pair and their pups. Sometimes, especially in winter, other relatives join up to form a larger pack, but packs seldom exceed six individuals. Their calls consist of a quick series of yelps, followed by a falsetto howl, given usually in the evening, at night, or in early morning.

For hunting, coyotes rely on their sharp hearing and acute sense of smell. They can run between 60 and 70 kilometres an hour and cover up to 4 metres in a single bound. Hunting is usually carried out at night. Coyotes feed upon small **mammals** and carrion, but will also kill **birds,** deer, **pronghorns,** and insects. They will even eat vegetation. The diet of a coyote varies dramatically depending on food availability.

Coyotes have historically been disliked by farmers and ranchers because they have a taste for domestic livestock. Consequently they have been hunted ferociously with guns, traps, and poisons, but with only minimal success. Where their populations have been thinned out, farmers usually end up with increased crop damage from mice, gophers, and other small mammals because the coyotes no longer control the size of these animal populations.

Like coyotes, wolves have traditionally ranged throughout all of Alberta. Unlike coyotes, however, this species has been largely extirpated from the southern and central parts of the province and is now confined to the northern **boreal forest, Canadian Shield** fragment, and the Rocky Mountains. In the Rockies they are most common north of **Jasper National Park,** where humans become less common. Between the 1950s and the mid-1980s wolves were extirpated from **Banff National Park** through a government-sanctioned vermin elimination policy. Since the error of this practice was recognized small numbers of wolves have returned to the park.

Male wolves weigh between 35 and 60 kilograms, while females are slightly smaller and lighter. There is great colour variation, ranging from black to white, with most being a dull brown or grey. They have a broader face than a coyote and eyes always shaded a tinge of yellow.

Like coyotes, wolves are pack animals, running in packs composed of a mating pair, pups, and close relatives. Numbers average four to seven but can reach 14. Packs have set territories that vary in range from 130 to 1,500 square kilometres. Their tireless gait can carry them over 30 to 40 kilometres a day.

Their senses of smell and hearing are extremely keen, while eyesight is good. A wolf howl is best described as "a long, guttural, quavering wail," a sound humans often find threatening.

Wolves primarily hunt big game, accounting for about 80 percent of their total diet, including moose, caribou, elk, deer, mountain sheep, and **bison.** They also eat rabbits, marmots, mice, and other small mammals.

Hampering their hunting effectiveness is the fact that, over short distances, wolves are slower than many of their regular prey. They make up for this by being stealthy and cunning hunters that work well as a team. Wolves have been known to split into units, with one driving the prey directly into an ambush set by the rest.

In contrast to wolves and coyotes, Alberta's two fox species remain solitary for half the year and link up only as small family units for the other half. Red foxes are relatively common in Alberta, except in the southern **prairie** regions where hunting and habitat change have largely pushed them out. Swift foxes were extirpated from the province but have been reintroduced in the southeastern short-grass prairie near **Medicine Hat.**

Red foxes are shy, nervous, nocturnal animals. They weigh about five kilograms and are between one-third and one-quarter the size of coyotes. In their most common colour phase (they have three denoted by season) red foxes have long, thick underfur that is grey at the base and buff-coloured toward the tips. This is the red phase.

During a nocturnal forage, red foxes can travel up to eight kilometres within their normal home range of about seven square kilometres. Like humans, they are largely omnivorous, eating whatever is readily available. In winter this is usually meat; in summer **invertebrates** and vegetable matter dominate their diet. Small mammals, such as moles, mice, and hares, are their most common source of meat. Birds and snakes are also preferred prey. Grasshoppers, beetles, and caterpillars are favoured invertebrates, with acorns, grasses, and corn figuring high in their vegetable diet.

The smallest Canadian fox, the swift fox, historically occurred from southern Alberta to southwest Manitoba. By 1970, however, trapping of the species and plowing of prairie into agricultural land resulted in it being declared extinct in Canada. In 1972, individual swift foxes were captured in Colorado and raised in captivity. Offspring from this captive population began to be released in 1980 in the short-grass prairie of southeastern Alberta. First releases were near Manyberries and Medicine Hat. Since then, evidence shows that some animals are successfully breeding in the wild and the population is slowly growing.

Swift foxes are about the size of a large house cat. Their flanks are yellowish grey, and the forehead, back, and tail a grizzled grey. They are timid creatures and solitary except during breeding season. Hunting and foraging is primarily carried out at night. Their name derives from their swift running speed, reaching up to 40 kilometres per hour. They can dart rapidly from one direction to another and this is their chief defence against predatory attacks by coyotes and domestic dogs. They live in dens or burrows dug into sandy soil on open prairie.

The food of swift foxes consists of small mammals, some birds, a few invertebrates, the odd lizard or **fish,** and vegetable matter such as grasses and berries. In winter they cache food, such as dead mice, under snow.

Wild Horses

Although horses are an introduced species to North America, having most likely been brought here by Spanish Conquistadors in the 1500s, they are actually native to North America and believed to have spread to the rest of the world from this continent. It appears horses first trod Alberta some 65 million years ago during the Tertiary Period (*see* **Ancient Alberta**). At that time they bore little resemblance to the modern horse, as they were about the size of a wire-haired terrier, and the small animal was also probably omnivorous (supported by the presence of carnivorous teeth even today in the mouths of horses).

At some point after prehistoric **First Nations peoples** arrived on this continent horses were extirpated here but managed to survive extinction by crossing the land bridge connecting Asia and North America in opposition to the human traffic. They flourished in China and were first domesticated there. Eventually they spread through Asia to the Mediterranean and North Africa, and were then returned (as a much enlarged and developed species) to North America by either Christopher Columbus in 1493 during his second voyage or by Hernando Cortez in 1519.

The Spanish introduction eventually transformed the First Nations peoples' way of life on the Great Plains by providing mobility. The entire culture of the plains peoples became dependent on the ability to use horses for transportation, hunting **bison,** and conducting military campaigns and raids against other nations. With the coming of Europeans to North America more horses were introduced from a variety of strains, including heavy draught stock and thoroughbreds.

Horses are not naturally domestic. Various animals escaped over the centuries, roaming free across the continent. In the plains country they thrived. By 1920 it was estimated that domestic horse populations in Alberta had peaked at 800,000 animals. From these a certain number disappeared each year to run wild. Others were turned loose when settlers could no longer afford their maintenance. From these stocks herds of wild horses (properly called feral horses) developed.

As settlement expanded through the southern portions of Alberta the wild horses were pushed west into the **foothills** of the **Rocky Mountains.** By the 1950s, however, wild horse populations were declared to have reached an all-time high, although no concise calculation of numbers exists and figures range from several thousand to absurdly high levels. They were accused of eating grass that was consequently denied cattle, of competing unfairly with deer and elk for graze, and of trampling seedlings on refor-estation plots.

In 1956, the Alberta government decided to completely eradicate wild horses from Alberta. Permits were issued allowing people to round up wild horses and dispose of them as they saw fit. Thousands were killed under this policy. Most wild horse carcasses were turned into dog food; the few spared were used as pack horses or put to bucking on the **rodeo** circuits. About 200 horses were slaughtered annually until public sentiment cur-tailed the practice in 1973. After that only the provincial forest superinten-dent had the authority to implement a roundup and culling.

In 1982, Calgary-based Animal Rights Concern demanded a stop to the occasional roundups. The public pressure raised by this group led to can-cellation of a planned roundup in 1983. Since then the government has largely assumed a hands-off position toward wild horses, which has done little to help researchers gain an understanding of how large their popula-tion is or how they affect the ecology of foothills ranges, where they are largely confined.

The last major wild horse study in Alberta was conducted in 1977. It concluded that there were about 900 animals ranging through the foothills country. Up to 1,100 were believed to exist elsewhere in the province, but no hard data supported this conclusion. All were at least one generation removed from domestication. One colony of wild horses existed on Suffield Canadian Forces Base—the largest armed forces base in Canada—but in the late 1980s this herd was rounded up and relocated because of herd man-agement concerns.

Wild horses remain a species in Alberta for which there is no clear gov-ernment policy of protection. Little attention is given to quantifying their numbers or considering how to preserve their populations without endan-gering the habitat of other species—especially cloven-hoofed species such as elk, caribou, and deer—or increasing the problems of wild horse incur-sions, and raids on domestic stock for brood mares.

Average herd size consists of about 17 mares and foals, led by one stal-lion. Most wild horses are compact in build, but because of intermixing with domestic stock some are tall and sturdy. The majority observed in the foothills during one study were bays, with the rest evenly mixed blacks, red roans, chestnuts, browns, and greys. All had full tails brushing the ground, and long manes, characteristics uncommon among domestic breeds where trimming is practised. Contrary to some myths about wild horses, there is no evidence to suggest that the animals are half-starved and that their extirpation would be a kindness to a suffering species. On the contrary, wild horses seem to thrive well in areas where they can compete with other cloven-hoofed species for graze and range that has been largely undisturbed by humans.

Wind Turbines

On Cowley Ridge, west of Pincher Creek, 52 wind turbines dominate the skyline. They are part of a unique technological experiment aimed at using Alberta's prevailing westerly winds to generate a stable, continuous source of electric power.

The complex is composed of two Windplants™ which have a combined capacity of 18.9 megawatts. This is enough to meet the peak demands of a community of 16,000 people.

The first project, consisting of 25 turbines, is called the Cowley Ridge 9.0 Mega-Watt Windplant. It was developed by KENETECH Ltd. of San Francisco in 1993. The second project, consisting of 27 turbines, is the 9.9-megawatt Pe-Kunnee Project. This project, codeveloped by Chinook Project, Inc. of **Calgary** and the Peigan Nation, was completed in 1994. Both were built by KENETECH at a total cost of approximately $26 million.

The turbines in these projects are KENETECH Model 33M-VS, the first variable-speed, variable-pitch machines to be used in a commercial setting in Canada. Their reinforced fibreglass blades are 16 metres long and weigh more than 900 kilograms. The towers are 24 metres high. These horizontal axis turbines must face into the wind in order to turn. They start turning when wind speed exceeds 105 kilometres an hour.

The electricity produced is sold to TransAlta Utilities Ltd. under the Alberta Small Power Research and Development Program. These projects, and several other renewable energy projects in the area, were assisted with funding from the Southwest Alberta Renewable Energy Institute.

Three kilometres east of Pincher Creek on Oldman River Dam Road is the Adecon Alberta Inc. wind plant. This plant uses a Darrius-type vertical axis wind turbine—looking remarkably like an upturned egg-beater supported by guy-lines—developed by the National Research Council in the early 1980s. The unique four-bladed design will turn at lower wind speeds than most other wind turbines. It produces 1.5 megawatts of power, which is also sold to TransAlta Utilities.

Wolves. *See* **Wild Dogs.**

Wood Buffalo National Park

Canada's largest national park, Wood Buffalo National Park, sprawls over 44,840 square kilometres. It is the second-largest national park in the world. Straddling the Alberta–Northwest Territories border, the park encompasses one of the world's largest freshwater deltas—the Peace-Athabasca Delta. It is also the last natural nesting habitat of the rare whooping crane.

The park was established in 1922 to protect the world's last surviving herd of wood **bison,** believed at the time to number between 500 and 1,500. A few years after the park was created, surviving members of the disease-ridden population of plains bison were moved here from the abandoned Wainwright Buffalo National Park. Soon the diseases—principally brucellosis and tuberculosis—were devastating the park's bison population, which also became cross-bred so that the wood bison were no longer pure stock.

By the 1950s, disease was so rampant among the bison population that large-scale roundups were organized in the Sweetgrass area of the delta. The diseased bison rounded up were herded into a 30-kilometre network of corrals and systematically slaughtered. The last of these roundup-slaughters took place in 1967 and the corrals have not been used since 1976 when bison herded into them were vaccinated against anthrax.

Because of disease and cross-breeding with plains bison, park officials thought by the 1950s that the wood bison had ceased to exist as a unique species. But in 1957 parks staff discovered a small herd of about 200 wood bison in the remote Nyarling River area of the park. Twenty-three of these animals were relocated to **Elk Island National Park** in 1965 to form the nucleus for a new herd that would safeguard the species from the diseases plaguing Wood Buffalo National Park.

The population of about 3,500 bison in Wood Buffalo remain threatened by disease. Some government environmental advisory boards have even recommended the slaughter of the park's entire population to permanently eradicate the diseases.

Besides the bison, Wood Buffalo is home to caribou, wolves, black **bears,** and moose. In the vast wetlands, beaver, mink, and muskrat are common. The forests support populations of fox, lynx, ermine, and red squirrels. More than one million ducks, geese, and swans migrate through the delta—many remaining to nest there.

The Peace-Athabasca Delta is silt-laden and slow draining. Over thousands of years, spring flooding created a wetlands that extended over hundreds of kilometres. The 1960s construction of the W.A.C. Bennett Dam more than 1,000 kilometres away on the **Peace River** in British Columbia has regulated **water** flow so this flood-cycle has been broken. Parts of the delta are consequently threatened with protein-rich sedges found alongside the sloughs and marshes being replaced by silverweed and thistle. Large sections of marshland have been reduced to dried-up mudflats. Water contamination from sawmills upstream is also causing environmental problems.

In the northeast corner of the park lies an expansive, naturally formed salt-encrusted plain. Underground water flows through salt deposits left by an ancient ocean. Where the water reaches the surface salt springs form. These springs are surrounded by large mounds of salt, which attract bison, wolves, foxes, and black bears.

Also found in the park is the best example in North America of karst terrain—an area where the landscape has been altered markedly by the dissolving of bedrock by water. In this case the bedrock is composed of gypsum, which is highly water soluble. The underground water here has created huge caverns that are highly unstable and prone to collapse of the covering layer of gypsum, leaving large depressions known as sinkholes. Thousands of sinkholes exist in this part of the park, some up to 100 metres in circumference.

Until March 7, 1991, Wood Buffalo National Park was not completely protected from logging. A remote region of the park, known as Timber Berth 408, had been logged for 30 years prior to the moratorium. The result was massive clear-cut logging of a 500-square-kilometre old-growth spruce forest. Logging continued here despite many violations by successive logging companies of lease conditions. Finally these continued violations led to the cancelling of the leases and there has since been no further logging inside the park boundaries.

Access to the park from within Alberta is extremely limited. The tiny settlements of Fort Chipewyan and Fort Fitzgerald are virtually the only communities bordering the park boundaries. The usual access for visitors is via Fort Smith in the Northwest Territories. Roads are limited to the eastern border.

Woodland Caribou

Although the woodland caribou's range extends from northern British Columbia and the Yukon Territory to Labrador, its range in Alberta is relatively small. It is found in the most northerly extent of the **boreal forest,** the remnant of **Canadian Shield** in the province's northeastern corner, and in the more northerly ranges of Alberta's **Rocky Mountains.** The Rocky Mountain population was isolated from the species' greater northerly range by habitat changes following the end of the last ice age about 11,000 years ago.

Woodland caribou are one of five subspecies of caribou (also called reindeer) historically found in Canada. One of these subspecies, a small mouse-coloured race previously found on Graham Island of the Queen Charlotte Islands, has been extinct since 1910. Although the woodland caribou is not in threat of extinction in most of Canada, its numbers are relatively small, probably no more than 40,000 nationwide. In Alberta, they may number fewer than 1,500. It is estimated, for example, that only about 500 survive in the isolated pocket along the Alberta side of the Rockies.

This group has in recent years extended its range, despite a declining population, along the **Icefields Parkway** to the **Lake Louise** area during summer months. Their decline has been noted since the 1950s and is largely attributed to logging of old-growth forest and increased human pressure, including hunting. Old-growth trees are rich in tree-lichen, one of the principle sources of food for woodland caribou during the winter.

The name caribou derives from French pronunciation of *xalibu,* an Algonquian word meaning "the one that paws or scratches." This reflects upon the animal's major food source—ground-growing lichen, which it unearths by pawing with its cloven hoofs. Caribou also eat grasses, sedges, horsetails, forbs, and twigs and leaves of willow and birch. About 4.5 kilograms of lichen a day is needed to fuel a full-grown woodland caribou. In winter, if snow is too deep for digging up ground lichen, tree lichen will suffice. Discarded antlers are chewed as a source of dietary minerals.

In a remarkable adaptive process, caribou hoofs grow larger and more splayed in winter, with thick stiff hair underneath. This enables them to move more easily over snow, as if they had donned snowshoes. Woodland caribou do not migrate as far as other caribou, but still move in annual migrations from lower fens to drier open ranges as summer progresses.

Adult males, or bucks, weigh between 120 and 250 kilograms. Does are about 25 percent smaller. They are similar in size to mule deer, but much more heavily built. Their necks are thick and their heads ponderous, like those of moose. Males have large, curved antlers; females do not always have antlers. All caribou have poor eyesight, depending almost entirely on their acute sense of smell to identify the presence and location of predators, other caribou, and food.

Bucks gather harems, usually numbering no more than 15. Calves are born between May and July. Their average lifespan is about nine to ten years.

Woodland caribou, like all caribou, can achieve remarkable, sustained speeds of between 60 and 80 kilometres per hour. Between their speed and the deadly thrust of the bucks' antlers, predators have a hard time closing for a successful kill. Wolves are their main predators, but a healthy caribou can easily outrun them and a caribou herd usually can successfully protect itself from a wolf pack. Grizzly **bears,** cougars, wolverines, and lynxes are also a threat. But the major predators of caribou are humans, originally **First Nations peoples** and later, before their protection in Alberta as an **endangered species,** trophy and game hunters.

Writing-On-Stone Provincial Park

The area of sandstone cliffs overlooking the **Milk River** at Writing-On-Stone Provincial Park was known to the Blackfoot **First Nations peoples** as *Áisinai'pi,* meaning "it is written." The park's boundary protects the largest number of **petroglyphs and pictographs** found in any one North American location. Almost 50 rock art sites have been found, ranging from a single petroglyph to sites containing hundreds of figures.

One of the most spectacular petroglyphs depicts a battle scene. It is one of the most elaborate rock art carvings ever found on North America's plains. The carving shows a large force of warriors attacking an encampment of **tipis,** defended by a gun line. While most of the attackers are on foot, there are 11 horses depicted on the attacking side. Some of these are dragging travois. In the centre of the carving, warriors from the two sides engage in hand-to-hand combat, next to several fallen corpses.

As horses did not appear in southern Alberta before 1730, it is believed this carving was created well after that date. Evidence suggests that it may show a great battle fought in 1866 between the Gros Ventre and Peigan (a Blackfoot tribe). Peigan legend holds that this carving appeared on the same day that the Gros Ventre were preparing to attack a Peigan camp just east of Writing-On-Stone. Warned by the mysterious appearance of the carving, the Peigans had time to prepare for the attack. The Gros Ventre were badly defeated during the ensuing battle.

Much of Writing-On-Stone's incredible rock art is far older than this battle scene. Some may predate 1,800 B.C., the time archaeological evidence first indicates this area was used by prehistoric First Nations people as a camp.

The majority of the rock art was probably created by members of the Blackfoot nation, for whom the valley was a sacred place—its cliffs and

hoodoos believed to be the home of powerful spirits capable of helping people who came to pray here. Hunting and raiding parties from other nations, such as the Gros Ventre, Cree, Assiniboine, Crow, Ktunaxa (formerly Kutenai or Kootenay), and Shoshone, also passed through the valley and these groups may have been involved in the creation of some of the rock art.

Writing-On-Stone's landscape is a majestic blend of sandstone cliffs, hoodoos, natural **prairie, coulees,** and **cottonwood forests** bordering the silt-coloured waters of the Milk River. Once plains grizzly bear and large herds of plains **bison** lived here, but today deer and **pronghorns** are the largest **mammals** living on the Milk River's shores. **Rattlesnakes** can be found, and yellow-bellied marmots are common on the rocky out-croppings.

Across the river from the picnic and camping area is a reconstructed **North-West Mounted Police** (NWMP) post. The post faithfully duplicates one built here in 1889, as part of the "Thin Red Line" stretching across the Canadian Prairies. Its primary purpose was to stem whiskey smuggling out of Montana and discourage First Nations horse-raiding parties. In 1897, this post was at its most active, with a garrison of five Mounties, 12 horses, and two hired range riders. The post remained in operation until May 1918. Later that year, the original fort was burned by vandals. Reconstruction of the buildings began after the site was archaeologically excavated as part of the NWMP centennial celebrations in 1973 and the post's rebuilding was completed in 1975.

York Boats

For many years the Canadian fur trade relied on canoes to bring furs east for shipment to European and other markets. But even large freight canoes could only carry relatively small loads of furs or the vital supplies that had to be moved west to sustain the operations of fur-trading posts that, by the 1780s, reached into present-day Alberta.

Competition between the North West Company (NWC) and Hudson's Bay Company (HBC) was fierce. The company able to move the most furs and supplies would clearly have the advantage. The HBC decided the solution was a larger boat than the canoe. In 1749, boatbuilders brought to

Canada from the Orkney Islands constructed the first York boat. Named after York Factory, the company's fur-trade trailhead on Hudson Bay, the boats carried twice the cargo of a canoe with no increase in crew size. The York boat was also less fragile than a canoe, more stable during lake crossings, and less prone to capsizing in storms. An experienced crew could match a canoe's average daily range of travel.

A typical York boat had a 9.1-metre keel, overall length of 12.6 metres, a beam of 2.7 metres, and inside depth of 0.9 metres. It could carry 2,700 kilograms and was typically crewed by six to eight men. The bow and stern were both high and sharply pointed. The crew generally sat in a single line, each man operating a set of oars. A man at the rear—usually the boat commander—used a long paddle as a rudder to keep the boat following a safe course.

Initially use of the York boat was limited to the Albany River link to James Bay, but in 1797, to supply its growing network of forts in Alberta, the HBC started using the boat on the run down the Hayes River route to the North Saskatchewan River. Soon York boats were plying the North Saskatchewan route all the way to **Rocky Mountain House,** established in 1799, and following the Slave River to Great Slave Lake and on up the Mackenzie River.

Each boat and crew would make one round-trip a year. Most boats were constructed at the forts during the winter. At Rocky Mountain House, located at the end of the North Saskatchewan River trade route, the annual boat-production quota was six.

In April, after winter breakup, crews loaded the boats with furs and started the long trip east. It was back-breaking work. Each crew member wielded a six-metre oar in a rhythmic motion that involved standing and sitting on each stroke as the oar dipped in and out of the water. At rapids, waterfalls, and where the water was too shallow for rowing, the heavy boats were heaved onto rollers and pushed around obstacles. At rocky shallows, ropes would be run from the boats to men on the river banks, and the boats would be slowly pulled to deeper water.

During the trip across Lake Winnipeg, the oarsmen often got a break from rowing. If the wind was right, sails could be raised. By summer, a great flotilla of York boats in from the forts congregated at Norway House in the northeastern corner of Lake Winnipeg before heading down the difficult Hayes River passage to York Factory. On their return trip, the boats were laden to the gunwales with supplies and trade goods to be used at the posts during the following year.

When the HBC and NWC merged in 1821, the York boat became the primary means of transportation for the fur trade in western Canada. Some York boats were still in use in the 1920s. But by 1852, because the company had shifted its main trailhead destination from Hudson Bay to St. Paul, Minnesota, the York boat began to be displaced by a new innovation in transportation technology—the **Red River cart.**

About the Author

Mark Zuehlke's family roots in Alberta reach back three generations, his grandparents on both sides settling there in 1905, the same year the province was created and entered Confederation. They settled primarily in the Bashaw and Donalda area, near Buffalo Lake, and established a number of farms.

Frances Backhouse

Mark has been a full-time writer since 1981. His other books include *The B.C. Fact Book*, for which this book is a companion volume, *Fun B.C. Facts For Kids*, and *The Vancouver Island South Explorer: The Outdoor Guide*. He is also the author of Book-of-the-Month Club selections *The Gallant Cause: Canadians in the Spanish Civil War, 1936-1939* and *Scoundrels, Dreamers & Second Sons: British Remittance Men in the Canadian West*.

He lives in Victoria, B.C.